Oxford Studies in Experimental Philosophy

Oxford Studies in Experimental Philosophy

Volume 3

Edited by

TANIA LOMBROZO, JOSHUA KNOBE,
AND SHAUN NICHOLS

OXFORD
UNIVERSITY PRESS

OXFORD

UNIVERSITY PRESS

Great Clarendon Street, Oxford, OX2 6DP,
United Kingdom

Oxford University Press is a department of the University of Oxford.
It furthers the University's objective of excellence in research, scholarship,
and education by publishing worldwide. Oxford is a registered trade mark of
Oxford University Press in the UK and in certain other countries

Published in the United States of America by Oxford University Press
198 Madison Avenue, New York, NY 10016, United States of America

British Library Cataloguing in Publication Data
Data available

Library of Congress Control Number: 2019954873

ISBN 978-0-19-885240-7 (hbk.)
ISBN 978-0-19-885252-0 (pbk.)

Printed and bound in Great Britain by
Clays Ltd, Elcograf S.p.A.

Contents

Introduction

Tania Lombrozo
Princeton University

Joshua Knobe
Yale University

Shaun Nichols
Cornell University

The chapters collected in this third volume of *Oxford Studies in Experimental Philosophy* illustrate the ways in which the field continues to broaden, taking on new methodological approaches and interacting with substantive theories from an ever wider array of disciplines. As the chapters themselves clearly show, some recent research in experimental philosophy is going more deeply into well-established questions in the field, but at the same time, other strands of research are exploring issues that hardly appeared at all in the field even a few years ago. Thus, we see the introduction of new empirical and statistical methods (network analysis), new theoretical approaches (formal semantics), and the development of entirely new interdisciplinary connections (most notably, in the emerging field of "experimental jurisprudence").

1. New Questions, New Methods

Illustrating experimental jurisprudence is a contribution by **Raff Donelson and Ivar Hannikainen**. Philosophers of law have long been concerned with the question as to whether it is built into the very concept

Tania Lombrozo, Joshua Knobe, and Shaun Nichols, *Introduction* In: *Oxford Studies in Experimental Philosophy.*
Edited by: Tania Lombrozo, Joshua Knobe, and Shaun Nichols, Oxford University Press (2020).
© Tania Lombrozo, Joshua Knobe, and Shaun Nichols.
DOI: 10.1093/oso/9780198852407.003.0001

of law itself that it meet certain normative requirements. Would something even count as a law at all if it was secret, or unintelligible, or not entirely prospective? Donelson and Hannikainen investigate people's intuitions on these questions, and obtain a surprising result. People are actually more inclined to say that it is *necessarily* the case that laws fulfill these normative requirements than that it is *actually* the case that laws fulfill these normative requirements. This finding sets up an intriguing puzzle for future work in experimental jurisprudence.

Emily Sullivan and colleagues take up a method that has not been used extensively in experimental philosophy research thus far, namely, *network analysis*. They use this method to explore the degree to which actual networks make possible the "wisdom of crowds." Taking as a case study the discussion of vaccination on Twitter, they show that the actual properties of the network do not facilitate wisdom of crowds. This chapter not only provides evidence for this particular conclusion but also illustrates a new way in which research in experimental philosophy can contribute to questions in social epistemology.

Dylan Murray explores questions related to disagreement and truth, which have been prominent in formal semantics. Judgments of taste seem to be subjective—based on our individual feelings. But it also seems that we find genuine disagreement on matters of taste, as when John says "the dessert was tasty" and Mary replies "no it wasn't." Many theorists think that such disagreements must involve contradictory contents— contents that cannot both be true. This is a key part of "truth relativism." Murray explores such putative disagreements of taste over three experiments. He finds that most people think they can disagree about taste and aesthetics, but they do not generally treat disagreements on matters of taste as involving contradictory contents.

Mario Attie-Picker helps expand the scope of experimental philosophy by considering how affective responses relate to epistemic commitments. Pyrrhonian Scepticism, as described by Sextus Empiricus, maintains that dogmatic belief causes anxiety. Attie-Picker argues that this claim plays an essential role in Sextus's philosophy and proceeds to test it empirically. Across three studies Attie-Picker finds that, contrary to the claim that dogmatism causes anxiety, dogmatism is actually associated with *lower* anxiety. This raises more general questions about how to understand the role of affect in philosophical commitments.

2. Emerging Trends: The Experimental Philosophy of Identity

A notable trend in this volume is the attention to questions surrounding the philosophy and psychology of identity. Traditional work on the problem of personal identity led to the development of a number of different theories (the psychological theory, the biological theory, etc.). Strikingly, research within experimental philosophy has provided at least some support for each of these theories. That is, some studies indicate that people hold a psychological conception, while others indicate that people hold a biological conception. **Hannah Tierney** argues for a new view that makes sense of this apparently conflicting evidence. On this 'Subscript View', there are actually two individuals where we thought there was just one: a psychological individual ($self_p$) and a biological individual ($self_b$). As Tierney explains, the Subscript View allows us to see each strand of people's apparently conflicting intuitions as getting at something real about one of these two selves.

Moving beyond the identity of people, the Ship of Theseus is thought to present a puzzle regarding identity even for physical objects. **David Rose and colleagues** report a large cross-cultural study on the issue. They find that across cultures people do find the Ship of Theseus scenario puzzling. The results also indicate that there are two criteria—"continuity of form" and "continuity of matter"—implicated in judgments of persistence and that these two criteria receive different weightings in different cultural settings.

Finally, **Vilius Dranseika** explores the relation between memory and personal identity. Memory is often thought to carry the presupposition that it is factive (such that if it's true that a person remembers p, p must be true) and that it involves previous awareness (such that if it's true that a person remembers an event, that person must have experienced the event). Dranseika reports studies involving scenarios of misidentified dream memories, memory transfer, and artificial memories and finds that neither of the presuppositions are essential to ordinary use of 'remembering' and 'having a memory.'

3. Revisiting Foundational Topics: Epistemology, Moral Judgment, and Beyond

The final chapters in this volume revisit foundational topics that have been prominent since the emergence of experimental philosophy, including epistemology, moral judgments, and the status of intuition.

Within the experimental philosophy of epistemology, a series of recent studies have called into question the traditional view that justification is a necessary condition in the ordinary concept of knowledge. **Gonnerman and colleagues** provide evidence against one possible deflationary interpretation of the results of these studies. Specifically, they provide evidence that previous results were not due to protagonist projection. Although this new finding sheds valuable light on the question, it also leaves open a number of different possible explanations, and the authors survey these possibilities in the closing section of their chapter.

Shaylene Nancekivell and Ori Friedman investigate norms of explanation, as understood by young children. They observe that we are sometimes obligated to explain our actions to other people, and that these obligations are in part governed by social norms. When and how does the ability to understand these norms develop? Across three experiments involving children aged 3–6 years old, they find that even young children judge that agents have to explain their actions when those actions interfere with another's goal, and that the explanation is owed to the agent whose goal was frustrated. These findings shed light on the developmental origins of the role of norms in governing the content of utterances, and additionally highlight a norm that is especially important to cohesive interaction with others: when we owe explanations.

Pascale Willemsen takes up a puzzle in attributions of moral responsibility. Many cases are taken to show that for an agent to be held morally responsible for the consequences of some action, it must have been possible for the agent to have acted otherwise. Yet other cases are taken to show that when it comes to the *omission* of an action, this requirement does not hold. Willemsen aims to resolve this puzzle by examining classic cases from the literature as well as novel scenarios in which actions and omissions are better matched to achieve greater experimental control. Across three experiments, he finds that the resolution to this puzzle is more nuanced than the literature may have suggested: the emergence of an action/omission asymmetry depends on the type of moral judgment elicited and how participants indicate their response.

Finally, **Alex Wiegmann, Joachim Horvath, and Karina Meyer** explore questions at the heart of experimental philosophy's inception: the role of intuition. One long-standing debate in the literature concerns the extent to which "expert intuitions" (e.g., the intuitions of philosophy professors) might evade the sorts of errors that plague more ordinary intuitions. Horvath and colleagues explore this question by examining the degree to which expert versus ordinary intuitions can be shifted by introducing irrelevant options. Interestingly, experts were just as susceptible to the presence of irrelevant options as non-expert participants were. In combination with a host of results from previous research, this finding provides evidence that expertise does not lead to a diminished impact of irrelevant factors.

1

Fuller and the Folk

The Inner Morality of Law Revisited

Raff Donelson
Penn State Dickinson School of Law

Ivar R. Hannikainen
Pontifícia Universidade Católica do Rio
de Janeiro & Universidad de Granada

The philosophy of law, or jurisprudence, is an area of study wherein experimental methods are largely absent but sorely needed. It is puzzling that the experimental turn has been slow in coming to jurisprudence, as the field straddles two disciplines where empirical evidence is increasingly common. On one flank, empirical studies have long been popular among non-philosophers in law departments; on the other, experimental methods now abound in many areas of philosophy.

While it is difficult to understand why few have adopted an experimental approach to jurisprudence, it is clear why experimental jurisprudence should be on the agenda: legal philosophers routinely ask questions that are explicitly empirical. To give just one brief example, consider the fact that in contemporary jurisprudence, some philosophers are concerned, in part, to give the correct account of *our* concept of law or *our* concept of a legal system (Raz, 2009), while others are anxious to show that there is no single concept of law (L. Murphy, 2005; Priel, 2013). It would seem that this empirical debate—about whether *we* have a shared concept of law at all, and if so, what contours that concept has—would benefit from empirical research. In particular, we might seek out folk

Raff Donelson and Ivar R. Hannikainen, *Fuller and the Folk: The Inner Morality of Law Revisited* In: *Oxford Studies in Experimental Philosophy*. Edited by: Tania Lombrozo, Joshua Knobe, and Shaun Nichols, Oxford University Press (2020).
DOI: 10.1093/oso/9780198852407.003.0002

psychological evidence, predicated on the positive impact such evidence has had in other domains of philosophy.

The foregoing may not be convincing. Traditional legal philosophers who do not use empirical methods will need to hear more to appreciate why strange, new techniques might be appropriate. Experimental philosophers who have yet to consider jurisprudence will need to hear more about the subfield and its issues to understand how they might contribute. We hope to address such philosophers and others, but not with a purely metaphilosophical tract. Instead, our chapter aims to exemplify the potential for experimental approaches to jurisprudence. As such, we focus on a narrow issue in jurisprudence. We appraise Lon Fuller's procedural natural law theory using experimental techniques. Admittedly, his is just one of many theories about law; however, it is a prominent theory, and legal philosophers have written extensively to criticize (Hart, 1965; D'Amato, 1981), defend (C. Murphy, 2005), and extend that theory (Winston, 2005). If our experiments usefully add to this debate, we hope to thereby have illustrated the legitimacy and value of experimental jurisprudence.

The trajectory of the chapter is as follows. We begin with background on Fuller's theory of law and on the state of jurisprudence. For those well-versed in those debates, this can be skimmed or skipped. Next, we offer an overview of the studies that we performed. In this overview section, we state with precision how our experimental approach helps to assess Fuller's theory. After the overview, we present each of the three studies themselves. For each study, we discuss our predictions, the motivating thoughts behind those predictions, the manner by which the experiment was performed, and the results. In the final section of the chapter, the general discussion, we elaborate on the results of our research, explore their limitations, and muse in a more broad-minded way about the future of experimental jurisprudence.

1. Fuller's Procedural Natural Law Theory

The key discussion in jurisprudence concerns the necessary and sufficient conditions something must satisfy in order to count as a law or a legal system. Fuller (1969) offered a major contribution to this discussion when he proposed a novel set of necessary conditions. Specifically, Fuller argued that a social arrangement is a legal system insofar as that arrangement satisfies eight principles that he collectively called "the inner morality of law." These principles include the generality principle (that legal systems must have general rules of conduct), the publicity principle (that legal rules of conduct must be made public for those regulated to learn of their rights and duties), and the prospectivity principle (that a legal rule of conduct may only regulate conduct performed after the promulgation of said rule of conduct).[1] Since its initial formulation in the 1960s, Fuller's theory has been widely discussed and continues to enlist new adherents. This is not surprising because the view has certain theoretical virtues, virtues one can identify upon reviewing other well-known views in this debate.

If the key discussion in jurisprudence is the search for necessary and sufficient conditions for law, the most notorious debate within that key discussion concerns whether a norm has to have particular content in order to count as legal norm. Legal philosophers have been especially interested in whether a norm's content has to comport with the strictures of morality in order to be a legal norm. *If a norm permits or even requires those subject to it to perform grossly immoral acts, can that norm be a legal norm?* That kind of question has long been the hot-button issue in jurisprudence. Those who answer in the affirmative are, roughly speaking, legal positivists; whereas, those who answer in the negative are, roughly speaking, natural law theorists. Legal positivism has a long list of famous proponents (e.g., Kelsen, 1967; Hart, 1994; Waluchow, 1994; Austin, 1998; Raz, 2009; Shapiro, 2011); while natural law theory has its own list of famous proponents (e.g., Finnis, 1980; Dworkin, 1986; King, 1986; Aquinas, 1994; Murphy, 2011). Fuller set himself apart by straddling the divide between the two camps.

Scholars are often drawn to natural law theory because they hold as a considered judgment the thought that, prima facie, those subject to a law's provisions have a moral reason to obey it. Or to put this considered judgment another way, prima facie, law deserves subjects' respect. If this

---

[1] We reproduce the full set of Fullerian principles below and only offer this abbreviated list to help fix ideas.

considered judgment is used as a desideratum for selecting one's theory of law, one will endorse some content restriction as a condition for some norm to count as law. On the other hand, scholars are often drawn to legal positivism because they hold as a considered judgment the thought that some laws are unjust, such as those of the Third Reich, apartheid South Africa, and the antebellum American South.

Because, for Fuller, a norm can be law only if it has certain content (e.g., it is prospective and not retrospective), his view is often classed as a version of natural law theory. However, Fuller's natural law theory differs from more familiar versions of natural law theory which claim that a norm is a law only if the norm is just (King, 1986; Aquinas, 1994) or claim that unjust norms can, at best, be defective instances of law (Finnis, 1980; Murphy, 2011). Fuller's conditions only disqualify norms which exhibit certain *procedural* failings from being laws. Thus, for Fuller, many unjust norms can be laws, and only some unjust norms would fail to be laws. For this reason, commentators often label Fuller's view an instance of *procedural natural law theory*.

Fuller's procedural natural law theory might be thought to enjoy theoretical virtues of both traditional natural law theory and legal positivism. Fuller's view can countenance the considered judgment that law, prima facie, deserves subjects' respect. Given the procedural constraints that Fuller sees as necessary features of law, laws minimally treat people fairly. Arguably, this feature of law would deserve respect and would give subjects some moral reason to comply with law. To illustrate the minimal sense in which law treats people fairly on Fuller's theory, consider two of his principles. The publicity principle (that legal rules of conduct must be made public for those regulated to learn of their rights and duties) and the prospectivity principle (that a legal rule of conduct may only regulate conduct performed after the promulgation of said rule of conduct) together imply that law necessarily gives subjects fair notice of which behavior will elicit adverse state responses. The foregoing explains how Fuller can accommodate one of the driving thoughts behind traditional natural law theory, but he does not incur that theory's key theoretical cost, denying that there are unjust laws. It is to Fuller's theoretical advantage over other natural lawyers that he can claim with legal positivists that some norms are both unjust and legal in the fullest sense.

Before concluding this section on Fuller's work and its place in contemporary jurisprudence, we summarize the eight principles which comprise Fuller's inner morality of law. The principles are as follows. (For ease of exposition, n will signify some norm, L will signify law, and all claims concern a single jurisdiction.)

CONSISTENCY: n_1 and n_2 are both L only if n_1 and n_2 are mutually consistent.

ENFORCEMENT: n is L only if the published version of n accords with how n is enforced.

GENERALITY: n is L only if n is a general rule of conduct.

INTELLIGIBILITY: n is L only if n can be understood by subjects.

POSSIBILITY: n is L only if n requires only those acts subjects are physically capable of performing.

PROSPECTIVITY: n is L only if n regulates only conduct performed after the promulgation of n.

PUBLICITY: n is L only if n is publicly announced.

STABILITY: n is L only if n does not change too frequently.

2. Overview of the Studies

Having outlined our general ambitions and offered a sketch of Fuller's position, we now must explain our experiments. This explanatory task is twofold: to chart the specific steps we took and to justify using these experiments in appraising Fuller's procedural natural law theory.

Broadly, our experiments attempt to ascertain the extent to which Fuller's inner morality of law reflects the folk understanding of law. The folk understanding of law can be important for assessing Fuller's theory in two different ways, depending on how one understands his effort.

Following Haslanger (2012a, 2012b), philosophical analysis of the kind that Fuller and others engage usually proceeds in one of two modes, either as *conceptual analysis*, analysis of what 'we' take the analysandum to be, or as *descriptive analysis*, analysis of what the analysandum actually is, irrespective of how we see it. If Fuller was engaged in conceptual analysis, he was trying to characterize 'our' concept of law. As such, his theory is, more or less, a prediction of what those who possess the concept of law would say. Therefore, folk intuitions bear directly on whether his attempt has been successful. The folk intuitions are the very subject of Fullerian claims on this construal. Alternately, insofar as Fuller attempts to do *descriptive* analysis of law, analysis of what law actually is, folk intuitions bear indirectly on whether Fuller is right. It is a familiar epistemic principle that views requiring a massive error theory, that is, views that imply that most people have false beliefs with respect to a given proposition, are to be regarded skeptically (Wright, 1994; Jackson, 1998). To be fair, this epistemic principle has its detractors (Frances, 2013), but generally, philosophers hold that extraordinary evidence is needed to overturn widespread, commonsense views. Given that, determining what people believe is essential to determining whether the presumption against error theories weighs for or against Fuller's theory.

Whether one understands Fuller's effort as an instance of conceptual analysis or descriptive analysis, experimental data would best bolster his account if it demonstrated that the folk *widely* and *reliably* agree with his principles. This implies that there are two ways that the data could cause trouble for the account: Folk support for Fullerian principles might be modest or even meager, or folk support for Fullerian principles might be unstable. If the data should reveal modest support, his account faces problems, whether construed as conceptual or descriptive analysis. If few share his view and Fuller is attempting to predict our shared concept of law, we may have to reject the account entirely as an inaccurate prediction. If we view the theory as descriptive analysis, the presumption against error theories may tell against him. If the data should reveal unstable support among the folk—presented in one fashion, Fullerian principles garner widespread support; presented another way, they are roundly rejected—supporters of Fuller would need to explain away the Fuller-unfriendly response pattern. Otherwise, some of Fuller's opponents will attempt to explain away the Fuller-friendly response pattern, thereby saddling the view with the previous problem, that of modest support.

With the foregoing in mind, we developed three experiments in which we probe folk (Studies 1 and 2) and expert (Study 3) concepts of the law. Our studies aim to capture the levels of support that Fullerian principles garner while also examining two kinds of effects on judgments about the nature of law. These effects, of *construal level* (Trope and Liberman, 2010) *evaluation mode* (Hsee, Loewenstein, Blount, and

Bazerman, 1999), have already been observed in other areas of judgment and decision-making. Below, we briefly describe both effects and summarize evidence of their impact upon decision-making at large.

2.1 Construal level

The theory of construal level posits that mental representations (e.g., of a soccer player scoring a goal) can occur at different construal levels: Higher-level construal focuses on the abstract and functional properties (e.g., whether it was a winning goal, or a beautiful goal), while lower-level construal highlights the concrete, sensorimotor, and/or descriptive properties (e.g., whether it was a shot or a header, whether it had spin, etc.). Psychological distance is closely linked to construal level (Trope and Liberman, 2010) because events that are closer to us in some respect, whether temporally, spatially, or socially, are construed at lower levels. Distant events, by contrast, tend to be construed at higher levels.

Throughout our studies, we investigate whether intuitions about Fuller principles are susceptible to effects of construal level—in the contrast between (i) hypothetical (higher-level) versus actual (lower-level) laws in Studies 1 and 3, and (ii) between the essence of law (higher-level) and concrete instances of law (lower-level) in Study 2.

2.2 Evaluation mode

Judgments and decisions can be made in one of two evaluation modes (Hsee, Loewenstein, Blount, and Bazerman, 1999): *separate evaluation*, in which a single option or alternative is evaluated, or *joint evaluation*, in which various options are presented and evaluated at once and often by comparison to each other.

A wealth of studies has shown that our preferences and judgments can vary as a function of evaluation mode—perhaps because judgments in separate evaluation depend on more spontaneous impressions and easily evaluable features, while in joint evaluation, secondary characteristics that are harder to evaluate can be taken into account (see, e.g., Hsee, 1996).

In an oft-cited example, when asked *separately*, participants offered to pay more for a new dictionary with only 10,000 entries than for a dictionary with 20,000 entries and a torn cover. Then, when asked *jointly*, participants were willing to pay more for the dictionary with more entries. Thus, it is sometimes argued that joint evaluation provides the opportunity for spontaneous assessments—i.e., assigning more weight to the defective cover than to the number of entries—to be checked against subjects' own normative benchmarks—i.e., believing that one ought to value the number of entries more than the condition of the cover (Bazerman, Gino, Shu, and Tsay, 2011).

In Study 1, we examine whether the folk conception of law varies as a function of evaluation mode. In particular, we test whether the folk endorse the procedural natural lawyer's view—that laws necessarily observe Fullerian principles—more in separate or joint evaluation.

3. General Methods

Our studies were conducted on samples drawn from two populations: (1) United States adults ($N = 242$) with no specific training or knowledge of the law, and (2) bar association members ($N = 73$) with training and substantial experience in the legal profession. Complete study materials, data and scripts are available at https://osf.io/my2xe/.

3.1 Lay sample

242 participants (39% women; Age: $Q_1 = 27$, $Mdn = 31$, $Q_3 = 40$) were recruited from Amazon Mechanical Turk to take part in Studies 1 and 2. All participants were US residents with a 90% approval rate and were compensated for their participation (at \$7.25/hour, based on median completion time during pre-testing).

3.2 Law professionals

73 participants (56% women; Age: $Q_1 = 38$, $Mdn = 52$, $Q_3 = 63$) were contacted via state bar associations. All participants were members of bar associations, and most (87%) were lawyers. Median years of experience doing law-related work was 25 ($Q_1 =$ "10"; $Q_3 =$ "30 or more").

4. Study 1: Necessary or Actual? Fullerian Principles in Separate and Joint Evaluation

In our first study, we sought to determine the degree of support Fullerian principles enjoy among the folk. In particular, we sought to determine how likely the folk were to endorse these principles in the manner set forth by Fuller, as necessary conditions for something to count as a law. We also sought to determine how likely the folk were to endorse these principles, if understood as mere contingent truths. Finally, we also sought to explore the effect of evaluation mode.

In this and the subsequent studies, we test whether Fullerian principles enjoy endorsement at the 2:1 supermajority level. A case can be made that "widespread support" is satisfied at any level of support at or above a simple majority. For that reason, our choice of 2:1 may appear arbitrary. Several considerations recommend this level of support. A bare majority is consistent with rife disagreement. If, for instance, 50.1% of the folk endorsed Fullerian principles, it would seem premature and perhaps even misleading to claim that Fuller's theory comports with the folk conception of law. It may even be premature to posit a univocal folk conception of law in the face of such disagreement. At the other extreme, requiring unanimity seems unduly onerous and uncharitable to Fuller's view. If all but a small fraction of participants endorse Fullerian principles, it would be unreasonable to claim that Fuller's theory fails to track folk intuitions. With both simple majority and unanimity ruled out as reasonable options, both the 2:1 and the 3:1 levels recommend themselves. The 3:1 level looks particularly attractive because it seems to "split the difference" between simple majority and unanimity. However, because we predicted that Fullerian principles would not even garner support at the 2:1 level, we chose this level as opposed to the more demanding 3:1 level.

To continue about our predictions, we predicted that Fullerian principles would garner only modest support, falling below the 2:1 level, whether the principles were understood as necessary claims or claims about the actual world. This skeptical prediction is motivated by general skepticism that Fuller's theory reflects folk intuitions as well as some concern that there is a univocal folk conception of law to be tracked. We also predicted that the folk would be more likely to endorse Fullerian principles as true of the actual world than as true necessarily. Two reasons backed this prediction. First, since necessity entails actuality but not vice versa, the necessity claim is the more ambitious. Second, we expected that participants' own experience living in polities that observe the rule of law would dispose them to claim that actual legal systems often do respect Fullerian principles; however, we also expected participants to be familiar with political orders—historical, contemporary, and even fictional—with little respect for the rule of law, and this familiarity would dispose them to reject the idea that Fullerian principles are necessary truths.

4.1 Study 1a: Fullerian principles in separate evaluation

In this part of our first study, we ask one group of participants to evaluate Fullerian claims as actually true, and another group to evaluate whether they are necessarily true.

4.1.1 Procedure

Participants were randomly assigned to one of two conditions, Actual or Necessary. In the Actual condition, participants read:

In this survey, we will ask you eight questions regarding the law.

Meanwhile, in the Necessary condition, participants read:

Imagine that anthropologists discover a few previously unknown societies on Earth, referred to as the Faraway nations. Their inhabitants are Homo sapiens like us and, though their customs and traditions are unique, they have government and laws much like the rest of nations on Earth. In this survey, we are interested in what you suppose Faraway nations are like. Specifically, we will ask you eight questions about their laws.

Next, participants were shown pairs of statements for each Fullerian principle and were asked to endorse one statement from each of the eight pairs. In each pair, one statement was a Fullerian principle, phrased either as an empirical claim ("The law as enforced does not differ much from the law as formally announced") or as a necessary claim ("The law as enforced [in Faraway nations] could not differ much from the law as formally announced"). The other statement in the pair was the negation of the Fullerian principle.

4.1.2 Results

There was substantial variation in endorsement by principle: Some principles, like the publicity principle and the possibility principle, garnered endorsement by a supermajority; others, such as the consistency principle, fell even below a simple majority view (see Figure 1.1 and Table 1.1).

To generate an overall measure of support for Fullerian principles, we first averaged participants' responses across all eight principles: Agreement

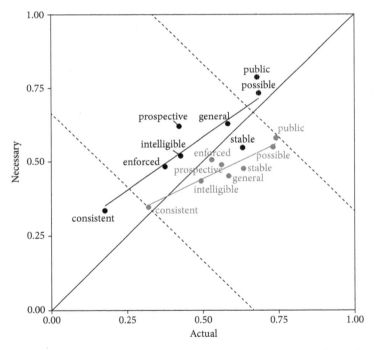

Figure 1.1 Actuality (x-axis) and necessity (y-axis) judgments for each Fuller principle under separate (black) and joint (gray) evaluation.

Note: The solid diagonal line highlights the judgment reversal between conditions. The diagonal dashed lines correspond to supermajority disbelief (1:2) and belief (2:1) averaging across judgment types.

Table 1.1 Endorsement of Fuller principles (in descending order) and effects (odds ratio and 95% confidence interval) of statement modality, evaluation mode, and their interaction derived from mixed-effects logistic regression models on agreement.

	Weighted prop.	Model 1		Model 2
		Necessity	Joint Evaluation	Necessity × Joint Evaluation
Publicity	0.70	0.89	0.71	0.28 **
	[0.65, 0.75]	[0.56, 1.43]	[0.44, 1.14]	[0.11, 0.73]
Possibility	0.68	0.70	0.71	0.30 *
	[0.63, 0.73]	[0.42, 1.18]	[0.42, 1.20]	[0.11, 0.88]
Stability	0.57	0.57 *	0.85	0.71
	[0.52, 0.63]	[0.34, 0.94]	[0.51, 1.42]	[0.27, 1.87]
Generality	0.57	0.81	0.69	0.46
	[0.52, 0.63]	[0.51, 1.30]	[0.43, 1.10]	[0.18, 1.18]
Prospectivity	0.53	1.29	1.01	0.33 *
	[0.48, 0.59]	[0.83, 1.99]	[0.66, 1.57]	[0.13, 0.82]
Enforcement	0.49	1.18	1.43	0.59
	[0.43, 0.54]	[0.77, 1.82]	[0.93, 2.21]	[0.25, 1.40]
Intelligibility	0.46	1.06	0.96	0.53
	[0.41, 0.52]	[0.68, 1.65]	[0.61, 1.65]	[0.22, 1.31]
Consistency	0.29	1.56 #	1.46	0.49
	[0.24, 0.34]	[0.96, 2.52]	[0.90, 2.35]	[0.18, 1.30]
Model 1:		0.87	0.94	–
Main effects only		[0.73, 1.05]	[0.74, 1.19]	
Model 2:		1.60 **	1.45 *	0.42 **
+ Necessity × Joint interaction		[1.26, 2.04]	[1.05, 2.01]	[0.28, 0.62]

Note: #: $p < 0.10$, *: $p < 0.05$, **: $p < 0.005$.

with Fullerian views ranged between 46% and 54% in the Actual condition ($M = 0.50$, $SD = 0.21$), and between 52% and 64% in the Necessary condition ($M = 0.58$, $SD = 0.27$). One-sample t-tests against the 2:1 supermajority level revealed that support for Fuller principles fell short of a supermajority in both conditions: Actual $t(82) = 7.16$, $p <0.001$; Necessary $t(80) = 2.81$, $p = 0.006$.

Surprisingly, agreement with Fuller principles appeared to be *higher* in the Necessary than in the Actual condition—opposite to our original prediction. A mixed-effects logistic regression confirmed this result: We entered condition as a fixed effect, and participant and principle as random effects, while allowing the slope of condition to vary across principles. The model revealed a significant effect of condition, $OR = 1.55$, 95% CI [1.04, 2.34], $t = 2.21$, $p = 0.027$. In other words, participants were more likely to believe that Fuller properties are necessary for law (when thinking about hypothetical legal systems) than that they are actual properties of laws.

It is unclear why a majority of participants treated Fullerian principles as necessarily true with regard to hypothetical laws, but not empirically true of the laws they know. First, it could be that participants do not fully understand necessity and possibility ($\Diamond A \rightarrow \sim\Box \sim A$). Alternatively, by appealing to hypothetical laws in one condition and known laws in another, perhaps we inadvertently asked participants to report on distinct concepts (Knobe, Prasada, and Newman, 2013).

If, however, participants view these distinct intuitions as conflicting or inconsistent, then the difference in participants' judgments regarding actual versus hypothetical laws ought to vanish (or even reverse) under joint evaluation—a hypothesis we pursue in Study 1b.

4.2 Study 1b: Joint evaluation

In this second part of the study, we asked a single group of participants to assess whether Fullerian principles actually hold, and whether they hold necessarily. We predicted that the surprising result we obtained in Study 1a would dissipate when participants make both judgments at once. Joint evaluation, we surmised, would help participants to spot the seeming inconsistency in claiming that laws obey Fullerian principles by necessity though many laws fail to do so in practice.

4.2.1 Procedure
Participants were asked to make both types of judgments (actuality and necessity) regarding each Fuller principle. A short introduction to the study made this clear.

4.2.2 Results

Agreement with Fuller principles ranged between 53% and 63% in the Actual condition ($M = 0.58$, $SD = 0.24$), and between 42% and 54% in the Necessary condition ($M = 0.48$, $SD = 0.26$), once again significantly below supermajority support in one-sample t-tests: Actual $t(77) = 3.18$, $p = 0.002$; Necessary $t(77) = 6.33$, $p < 0.001$.

Indeed, prompting participants to evaluate Fuller principles simultaneously as empirical and necessary claims reversed the distinction we saw under separate evaluation. In a mixed-effects model, the effect of condition was highly significant, $OR = 0.64$, 95% CI [0.46, 0.89], $z = 3.00$, $p = 0.003$. This time, laws were seen as observing Fullerian principles de facto (by a simple majority), but not necessarily in a hypothetical legal system—as we originally predicted.

Table 1.1 summarizes Fuller principles by endorsement and compares the results of Studies 1a and 1b, through additive (Model 1) and interactive (Model 2) models with evaluation mode and statement modality as fixed effects. The Necessity × Joint Evaluation interaction represents the judgment reversal across conditions: Overall, participants were more likely to treat Fuller principles as necessarily (but not actually) true when judged in isolation, and as actually (but not necessarily) true when making both judgments at once.

5. Study 2: The Abstract Essence versus Concrete Instances of Law

The previous study focused on attitudes toward Fullerian principles when stated in abstract terms. Next, we introduce concrete violations of Fullerian principles and ask participants to assess whether they constitute law. By comparing participants' endorsement of abstract principles to their assessments of concrete laws, we aim to conceptually replicate the effect of construal level on Fullerian intuitions.

We predicted that the folk would be more likely to endorse Fullerian principles when the principles are stated abstractly than when grappling with the principles in concrete situations. This prediction is undergirded by the thought, expressed by others (e.g. Hart, 1965), that Fuller's principles express reasonable rules-of-thumb to make legislating rational and efficient. As such, it may be hard—when thinking abstractly—to imagine how one would engage in lawmaking in any other way. However, if one is invited to consider concrete cases of lawmaking that run afoul of the Fullerian principles, this difficulty in imagining dissipates, which should lead to lower rates of endorsement.

Finally, we also investigate whether judgments on either task, the concrete or the abstract, are impacted by the order in which the tasks are presented. In our opening study, we found evidence that participants treated their judgments at different construal levels as contradictory. Specifically, they appeared to 'correct' their spontaneous Fullerian intuition—that hypothetical laws necessarily observe Fuller principles—when prompted to consider also whether actual laws in fact observe them. Analogously, we might expect that beliefs about the essence of law, stated in abstract terms, might depend on whether participants previously considered specific violations of Fuller principles (i.e., an effect of order on judgments in the abstract condition).

5.1   Procedure

In a 2 (construal: *abstract, concrete*) × 2 (order: *abstract-first, concrete-first*) mixed factorial design, 104 participants were randomly assigned to one of two orders. Every participant completed two tasks—an abstract task and a concrete task—in a counterbalanced order across participants.

In the abstract section, participants were asked whether laws 'must' observe a given Fuller principle *P* or if they 'can' violate *P*, for example:

Can there be laws that contradict one another or must laws be consistent?

The dependent measure in the abstract condition was participants' endorsement of one of two statements:

There can be laws that contradict one another in a single jurisdiction (0: non-Fullerian),

or

There must not be any laws that contradict other laws in a single jurisdiction (1: Fullerian).

In the concrete section, participants read about a city ordinance, policy proposal, or bill that violated a certain Fuller principle *P* and were asked whether it was 'truly a law' or not. For example:

In a hypothetical country, a state legislature passes two bills that the governor eagerly signs. The first bill is a speed limit bill. It says that driving along Highway 1 at speeds over 80 kilometers per hour is forbidden and that anyone found driving at speeds over 80 kilometers per hour on Highway 1 will be ticketed.

The second bill is a speed minimum bill. It says that driving along Highway 1 at speeds under 85 kilometers per hour is forbidden and that anyone found driving at speeds under 85 kilometers per hour on Highway 1 will be ticketed. As a result of the two bills, many tickets are issued and the state revenues increase dramatically.

In the above example, we then asked *"Are these two bills truly laws?"* Fullerian judgments (that they are *not* laws) were coded as *1*s, while non-Fullerian judgments that they are laws despite violating the consistency principle were coded as *0*s.

5.2   Results

As predicted, we observed an effect of construal level, $OR = 7.51$, 95% CI [3.75, 15.03], $z = 5.69$, $p < 0.001$. Participants were much more likely to endorse Fuller principles in the abstract. When stated abstractly, participants endorsed Fullerian principles approximately 67%, 95% CI [64%, 69%] of the time. When assessing concrete violations of Fuller principles, participants largely reported that they were truly laws nonetheless, with only 21%, 95% CI [19%, 24%] reporting Fullerian judgments.

Unexpectedly, there were no effects of order in either condition, $|z| < 1$, ps > 0.50. Exposure to violations of Fuller principles did not affect beliefs about the inner morality of law, and reflection on the essence of law in the abstract did not promote Fullerian reactions to concrete violations of procedural principles.

6. Study 3: The Expertise Defense

So far we have assessed views about the inner morality of law in a sample of participants who lack technical knowledge of the law. In reaction to past folk psychological evidence, philosophers have sometimes argued against drawing any major conclusions from laypeople's use of technical concepts (Sosa, 2007). On this view, evidence of *experts'* beliefs is needed to understand whether law truly observes Fuller's inner morality of law. In Study 3, we examine whether professionals with legal training and experience reveal distinct intuitions about the nature of law.

6.1   Procedure

For this study, lawyers were contacted through their bar association mailing lists and assigned to one of two conditions, Actual or Hypothetical, as in Study 1a. The materials were identical to Study 1a, except we added specific questions about participants' experience in the legal profession to the demographic information section.

6.2   Results

Averaging across principles, overall agreement with Fullerian views ranged between 39% and 54% in the Actual condition ($M = 0.47$, $SD = 0.22$), and between 57% and 78% in the Necessary condition ($M = 0.67$, $SD = 0.32$). Like lay participants, legal professionals did not tend to think that actual laws observe Fuller principles at the 2:1 supermajority level, Actual, $t(34) = 5.26$, $p <0.001$. However, they did tend to judge that hypothetical legal systems would necessarily observe Fuller principles at approximately a 2:1 ratio, $t(37) = -0.08$, $p = 0.93$.

Replicating the results of Study 1a, law professionals tended to demonstrate the effect of construal level observed in laypeople, $OR = 4.05$, 95% CI [1.15, 15.08], $z = 2.29$, $p = 0.022$. When thinking about hypothetical legal systems, Fuller principles were viewed as necessary properties although they were not viewed as properties of actual law.

We then compared the responses of legal professionals to those of lay participants. No simple effects of expertise emerged in either modality: Professionals were no more likely to judge that Fuller principles are actually observed, $OR = 0.81$, 95% CI [0.33, 1.97], $z = -0.51$, $p = 0.61$, or that they are necessarily observed by hypothetical legal systems, $OR = 1.86$, 95% CI [0.84, 4.28], $z = 1.57$, $p = 0.12$.

Much like lay respondents, experienced lawyers exhibited the core intuition that Fuller's procedural principles are necessary for law, while at the same time believing that laws in practice fail to observe them.

7. General Discussion

In three studies, we found limited support for Fuller's (1969) procedural natural law theory. As we noted at the outset, in the best case for Fuller, we would see widespread and reliable folk endorsement for his principles. This is not what we see.

First we consider the *widespread* front. Though some individual principles were widely endorsed by the folk, others were not, and as a set, the inner morality of law did not garner 2:1 supermajority level support from the folk. Insofar as Fuller aimed to capture 'our' concept of law, his theory misses the mark at least in part. Because many of his principles garner a slim majority support (when construed the right way), worries about the presumption against error theories probably do not obtain. Thus, if Fuller's venture is what we called descriptive analysis, he may be largely safe. However, as some of his principles did not gain supermajority level support (particularly the consistency principle which has 2:1 supermajority level opposition), perhaps that needs to be modified.

There are larger problems on the *reliability* front. In conjunction, Studies 1a and 1b show that participants' views about Fullerian principles shift depending on the conditions in which they are evaluated. Instability of this kind is problematic for Fuller, because, as we argued above, when there are two conflicting reports of the level of endorsement, Fuller's defenders are now saddled with data to explain away. This general problem looks particularly worrying given the precise way that results turned out, since non-Fullerian reactions look like they emerge in the epistemically preferable circumstance, i.e., joint evaluation in Study 1b. In joint evaluation, as opposed to separate evaluation, arguably one's views are more likely to reflect one's more settled opinion. Study 2 looks similar, for it shows that when we vary construal levels from high to low, participants are more likely to doubt Fullerian principles. Again, Fuller is saddled with something to explain away; and again, there is room to argue that the non-Fullerian response pattern is formed in the more epistemically ideal setting. Such an argument might begin by noting that our intuitions are sharpest when considering more everyday things.

On closer inspection, our experiments also point toward effects of construal level on the propensity toward Fullerian views. When asked to reason about the law at a higher construal level, a majority of respondents demonstrated Fullerian intuitions. This was true when participants reasoned about hypothetical legal systems instead of actual legal systems (Studies 1 and 3), and when they described the abstract essence of law instead of concrete instances of law (Study 2).

Taken together, the evidence we presented casts doubt upon the notion that we have a stable and univocal concept of law. Rather, our evidence suggests that natural law and positivist concepts of law are supported by thinking at different levels of construal. If so, the philosophical debate concerning the role of morality in law may in part arise from the psychological capacity to oscillate between two conflicting concepts of law (see also Struchiner, Hannikainen, and Almeida, ms.).

Our results also speak to two common objections levied against folk psychological evidence on philosophical issues: the *expertise* defense and the *reflection* defense.

Regarding the former, did experienced legal professionals reveal different intuitions? They did not; legal professionals were also divided with regard to the truth of Fuller principles and susceptible to the effect of construal level. If anything, under separate evaluation, legal professionals were somewhat *more* likely to treat Fuller principles as necessary properties of hypothetical laws despite recognizing that the principles are flouted by actual legal systems. One may wish to push back at this point by contending that legal professionals are not the relevant sort of experts for the expertise defense. On this refurbished version of the expertise defense, legal philosophers, not lawyers, are the true experts. We do not and need not deny that our attack on the expertise defense would be *better* if we also surveyed legal philosophers. Nevertheless, trained lawyers do not have untutored minds about the law, such that one can just dismiss their intuitions. These professionals have expertise vis-à-vis the folk regarding a wide range of norms that purport to be law, and frankly, many trained lawyers have expertise vis-à-vis legal philosophers.

Regarding the reflection defense, did conditions favoring more careful reflection influence beliefs about the inner morality of law? Indeed, our evidence indicated that, when prompted to resolve the tension between their conflicting intuitions, individuals were more likely to conclude that Fuller principles are contingent, not necessary, properties of law.

However, we must draw attention to important limitations of our studies. First, our sample of legal professionals was smaller than one would hope. As a consequence, our claims regarding the expert concept of law should be treated as provisional and subject to confirmation in future research. Second, we did not succeed in eliciting a distinction between necessary and contingent truth overall, which may somewhat compromise our conclusions regarding the modality of Fuller principles.

We close by re-emphasizing the broad ambition of this chapter. As the article actually proceeded, it was largely a piece which offered new reasons to doubt Fuller's procedural natural law theory. As such, one might be led to believe mistakenly that the interest of this chapter lies solely in point-scoring for particular sides in a narrow debate. One of our broader ambitions was to demonstrate that, by using empirical methods, we can contribute to core debates in jurisprudence. Thus, this work hopes to make a significant methodological point about jurisprudence, that experimental methods are viable. We also hope that this chapter provides a blueprint to others (to revise and improve!) on gathering information about folk intuitions about the nature of law. At present, little such evidence is available (but see, e.g., Tobia, 2018; MacLeod, 2019). Thus, this venture and others it inspires will be helpful to many philosophers.

To see this, we mention just three groups that stand to benefit from more experimental jurisprudence projects. There are philosophers of law engaged in conceptual analysis of law (e.g., Raz, 2009); for them, folk intuitions are the very thing they aim to discover. Experimental jurisprudence will provide more reliable access to the truths they seek. Other philosophers contend that we have no shared concept of law (e.g., L. Murphy, 2005); for them, access to good data about folk intuitions could help to decide that matter. Our data might be suggestive on this front, but much more evidence is needed. Still other philosophers argue that our task as philosophers of law should include (or even wholly comprise) advocating that people accept particular conceptions of law for practical reasons (L. Murphy, 2005; Stoljar, 2012; Donelson, in press); for them, data about which views already have currency might influence the views that these philosophers recommend. These are just some of the theorists who stand to gain from more of these projects. We can only hope that others will continue in our stead and that this will yield a new, experimental jurisprudence.

Acknowledgements

We thank Guilherme Almeida, Joshua Knobe, Noel Struchiner, Dietmar von der Pfordten, and three anonymous reviewers for feedback on earlier versions of this chapter. We also thank Mihailis Dimantis for the invitation to present our work in his experimental jurisprudence seminar at the University of Iowa College of Law and participants at the New Frontiers of Experimental Jurisprudence conference, held at the University of Chicago Law School. Raff Donelson's work on the project was supported by an LSU Manship Summer Research Grant.

References

Aquinas, T. (1994). *The Treatise on Law*. Ed. R. J. Henle. Notre Dame: University of Notre Dame Press.

Austin, J. (1998). *The Province of Jurisprudence Determined*. Indianapolis: Hackett.

Bazerman, M. H., Gino, F., Shu, L. L., and Tsay, C. J. (2011). Joint evaluation as a real-world tool for managing emotional assessments of morality. *Emotion Review*, 3(3), 290–2.

D'Amato, A. (1981). Lon Fuller and substantive natural law. *American Journal of Jurisprudence*, 26(1), 202–18.

Donelson, R. (in press). Describing law. *Canadian Journal of Law and Jurisprudence*.

Dworkin, Ronald (1986). *Law's Empire*. Cambridge, MA: Harvard University Press.

Finnis, J. (1980). *Natural Law and Natural Rights*. Oxford: Oxford University Press.

Frances, B. (2013). Philosophical renegades. In *The Epistemology of Disagreement: New Essays*, 121–66. Eds. Jennifer Lackey and David Christensen. Oxford: Oxford University Press.

Fuller, L. L. (1969). *The Morality of Law*, rev. edn. New Haven: Yale University Press.

Hart, H. L. A. (1965). Review of *The Morality of Law*. *Harvard Law Review*, 78(6), 1281–96.

Hart, H. L. A. (1994). *The Concept of Law*, 2nd edn. Eds. Penelope A. Bulloch and Joseph Raz. Oxford: Oxford University Press.

Haslanger, S. (2012a [1999]). What knowledge is and what it ought to be: Feminist values and normative epistemology. In *Resisting Reality*, 341–64. Oxford: Oxford University Press.

Haslanger, S. (2012b [2005]). What are we talking about? The semantics and politics of social kinds. In *Resisting Reality*, 365–80. Oxford: Oxford University Press.

Hsee, C. K. (1996). The evaluability hypothesis: An explanation for preference reversals between joint and separate evaluations of alternatives. *Organizational Behavior and Human Decision Processes*, 67(3), 247–57.

Hsee, C. K., Loewenstein, G. F., Blount, S., and Bazerman, M. H. (1999). Preference reversals between joint and separate evaluations of options: A review and theoretical analysis. *Psychological Bulletin*, 125(5), 576.

Jackson, F. (1998). *From Metaphysics to Ethics: A Defence of Conceptual Analysis*. Oxford: Oxford University Press.

Kelsen, H. (1967). *Pure Theory of Law*. Trans. M. Knight. Berkeley: University of California Press.

King, M. L. (1986 [1963]). Letter from Birmingham City Jail. In *A Testament of Hope*, 289–302. Ed. James M. Washington. New York: Harper & Row.

Knobe, J., Prasada, S., and Newman, G. E. (2013). Dual character concepts and the normative dimension of conceptual representation. *Cognition*, 127(2), 242–57.

MacLeod, J. (2019). Ordinary causation: A study in experimental statutory interpretation. *Indiana Law Journal*, 94(3), 957–1029.

Murphy, C. (2005). Lon Fuller and the moral value of the rule of law. *Law and Philosophy* 24, 239–62.

Murphy, L. (2005). Concepts of law. *Australian Journal of Legal Philosophy*, 30(1), 1–19.

Murphy, M. (2011). The explanatory role of the weak natural law thesis. In *Philosophical Foundations of the Nature of Law*, 3–21. Eds. Wil Waluchow and Stefan Sciaraffa. Oxford: Oxford University Press.

Priel, D. (2013). Is there one right answer to the question of the nature of law? In *Philosophical Foundations of the Nature of Law*, 322–50. Eds. Wil Waluchow and Stefan Sciaraffa. Oxford: Oxford University Press.

Raz, J. (2009 [2004]). Can there be a theory of law? In *Between Authority and Interpretation*, 17–46. Oxford: Oxford University Press.

Shapiro, S. J. (2011). *Legality*. Cambridge, MA: Harvard University Press.

Sosa, E. (2007). Experimental philosophy and philosophical intuition. *Philosophical Studies*, 132(1), 99–107.

Stoljar, N. (2012). In praise of wishful thinking: A critique of descriptive/explanatory theories of law. *Problema: Anuario de Filosofía y Teoría del Derecho*, 6, 51–79.

Struchiner, N., Hannikainen, I. R., and Almeida, G. (ms.) An experimental guide to vehicles in the park.

Tobia, K. (2018). How people judge what is reasonable. *Alabama Law Review*, 70, 293–359.

Trope, Y., and Liberman, N. (2010). Construal-level theory of psychological distance. *Psychological Review*, 117(2), 440–63.

Waluchow, W. J. (1994). *Inclusive Legal Positivism*. Oxford: Clarendon Press.

Winston, K. (2005). The internal morality of Chinese legalism. *Singapore Journal of Legal Studies*, December, 313–47.

Wright, C. (1994). Response to Jackson. *Philosophical Books*, 35(3), 169–75.

2

Can Real Social Epistemic Networks Deliver the Wisdom of Crowds?

Emily Sullivan
Eindhoven University of Technology

Max Sondag
Eindhoven University of Technology

Ignaz Rutter
University of Passau

Wouter Meulemans
Eindhoven University of Technology

Scott Cunningham
Delft University of Technology

Bettina Speckmann
Eindhoven University of Technology

Mark Alfano
Delft University of Technology and Australian Catholic University

1. Introduction

One of the central ways people gain knowledge is through the testimony of others. Despite this, the epistemology of testimony has made modest progress in addressing its inherently social components. The paradigm case of testimony in the philosophical literature consists of the transmission of

Emily Sullivan, Max Sondag, Ignaz Rutter, Wouter Meulemans, Scott Cunningham, Bettina Speckmann, and Mark Alfano, *Can Real Social Epistemic Networks Deliver the Wisdom of Crowds?* In: *Oxford Studies in Experimental Philosophy.* Edited by: Tania Lombrozo, Joshua Knobe, and Shaun Nichols, Oxford University Press (2020). © Emily Sullivan, Max Sondag, Ignaz Rutter, Wouter Meulemans, Scott Cunningham, Bettina Speckmann, and Mark Alfano. DOI: 10.1093/oso/9780198852407.003.0003 knowledge from *exactly one* person to *exactly one* other person, neglecting proximal and (even more so) distal social sources of knowledge. Only recently have philosophers moved beyond the hearer–speaker dyad. For example, in epistemology some have considered what it means for *groups* to testify (Tollefsen 2007; Lackey 2014, 2018). In the philosophy of science, others have started to explore which network structures are conducive to sharing knowledge within ideal communities of scientific researchers (Zollman 2007, 2010; Holman and Bruner 2015; Rosenstock et al. 2017). Still lacking is an evaluation of testimonial networks consisting of both experts and non-experts in non-ideal settings. In philosophy, Coady (1992) briefly considers the influence of network structure on the transmission of historical knowledge. However, he does not identify formal network features or structures that are likely to produce epistemic goods and avoid epistemic ills. In sociology, Senturk (2005) addresses the structure of the *hadith* transmission network from Muhammad's contemporaries to subsequent generations; this is arguably the longest extant intergenerational testimonial network of its sort, spanning 610 CE to 1505 CE. Senturk shows that participants in this network, known as *huffaz* (roughly "ones who memorize and protect" *ahadith*), aimed to learn *ahadith* from other *huffaz* with the shortest paths back to the prophet and his companions. In the terminology we use below, this means that the *huffaz* saw themselves as playing the role of epistemic conduits, and that they attempted to minimize the length of epistemic geodesics in the *hadith* transmission network. Minimizing geodesics is an epistemic strategy that can be formally modelled, but do modern advances suggest more epistemically promising strategies? In this chapter, we seek to make progress on this front. In particular, we are interested in identifying good sources and receivers of information based on the surrounding network structures of their epistemic community.

Consider a typical search engine. After a user enters a query, a series of links to presumed answers to the query are ranked and displayed to the user. There are several underlying mechanisms that give rise to the resulting list. Some of these mechanisms are inherently networked and constitute a link-based ranking. It is the interconnection among the links that helps determine which ones are displayed first. PageRank, developed by one of Google's founders, is one of these networked mechanisms (Brin and Page 1998). Importantly, one of the motivations behind PageRank is its epistemic benefits. The underlying assumption is that groups of individuals can be more reliable and converge on true answers more so than individuals acting in isolation. Following Masterton et al. (2016), we refer to this assumption as the *wisdom-of-crowds hypothesis*.[1] One of the distinguishing features of PageRank and algorithms like it is that, instead of determining rank solely based on the number of incoming links, it accounts for the *importance* of those links. For example, if a well-connected news source links to a particular webpage, that link is given higher weight than a link to the same webpage from an obscure blog. Such a ranking system has the potential to track epistemic importance. In fact, Masterton et al. (2016) and Masterton and Olsson (2017) have shown that PageRank can deliver epistemic benefits and justify a wisdom-of-crowds thesis, albeit in artificial or ideal cases.

There are many similarities between a large testimonial network and a network of webpages. Like webpages, individuals share novel information. Individuals also decide to share information with others by posting or linking to it. Thus, we can ask whether ranking individuals based on formal properties of their information-sharing network is truth-tracking or justifies a wisdom-of-crowds thesis of testimony. More precisely, can PageRank identify good sources of information and well-informed receivers of information in a testimonial network?

In order to shed light on this question and test the related wisdom-of-crowds hypothesis, we conducted two case studies involving non-ideal epistemic communities. Both studies involve discussions of vaccine safety on Twitter. The results of these studies indicate that, in non-ideal cases, PageRank is sufficient neither for identifying individuals who are good sources of information nor for identifying individuals who are likely to be well-informed receivers. We conclude by arguing that, in testimonial networks, considerations of source independence and source diversity are needed to give a fuller picture of the network structures conducive to knowledge transmission.

In what follows, we first expound on the nature of networks, especially how they can help answer epistemological questions by harnessing the wisdom of crowds. In Sections 3 and 4 we describe our two case

---

[1] Wisdom-of-crowds hypotheses are not unique to the web. They also underlie arguments for the epistemic value of democracy (List and Goodin 2001), the epistemic value of juries (Hedden 2017), and crowd wisdom more generally (Surowiecki 2004).

studies. We end with a discussion of our results and point to areas of future research for both philosophers and graph theorists.

2. Networks, Epistemology, and PageRank

A network or graph is an abstract mathematical object. The simplest networks represent nothing beyond the bare presence of nodes and whether, for each pair of nodes, there exists a connection between them. Connections between nodes can be directed or undirected. In an undirected network the connections between the nodes (edges) represent a bidirectional relationship. A network of connected cities is an example of an undirected network: the cities are the nodes and the highways or interstates are the edges that connect them. In a *directed* network, by contrast, each edge is unidirectional. A network showing the flow of money to politicians from campaign funders is an example of a directed network. Individual politicians and campaign contributors are the nodes, and the flow of money is represented by directed edges connecting the nodes. In this toy example, the direction of the edges is always *from* the campaign contributors *to* the politicians. Moreover, edges can be *weighted*. The weight of an edge indicates the varying strength of an edge. In a campaign contributions network, edge weights could represent how much money each contributor gives to a particular politician. The research question and the target phenomenon dictate how modelers determine which network parameters, such as edge weights and directions, to use.

As mentioned above, in this chapter we are interested in identifying good sources and receivers of information based on the surrounding structures of their testimonial network. In order to successfully model such a testimonial community we need to get clear on what the appropriate network structure is for our target phenomenon. In the remainder of this section, we discuss important testimonial concepts (2.1), their operationalization in a network (2.2), and the wisdom-of-crowds hypothesis regarding how to rank individuals within a network (2.3).[2] In what follows, "testimonial community" refers to the target phenomenon and "testimonial network" refers to the network-model of the community.

---

[2] Broadly, our research follows the workflow outlined in Alfano and Higgins (2019).

2.1 Testimonial concepts

In a community, an epistemic agent can play one or more roles. They can be a primary *source* of knowledge for others.[3] Alternatively, they can *receive* knowledge from others. Additionally, they can act as a *conduit* who passes along knowledge from a primary source (or another conduit) to a receiver (or another conduit). An agent is a powerful epistemic source if their messages are likely to be transmitted to others in the network. Likewise, an agent is a well-positioned receiver if messages in the network are likely to be transmitted to them. And an agent is a powerful conduit if they have the ability to control whether and which messages originated by others propagate through the network. In this chapter, we focus primarily on sources and receivers, leaving conduits to future research.

In each case of testimonial exchange, there is a single *testifies-to* relation that originates from the source to the receiver. The testifies-to relation between one source and one receiver has been explored in great depth in social epistemology. Considerations of trust, reliability, social power, and expertise are all present in a single case of testimony (Fricker 2007; Medina 2013). However, most discussions focus on whether one isolated source is trustworthy, reliable, or has power over the receiver, and how these considerations reflect on epistemic norms or virtues. Importantly, there are macro-level aspects to testimonial trust, power, and source reliability that are sure to be ignored, if we focus only on *one* source and *one* receiver. Consider, for example, epistemic power. A source of information can have great epistemic power not only in virtue of her social identity (i.e., occupying a role society deems valuable or important) but also simply in virtue of her *epistemic reach*: how many individuals in the community will or are likely to receive her testimony first-, second-, or third-hand. This latter sense of epistemic power captures how chains of information—*epistemic paths*—propagate through the community. Such paths of testimony can be short, as in the dyadic case of a single source transmitting to a single receiver. They can also be

---

[3] We begin by conceptualizing the research question and all variables involved because inadequate, imprecise, and ambiguous conceptualization is arguably one of the root causes of the replication crisis currently racking psychology (Lurquin and Miyake 2017).

indefinitely long, as when a source transmits through a string of conduits who together manage to convey the information to a receiver.

How much epistemic reach certain sources have is no doubt relevant to the epistemic norms and virtues surrounding testimonial knowledge. For instance, it seems plausible that someone with great reach should be more cautious in what they say, compared to someone with very limited reach. Likewise, it seems plausible that part of what it takes to embody the virtue of intellectual humility is to be disposed to notice gaps in one's testimonial network and make efforts to fill them, when those gaps are sufficiently large and important enough.

Questions of epistemic power go beyond epistemic sources. Epistemic receivers could also be well placed in a very direct way, if they receive testimony from a very large number of sources. However, most real epistemic communities are much sparser. In such communities, an agent might be a well-placed receiver, not due to a large number of sources, but simply in virtue of the fact that a large number of messages in the community eventually make their way to her—sometimes through short epistemic paths and sometimes through much longer ones.

These points, about the relation between epistemic power, on the one hand, and the source and receiver roles, on the other hand, hold *mutatis mutandis* for other epistemic phenomena, such as trust and reliability.[4] Thus, there are macro-level influences that are operative in large-scale epistemic communities that are not operative in a dyadic community. Attending to these phenomena, using the concepts and distinctions discussed here, makes it possible and worthwhile to explore what Alfano (2016) calls the *topology* of communities of epistemic trust, both from a normative and from a descriptive point of view.

In order to explore these macro-level dimensions of the testifies-to relation, it is paramount to investigate larger, more structured epistemic communities than have typically been studied by social epistemologists. Hence, in this chapter we model a non-ideal epistemic community. Such a model will help to inform us how we should think about macro-level aspects of epistemic trust and power, as well as what makes for a good source or receiver of information in an interconnected epistemic community.

---

[4] See Alfano and Huijts (forthcoming) for a discussion on how trust manifests in non-dyadic epistemic networks.

2.2 Testimonial communities as directed networks

As discussed above, the designation of nodes, edges, edge weights, and network directedness are central determinations to make when modeling a target phenomenon, such as an epistemic community, as a network.[5] In our testimonial network the nodes represent epistemic sources and receivers of testimony. The edges represent the *testifies-to* relation discussed above. However, in order to focus on the macro-level structural influences of testimonial networks we abstract away any details of trust or weighted reliability in the testifies-to relation. Thus, the weight of edges simply represents the number of messages from a source to a receiver. By first analyzing these simple structural relations, we will then be able to more clearly see how trust and reliability could function within macro-level structures.

Next, we need to determine whether a testimonial epistemic community is best modeled as a directed or undirected network. The information-sharing network models deployed in the philosophy of science are largely undirected models (Zollman 2007, 2010; Holman and Bruner 2015; Rosenstock et al. 2017). The use case for these models is how information is shared within a scientific community and how groups of researchers converge on a single plan of action, such as prescribing one medication over another. The acting assumption in these models is that testimonial exchanges are *symmetric*: agents jointly trade information with each other.[6] It is fair to say that in these models edges represent a testifies-*with* relation. For any pair of connected agents, each agent provides information to, and receives information from, the other. In contrast, if we consider a testimonial exchange between an expert and a non-expert, symmetry can no longer be presumed. In many cases, the non-expert does not offer testimony in exchange with the expert; the non-expert is merely a receiver of testimony. Thus, when modeling

---

[5] This is not meant to be an exhaustive list. For example, dynamic network models that involve agent-based simulation include node parameters that simulate agent decisions that update throughout the simulated run. For an information sharing example, see Zollman (2007, 2010), Holman and Bruner (2015), and Rosenstock et al. (2017).

[6] Holman and Bruner (2015) deploy a model where the testifying relationship is not entirely symmetric. In their agent-based model they simulate that researchers tend to rely on and trust some sources more than others. However, they model this through the dynamics of the agent-based system on how nodes update, not through introducing directed edges.

testimonial networks outside of an idealized community of near-peer researchers, where agents have different epistemic goals and projects, it is important to take into account the directional nature of the testifies-*to* relation. That said, the same individual can take on the source role as well as the receiver role in the larger community. However, each testifies-to relation remains an asymmetrical case of sharing information *to* someone who is presumed to lack information, and where the receiver is not presumed to give information back in response.

2.3   (Page)Ranking sources and receivers

Our main goal in this chapter is not simply to model a real epistemic community, but to explore how we can identify which individuals in the network are good sources of information by virtue of the surrounding network that links to (or shares) that information, and which individuals in the network are well informed by virtue of their position and the positions of their sources. PageRank offers a plausible approach.

Recall that PageRank was implemented in web-search technologies to help identify sources that are likely to have epistemic importance. Roughly, a webpage's PageRank is the probability that someone randomly clicking through webpages will end up visiting that page (Brin and Page 1998). The ranking is not based solely on the number of pages that link to it, but also includes the importance of the pages that link to it. Pages with several links "pass on" some of the value of those links to the pages they link to. One perhaps-counterintuitive result of this approach is that some pages with considerably fewer incoming links can be ranked higher than a page with far more links. The rationale is that if important webpages are linking to something, that in itself is an important indicator of the page's merit. For example, if *The New York Times* were to link to another source in its reporting, then that source may have a higher PageRank, even if it is a more obscure page. However, despite the page's obscurity, it does ground the *Times'* reporting, and thus the content of the page should seem to weigh heavier than the second-hand reporting from the *Times*. The same intuitions motivate testimonial exchanges. Sources of testimony that attract more trust are more likely sharing epistemically useful information, which is a strong though defeasible reason to give more weight to those sources. Thus, it seems that PageRank houses the theoretical tools not only to track epistemic importance on the web, but also to exploit the wisdom of crowds in testimonial networks (Masterton et al. 2016; Masterton and Olsson 2017).

Furthermore, there are practical benefits to applying link-based rankings to testimonial networks. Algorithms can be designed to increase the epistemic position of those in online testimonial communities, as they have in optimizing search queries. Thus, the time is ripe to ask whether PageRank actually lives up to its wisdom-of-crowds promise in non-ideal testimonial networks. In order to test this, we conducted two case studies consisting of real epistemic communities found on Twitter.

3. Study 1

In order to test the wisdom-of-crowds hypothesis in a non-ideal network, we needed to identify accessible data sources that we expect to contain a large number of epistemic agents acting as sources and receivers, potentially mediated by conduits. One of the largest social epistemic networks currently in existence is Twitter. Although the quality of discourse on this platform varies greatly, it provides a suitable source for exploring whether PageRank lives up to its promise of delivering the wisdom of crowds for real testimonial communities.

On the Twitter platform, users have the ability to compose new tweets of up to 280 characters; they also can see the tweets published by other users and can interact with these by "liking" them, retweeting them, or replying to them. The retweeting functionality, which is similar to functionalities on other platforms (e.g., "sharing" on Facebook) is especially interesting for our purposes. It enables a user to pass along content (and potentially whatever knowledge could be acquired from that content), making them a conduit. It also indicates (heuristically) that the person read the testimony and thought it was worth sharing. This suggests the testimony was a source of information for the retweeter, whether or not they ultimately accepted that testimony as true.

When user A gets retweeted by user B, that establishes a link *out* from A (and, by the same token, a link *in* to B). The number of links out from a given node is that node's out-degree; the number of links in to a given node is that node's in-degree. PageRankIn and PageRankOut are calculated using the PageRank algorithm (Brin and Page 1998) with $d = 0.85$ on the network of users and links, and the reverse of this network, respectively. We use *high PageRankOut* as a heuristic for identifying a good epistemic *source*; high PageRankOut indicates that the user's tweets tend to be retweeted to a wide audience. We use *high PageRankIn* as a heuristic for identifying well-placed epistemic *receivers*; high PageRankIn indicates that the user tends to retweet more messages, thus drawing on a wide number of sources. Table 2.1 shows the epistemic concepts to be modeled along with their operationalizations.

3.1 Data collection

We conducted a search query on the Twitter stream API that ran from March 5, 2017 to March 11, 2017. We explain how this is done below and provide our code in the Appendix. We were interested in seeing a discussion surrounding a controversial topic that would include information that varied along the dimensions of both quality and quantity. For this purpose, we chose to look at discussions of vaccine safety. We searched for tweets that used hashtags and text strings, such as #vaxxed, #vaccineswork, #vaccinesafety, 'vaccine,' and 'antivax.' In addition we collected tweets that were from, to, or mentioned specific users, such as @realnaturalnews and @CDCgov. These users were identified inductively: researchers searched for sources on both sides of the debate that were prominently involved in ongoing discussions of vaccine safety, then added those sources to a list. The full search query can be found in the Appendix. The search resulted in 60,230 tweets from 36,390 users.

Table 2.1 Definitions and operationalizations of key terms.

Concepts	Network Definitions	Formal Parameters
well-positioned epistemic source	a node that transmits new information into the network	high PageRankOut
well-positioned epistemic receiver	a node that receives information propagated from elsewhere in the network	high PageRankIn
epistemic path	a path through from a source through zero or more conduits to a receiver	chain of retweets between nodes
epistemic geodesic	the shortest epistemic path between a pair of nodes	shortest chain of retweets between nodes

3.2 Cleaning and processing the data

Data collected through the Twitter API contains several data points about each tweet, including the text of a tweet, whether it is a retweet or reply, how many likes and followers the user has, and sometimes the geographic location the tweet was made from, among (many) other data points. As discussed above, a retweet network is best-suited to our research questions.

Almost all the 36,390 accounts in our raw dataset are minimally connected to the discourse on vaccine safety. Thus, we proceed by isolating the core of the network in order to avoid imposing artificial boundaries, aid in network visualization, and analyze those who participate in ongoing engagement and discussion. Starting with the raw data, we repeatedly remove nodes (accounts) if they are only minimally connected. A node counts as minimally connected if the sum of its in-degree and out-degree is 0 or 1. In other words, we eliminate users who published one vaccine-related tweet that was retweeted exactly 0 or 1 times (and didn't retweet any other tweets about vaccines), as well as users who retweeted exactly 0 or 1 tweets about vaccine safety (and didn't publish any tweets about vaccines that were retweeted by others). We repeat this process in stages until zero accounts are removed in a stage, indicating that the core of the network is all that remains.

All actors removed from the original network were never engaged in the conversations of the core directly. They propagated the conversation of the core outwards in the unfiltered network, or supplied input to the core via proxy. After removing these actors, we have multiple networks consisting of only the important actors. We designate the largest of these networks as our core network. This process filtered out the vast majority of accounts from the raw data, leaving a core network of just 240 nodes.

3.3 Analysis

Our methodology for interpreting a network proceeds along two tracks. The first track is through inferences from the mathematical properties of the network. The second track, visualization, is discussed in Section 3.4.

The measures used to analyze networks are derived from the relational properties of nodes. As we explained above, the basic relational property is a node's *degree*, or the number of other nodes it is connected to. In directed networks, we can distinguish between a node's *in-degree* (the number of edges that point to it) and its *out-degree* (the number of edges that point from it). In our retweet network on vaccine safety a node with a high out-degree is one that has been retweeted often. A node with a high in-degree retweets others often. Degree is a local property of nodes: a node with three connections could exist at the periphery of a network or function as a significant bridge or bottleneck in the network, depending on how the rest of the network is structured. In order to better understand the roles played by different nodes, it's therefore helpful to employ more holistic properties. As mentioned above, for this purpose we use PageRankOut and PageRankIn because they informatively summarize holistic information.

As an initial check on the viability of our API query, two of the authors independently hand-coded random samples of tweets both from the unfiltered network (300 tweets) and from the core network (300 tweets). 28.8% of the tweets in the unfiltered network were deemed irrelevant, whereas only 7% of tweets in the core network were deemed irrelevant. Many of the irrelevant tweets were by (or retweets of, replies to, or mentions of) the specific accounts mentioned in Section 3.1. For this reason, in the second case study, we did not automatically include these accounts in our API query.

In addition, to further establish the viability of our approach, we use latent dirichlet allocation (LDA—Blei et al. 2003) topic modeling on the full collection of tweets, and define $C(u,v)$ as the union of the most dominant topic per tweet that is retweeting along edge (u,v). The LDA topic model reveals three main kinds of tweets: a predominately pro-vaccination set of tweets, a predominantly anti-vaccination set of tweets, and a set that represents alternative perspectives. The latter set includes topics surrounding alternative medicine and anti-establishment politics, among others. We surmise that this third group was responsible for the higher proportion of irrelevant tweets in the unfiltered network as compared to the core network. There were also more nuanced topic trends present in the data. For example, within the pro-vaccination tweets some users present a positive case for societal vaccination, while others present a negative argument against the viewpoints of those who are anti-vaccination (in other words, they are anti-anti-vaccination).

Next, because the number of nodes in the core network was of a manageable size, we labeled them by hand rather than using automated natural language processing. In line with the semantic broad topics identified by LDA, three independent coders labeled each of the nodes of the core network as being either pro-vaccine, con-vaccine, or neutral. No codebook was used; instead, the coders simply read with an eye to the opinions expressed in the tweets and any URLs they linked to. We observed adequate interrater reliability (Fleiss's $\kappa = 0.734$, $z = 29.7$, $p < 0.001$). The main source of disagreement was a set of accounts that could not easily be classified as pro-vaccine, con-vaccine, or neutral. Two researchers reviewed cases of disagreement and designated eighteen accounts as *irrelevant*; these accounts were removed from the core network, leaving 185 nodes. The average out-degree, in-degree, PageRankOut, and PageRankIn of nodes in each of the three camps is summarized in Table 2.2. For more detailed plots of the data, we refer to Figure 2.6 in the Appendix.

The number of pro- and con-vaccine accounts in the core of the network is nearly identical, and there is just one neutral account. The average out-degree, in-degree, and PageRankOut of con-vaccine accounts is higher, whereas the average pro-vaccine PageRankIn is higher. Because there are so few neutral accounts, we exclude them from significance testing. Kruskal–Wallis tests reveal that differences in out-degree ($\chi^2 = 16.17$, df $= 1, p = 0.001$), in-degree ($\chi^2 = 7.96$, df $= 1, p = 0.046$), and PageRankOut ($\chi^2 = 9.64$, df $= 1$, $p = 0.02$) are significant, whereas differences in PageRankIn are not ($\chi^2 = 1.80$, df $= 1, p = 0.62$). Together, these results suggest that there are very few neutral accounts tweeting about vaccine safety, and that the reach (out-degree & PageRankOut) of con-vaccine

Table 2.2 Mean degree and PageRank properties of pro-vaccine, neutral, and con-vaccine accounts.

	n	out-degree	in-degree	PageRankOut	PageRankIn
pro-vaccine	91	2.49	2.46	$10.4^*(10^{-6})$	$7.98^*(10^{-6})$
neutral	1	1	1	$4.35^*(10^{-6})$	$4.28^*(10^{-6})$
con-vaccine	93	8.69	8.73	$16.9^*(10^{-6})$	$13.5^*(10^{-6})$

accounts is greater. Regarding receptivity (in-degree & PageRankIn), the results are mixed: the con-vaccine community has significantly greater in-degree but statistically indistinguishable PageRankIn.

3.4 Visualization

In principle, everything that can be learned from a visualization could also be learned by analyzing the bare mathematics of the network itself. However, given the relative strengths and weaknesses of human cognition and perception, it is sometimes (though by no means always) advantageous to employ visualizations.[7] This is especially acute for analyzing nodes ranked by PageRank or degree. Importantly, visualization is a tool for analysis and understanding.

We first plot the network (Figure 2.1) using a simple force-directed layout as implemented in D3.js.[8] This gives the impression of two well-separated communities, one more tightly knit than the other, but we should keep in mind that a force-directed layout provides us with no guarantees about perceived and actual distance: nodes that are far apart in the visualization may in fact be fairly close in the network structure. Moreover, it is difficult to correlate PageRank scores with sentiment (being pro- or con-vaccine, etc.).

We therefore alter the layout and use the node positions to communicate these values. As position is the strongest visual variable (Munzner 2014), this allows us to best focus on and assess the values of PageRank and sentiment. Below are visualizations of users' attitudes toward vaccination based on the three independent coders, with all 185 accounts in the core network represented. Position on the x-axis is determined by averaging the sentiment scores of all three raters. We slightly offset these positions horizontally, to get a better sense of the number of accounts and a clearer view of the network: the horizontal position within a column is *not* indicative of strength of opinion. Position on the y-axis represents an account's reach (PageRankOut,

---

[7] Visualizations can also be misleading, so it's important to employ best practices as outlined in Munzner (2014).

[8] We used version 4 of D3.js by Mike Bostock. See http://www.d3js.org, accessed August 2018.

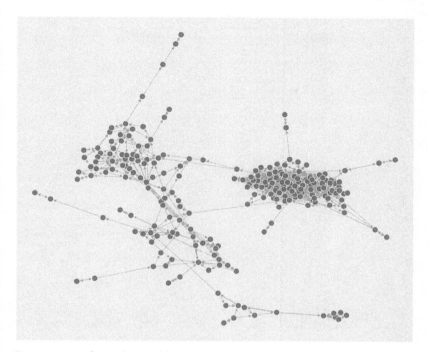

Figure 2.1 A force-directed layout of the graph.
Note: Nodes represent accounts and arrows represent retweeting.

Figure 2.2) or receptivity (PageRankIn, Figure 2.3). The properties of the most prominent pro and con accounts are summarized in the notes to the illustrations.

Figures 2.2 and 2.3 illustrate the reach and receptivity of both the pro-vaccine and con-vaccine camps. Communication between the camps is rare, and there are just a handful of neutral participants. To test this more formally, we use a *homophily* test, following the exposition of Easley and Kleinberg (2010). The main idea is to compare the fraction of cross-camp links to the expected fraction of such links if links were chosen randomly. To do so, let p denote the fraction of nodes in one camp, and $q = 1 - p$ the fraction of nodes that are not in this camp. A random link has probability p^2 of being within the considered camp, q^2 of being fully outside the camp, and $2pq$ of being between a node in the considered camp and one outside of it. As such, we can assess the homophily of the network by comparing the actual cross-camp links to

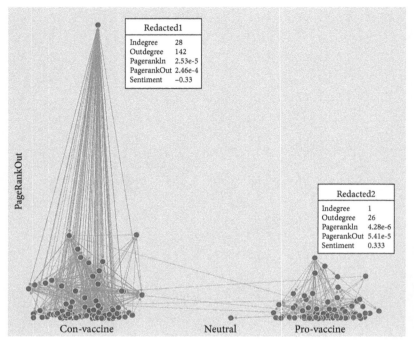

Figure 2.2 Active pro-vaccine, neutral, and con-vaccine Twitter accounts ranked by PageRankOut.

Note: Nodes represent accounts and arrows represent retweeting. We treat accounts as sources to the extent that they have high PageRankOut. The most prominent con-vaccine and pro-vaccine accounts are, respectively, @[REDACTED1] and @[REDACTED2]. Following the ethical considerations outlined in Townsend and Wallace (2016), we keep any non-public figure anonymous where possible. In this context, public figures are those who either have been verified by Twitter (i.e., have a blue check) or have a Wikipedia entry about them.

this threshold. Following Meulemans and Schulz (2015), we can extend this to a *degree of homophily*, defined as $1 - x/(4pq)$ if $x < 2pq$ and $(1 - x)/(2 - 4pq)$ otherwise, where x is the actual fraction of cross-camp links. The degree of homophily is 0 if there are only cross-camp links, 0.5 if there is no homophily at all, and 1 is there is a strong indication of homophily. We assess the homophily of each camp by lumping together the other two camps to assess the strength of preference of communicating within the camp to communicating between camps. For example, when considering the pro-vaccine camp, we treat both con-vaccine and neutral accounts as a single distinct camp. The homophily of the

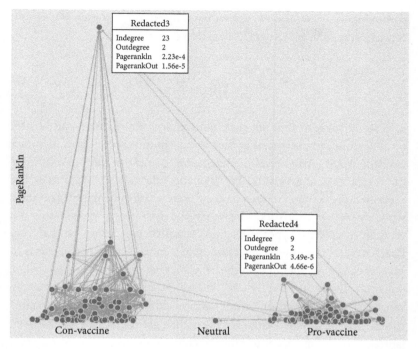

Figure 2.3 Active pro-vaccine, neutral, and con-vaccine Twitter accounts ranked by PageRankIn.

Note: Nodes represent accounts and arrows represent retweeting. We treat accounts as receivers to the extent that they have high PageRankIn. The most prominent con-vaccine and pro-vaccine accounts are, respectively, @[REDACTED3] and @[REDACTED4].

pro- and con-vaccine camps are 0.993 and 0.995 respectively, indicating a strong bias toward retweeting information from accounts that have the same viewpoint.

In addition, while the number of members in each camp is roughly equivalent, the communication pattern in the con-vaccine camp shows greater density, whereas the pro-vaccine community is more diffuse. This corroborates our analysis in Section 3.3, which showed higher PageRankOut and PageRankIn of accounts in the con-vaccine community. What accounts for this difference? One possibility is that con-vaccine accounts are solely or primarily focused on this one topic (as commentators, activists, etc.), whereas the pro-vaccine accounts are occasional commentators who also engage with a range of other topics. We explore this hypothesis in more detail in Section 5.

3.5 Discussion

This study suggests that network analysis and visualization can be used to better understand social epistemic communities. We have identified two important formal roles that epistemic agents can have in a community: sources and receivers. We then operationalized these roles and identified those who are seen as good sources of information and those who are active receivers. These are the first steps in assessing the wisdom-of-crowds hypothesis. Our tentative conclusion is that high PageRankOut is epistemically bivalent. Given the scientific consensus on vaccine safety, we operated on the heuristic that the pro-vaccine accounts are more likely to offer reliable testimony compared to anti-vaccine accounts. Our observations, from taking a close look at various accounts, stayed true to this heuristic. Nodes with high PageRankOut that were labeled pro-vaccine seem to offer reliable, expert testimony to others in their community. For example, Redacted2 is a medical doctor and the president of a prominent medical association. However, nodes labeled as anti-vaccine with high PageRankOut (including the node with by far the highest PageRankOut) spread misinformation and disinformation. The formal properties of the network under discussion here do not make it possible to distinguish between these. Likewise, we suggest that high PageRankIn is epistemically bivalent. Again after taking a close look at various accounts we saw that some nodes with high PageRankIn seem to be well positioned to learn that vaccines are generally safe, but others are liable to end up more misinformed or disinformed than they would have been if they simply disconnected from the testimonial network entirely. And as with the sources, the formal properties of the network under discussion here do not make it possible to distinguish between these cases. If this is right, then the wisdom-of-crowds hypothesis needs to be significantly curtailed. Using PageRankOut as a heuristic to identify trustworthy sources does not succeed in this network. Using PageRankIn as a heuristic to identify well-informed receivers does not succeed in this network. In Study 2, we replicate this study with a larger sample.

4. Study 2

Study 1 suggested that an unvarnished version of the wisdom-of-crowds hypothesis is false. Of course, that was based on one week's discussion of vaccine safety in English on Twitter. It would be rash to generalize from just a single case. To shed further light on this topic, we conducted a second study with a new and larger data set.

4.1 Data collection

As in Study 1, we conducted a search query on the Twitter stream API. This search ran from March 1, 2018 to March 31, 2018. These dates were selected to ensure that any seasonal effects on our data would be minimal, and to expand the amount of data under analysis by a factor of approximately 4. We searched for tweets that used the same hashtags and text strings as in Study 1. These include such hashtags and text strings as #vaxxed, #vaccineswork, #vaccinesafety, 'vaccine,' and 'antivax.' However, we did not automatically include all tweets from specific accounts because these seemed to be a source of noise in Study 1. The full search query can be found in the Appendix. The search resulted in 167,521 tweets from 156,932 users.

4.2 Cleaning and processing the data

Almost all the 156,932 accounts in our raw dataset are minimally connected to the discourse on vaccine safety. Thus, we again isolate the core of the network by repeatedly removing nodes (accounts) if they are only minimally connected. A node counts as minimally connected if the sum of its in-degree and out-degree is 0 or 1. We repeat this process in stages until zero accounts are removed in a stage, indicating that the core of the network is all that remains. After removing these actors, we again designate the largest remaining network as our core network. This process filters out the vast majority of accounts from the raw data, leaving a core network of 897 nodes.

4.3 Analysis

Two of the authors independently hand-coded random samples of tweets both from the unfiltered network (300 tweets) and from the core network (300 tweets). 12.8% of the tweets in the unfiltered network were deemed irrelevant, whereas only 1.8% of tweets in the core network were deemed irrelevant.[9] This indicates that ceasing to include all tweets from specific accounts greatly reduced the amount of noise in the data, and further corroborates our decision to focus the analysis on the core network rather than the unfiltered network.

Next, we assigned nodes to categories, as in Study 1. Some of the nodes from the core network of Study 1 were also part of the core network in Study 2. We did not re-label these nodes; instead, we carried over their labels from Study 1. For all 824 new nodes in the core network, two independent coders labeled each of the nodes of the core network as being either pro-vaccine, con-vaccine, neutral, mixed, or irrelevant. We observed adequate interrater reliability (Fleiss's $\kappa = 0.811$, $z = 26.4$, $p < 0.001$). The two labelers then reviewed cases of disagreement and designated a few accounts as *irrelevant*; these accounts were removed from the network before calculating the core, leaving 888 nodes in the core network. The average out-degree, in-degree, PageRankOut, and PageRankIn of nodes in each of the four camps is summarized in Table 2.3. For more detailed plots of the data, refer to Figure 2.6 in the Appendix.

Table 2.3 Mean degree and PageRank properties of pro-vaccine, neutral, and con-vaccine accounts.

	n	out-degree	in-degree	PageRankOut	PageRankIn
pro-vaccine	549	5.82	5.74	$2.98^*(10^{-6})$	$1.71^*(10^{-6})$
neutral	3	1.67	3.00	$1.64^*(10^{-6})$	$2.02^*(10^{-6})$
mixed	9	1.33	1.33	$1.78^*(10^{-6})$	$1.51^*(10^{-6})$
con-vaccine	327	17.42	17.52	$5.74^*(10^{-6})$	$2.31^*(10^{-6})$

[9] We further note that several of the tweets in the core network were in French, Italian, or Japanese. They ended up in our network primarily because they also included one or more of the hashtags in our API query. Further investigation may benefit from a multi-language approach.

As before, the number of neutral (and mixed) accounts in the core of the network is very small.[10] Unlike Study 1, however, Study 2 suggests that there are nearly twice as many pro-vaccine accounts as con-vaccine accounts in the core of the network. The two researchers who labeled the data noted a large number of pro-vaccine accounts that seemed to represent pediatricians and other types of physicians (as indicated by their account names). It is unclear whether Study 1 simply missed tweets from such accounts or whether instead an active campaign by pediatricians and other doctors is distinctive of the year 2018. Because there are so few neutral and mixed accounts, we exclude them from significance testing. Kruskal–Wallis tests reveal that differences in out-degree (χ^2 = 19.67, df = 1, p = 0.0002), in-degree (χ^2 = 41.99, df = 1, p < 0.0001), PageRankOut (χ^2 = 12.95, df = 1, p = 0.005) and PageRankIn (χ^2 = 11.80, df = 1, p = 0.008) are all significant. Together, these results suggest that there are very few neutral or mixed accounts tweeting about vaccine safety, and that both the reach (out-degree and PageRankOut) and the receptivity (in-degree and PageRankIn) of con-vaccine accounts is greater. It's noteworthy that these differences obtain despite the fact that there are almost twice as many pro-vaccine accounts in the core network. This is in keeping with the findings of Radzikowski et al. (2016), who studied Twitter discussions during a measles outbreak in February 2015. Their data "indicated that a bottom-up campaign [...] far outweighed the presence of official sources such as the top-down efforts of CDC and WHO." Our findings go further: even when individual pediatricians and doctors get involved in debates over vaccine safety (recall that pro-vaccine accounts far outnumber con-vaccine accounts in the core network), their reach and receptivity do not match the reach and receptivity of the con-vaccine accounts.

4.4 Visualization

As before, we also visualize the data to aid in interpretation. These visualizations are based on the core network, with 888 accounts represented.

---

[10] It is not clear whether distinguishing neutral from mixed views in this way is worth the effort when analyzing testimonial networks about vaccine safety. Perhaps in other testimonial networks on other topics, it would be so.

Position on the x-axis is determined by sentiment, with neutral and mixed accounts grouped together for convenience; again, we offset these horizontally for legibility but remind the reader that this offset within a column carries no meaning. Position on the y-axis represents each account's reach (PageRankOut, Figure 2.4) or receptivity (PageRankIn, Figure 2.5). We again see that communication between the camps is rare. We compute the degree of homophily and observe that with 0.988 and 0.983 for the pro- and con-vaccine camps, respectively, these values remain very high (recall that the maximum possible value is 1.0) and are only marginally lower than those for Study 1.

In addition, while there are more members of the pro-vaccine camp, the communication pattern in the con-vaccine camp shows greater

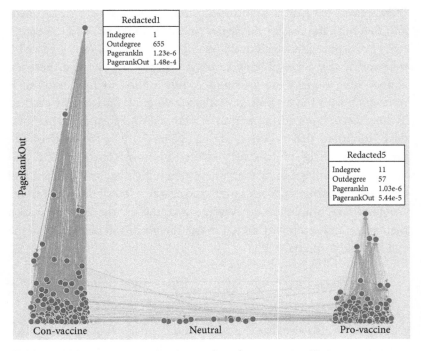

Figure 2.4 Active pro-vaccine, neutral, and con-vaccine Twitter accounts ranked by PageRankOut.

Note: Nodes represent accounts and arrows represent retweeting. We treat accounts as sources to the extent that they have high PageRankOut. The most prominent con-vaccine and pro-vaccine accounts are, respectively, @[REDACTED1] and @[REDACTED5].

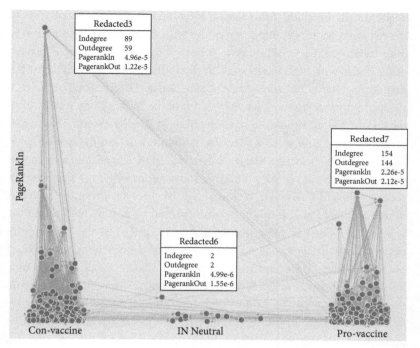

Figure 2.5 Active pro-vaccine, neutral, and con-vaccine Twitter accounts ranked by PageRankIn.

Note: Nodes represent accounts and arrows represent retweeting. We treat accounts as receivers to the extent that they have high PageRankIn. The most prominent con-vaccine, neutral, and pro-vaccine accounts are, respectively, @[REDACTED3], @[REDACTED6], and @[REDACTED7].

density, whereas the pro-vaccine community is more diffuse. This corroborates our analysis in Section 4.3 and in Study 1, which showed higher PageRankOut and PageRankIn of accounts in the con-vaccine community. In Section 5, we return to this finding.

4.5 Discussion

This study once again suggests that network analysis and visualization can be used to better understand social epistemic communities. As in Study 1, the wisdom-of-crowds hypothesis is not borne out by our data and analyses. Once again, it appears that high PageRankOut is epistemically bivalent. After taking a close look at various accounts in the network, we found that some nodes with high PageRankOut seem to offer reliable, expert testimony to others in their community. However, other nodes with high PageRankOut (including the node with by far the highest PageRankOut) spread misinformation and disinformation. In fact, the same misinformation account that had the highest PageRankOut in our first study, continued to have the highest PageRankOut. The formal properties of the network under discussion here do not make it possible to distinguish between these. Likewise, high PageRankIn is again epistemically bivalent. We found that some nodes with high PageRankIn seem to be well positioned to learn that vaccines are generally safe, but others are liable to end up more misinformed or disinformed than they would have been if they simply disconnected from the testimonial network entirely. For such actors, avoiding testimony altogether would both save them time and improve their epistemic position; this may hold more generally in the context of fake news and a polluted epistemic ecosystem (Levy 2017). And as with the sources, the formal properties of the network under discussion here do not make it possible to distinguish between these cases. In light of this replication with a new and larger dataset, the wisdom-of-crowds hypothesis needs to be significantly curtailed, especially in regard to polarized topics. Using PageRankOut as a heuristic to identify trustworthy sources does not work in the sorts of non-ideal epistemic networks found in the real world. Using PageRankIn as a heuristic to identify well-informed receivers also does not work in the sorts of non-ideal epistemic networks found in the real world.

5. General Discussion and Directions for Future Research

On its own, PageRank does not seem to deliver on the promise of harnessing the wisdom of crowds for agents in real testimonial communities. In both of our case studies, the nodes with highest PageRankOut were not reliable sources, the nodes with highest PageRankIn were not likely to be well informed, and both PageRankOut and PageRankIn were overall higher in the con-vaccine camp. Perhaps some other metric would do better in such an epistemically treacherous environment. In this section, we point to two such features that deserve further research.

First, most articulations of the wisdom-of-crowds hypothesis require that the crowd be structured in a way that preserves sufficient independence among the members of the community (Surowiecki 2004). One attractive way to spell out the independence criterion is in terms of the distance between the sources that a given receiver relies upon. The metaphors of the "filter bubble" and "echo chamber" (Pariser 2011) that are nowadays common in criticisms of public discourse on social media suggest a lack of independence. Perhaps if a formal definition of relying on multiple independent sources could be developed and operationalized for the study of real testimonial networks, it would fare better than PageRank in harnessing the wisdom of crowds.

Second, in this chapter we have noted that the discourse on vaccine safety is highly polarized and partisan. The proportion of discussants whose views could plausibly be considered neutral or mixed was very low. In Study 1, just 1 out of 185 accounts was not partisan. In Study 2, only 12 out of 888 accounts were not partisan. The cross-talk between the camps was also rare. In Study 1, the degree of homophily for the pro- and con-vaccines camps were .993 and .995, respectively. In Study 2, these values were .988 and .983, respectively, extremely close to the maximum of 1.0. This suggests that, in addition to purely structural metrics such as PageRank and source independence, assessments of the health of epistemic communities would do well to attend to diversity of viewpoint or content.[11] Indeed, Tafuri et al. (2014) advocate fostering diversity among news media to address anti-vaccine misinformation, and Dubois and Blank (2018) argue that citizens with sufficient curiosity operating in a diverse media environment typically manage to avoid getting trapped in echo chambers more generally.

However, measuring and improving viewpoint diversity is challenging for several reasons. While it is possible to delineate broad topical communities using LDA, as we did in Study 1, this is a very coarse way of

---

[11] It is also worth investigating how PageRank fares in non-ideal testimonial networks involving non-controversial topics that have a lower degree of homophily.

carving up the space of discussion. It is important to be able to assess not just how various camps disagree with each other but also their *reasons* for disagreeing. In other words, there is not simply diversity in viewpoint regarding diversity in the conclusion reached (either pro or anti-vax), but also diversity in the reasons given for a given conclusion. Furthermore, when taking a close look at the profiles of both the pro-vaccine and con-vaccine accounts with highest PageRankOut and PageRankIn, we found that the most prominent con-vaccine accounts in our data seem to have a single-minded focus on vaccines. We observed that the most prominent sources on the pro-vaccine side of the controversy were medical professionals and the most prominent receivers on this side of the controversy were non-medical accounts that engaged in a wide range of topics. By contrast, the most prominent sources on the con-vaccine side of the controversy include vaccination-related information in their account descriptions, along with references to homeopathy and alternative medicine. The most prominent receivers on this side of the controversy seem to be controlled by activists who believe that their children have been harmed by vaccination. These accounts are also more single-minded in their topic focus, with the vast majority of content referring directly or tangentially to vaccine safety, compared to the pro-vaccine accounts. Plausibly, this may lead them to seek out, attend to, interpret, and remember information about vaccine safety that makes them epistemically worse off. This suggests that beyond viewpoint- and reasons-diversity *between* individuals and groups, it may be important to attend to diversity of interests *within* individuals and groups. Measuring these three types of diversity (viewpoint-, interest-, and reasons-) is a tall order.

Moreover, there are at least two important caveats regarding the epistemic value of diversity that make harnessing a diversity metric in the wisdom of crowds even more challenging. First, regarding interest-diversity: we are well aware that activists are often criticized for lacking diversity in their interests or being obsessed by an *idée fixe*. We do not want to unthinkingly condemn all activism. Moreover, presumably, the vaccine skeptics in our data see themselves as being activists in exactly this way. This makes interest-diversity an ambivalent epistemic heuristic.

Second, in the case of vaccine safety, scientific evidence supports one side of the controversy. In such conditions, neutrality, ambivalence, or conciliation is not necessarily a virtue and may be a vice. As mentioned above, Levy (2017) argues that avoiding testimony is the correct response in these sorts of cases. However, inter-camp discussion does not necessarily require partisans to change their views, reduce their confidence, or conciliate epistemically in some other way. As John Stuart Mill (1859/1989) argued in chapter 2 of *On Liberty*, there is much to be said for the free expression of opinions, whether they are true, false, or partially true. According to Mill, false views are epistemically defensible because expressing false opinions leads to debate, which is one of our best methods for arriving at the truth on a given question. Mill famously indicts those who are unwilling to defend in open debate (what they take to be) the truth as being at risk of having their knowledge demoted to "dead dogma" and "phrases retained by rote." Furthermore, when the topic under discussion is complex—as is typically the case in the political, moral, and medical domains—it often happens that any given person's opinion contains some truth and some falsehood. For instance, health experts do not recommend that all populations receive all vaccines as early as possible; the measles–mumps–rubella (MMR) vaccine is generally not recommended for infants younger than twelve months.[12] In complex cases, universal generalizations (e.g., "All vaccines are safe for all populations") are almost always false. Debate, when it plays out well, helps to refine the proposition under discussion until it becomes epistemically acceptable.

That said, there are limits to the epistemic value of debate. In particular, the rise of trolling as a form of engagement means that many invitations to debate are not made in good faith. By good faith we mean, roughly, that one is willing to change their views in light of some conceivable evidence or argument that one's opponent might offer. Furthermore, it's important to recognize that engaging in debate often brings with it significant opportunity costs in terms of time, effort, and emotional engagement. Incessant, bad-faith invitations to engage in debate are a

---

[12] See http://www.immunise.health.gov.au/internet/immunise/publishing.nsf/Content/ Handbook10-home~handbook10part4~handbook10-4-9.

well-known tactic of trolls called 'sea lioning' (Poland 2016, 145). Trolls who engage in sea lioning might seem to have John Stuart Mill on their side: after all, can't they accuse their would-be opponents of adhering to "dead dogma"? On both this question and the question of interest-diversity, simple-minded maximization heuristics (*as many interests as possible! as many viewpoints as possible! as much debate as possible!*) are hopeless.

Thus, much needs to be done on how to establish a diversity of viewpoint metric that can harness the wisdom of crowds that can balance issues of when to cut off testimony and debate and when to engage in order to maintain and secure one's epistemic position. Articulating and defending operationalizable heuristics is a massive task that will require the expertise and input of philosophers, computer scientists, social scientists, and many others.

6. Appendix

6.1 Twitter search query for Study 1

text: vax, vaxxed, vaccine, vaxsafety, vaccineswork, vaccinesafety, vaccinesrevealed, novax, antivax, vaccination, vaccinations, immunization

hashtags: #vax, #vaxxed, #vaccine, #vaxsafety, #vaccineswork, #vaccinesafety, #vaccinesrevealed, #novax, #antivax, #vaccination, #vaccinations

mentions: @CDCgov, @drwakefield, @realnaturalnews, @drpanmd, @conservabotia, @WHO, @HHSGov, @DrRandPaul, @MicheleBachmann, @kwakzalverij, @rivm, @gezondheidsraad, @RolandPierik, @Gert_van_Dijk, @nvkp_nl, @VaccinatieRaad, @AnthonySc6, @LotusOak, @jelani9

from: @CDCgov, @drwakefield, @realnaturalnews, @drpanmd, @conservabotia, @WHO, @HHSGov, @DrRandPaul, @MicheleBachmann, @kwakzalverij, @rivm, @gezondheidsraad, @RolandPierik, @Gert_van_Dijk, @nvkp_nl, @VaccinatieRaad, @AnthonySc6, @LotusOak, @jelani9

to: @CDCgov, @drwakefield, @realnaturalnews, @drpanmd, @conservabotia, @WHO, @HHSGov, @DrRandPaul, @MicheleBachmann, @kwakzalverij,   @rivm,   @gezondheidsraad,   @RolandPierik,   @

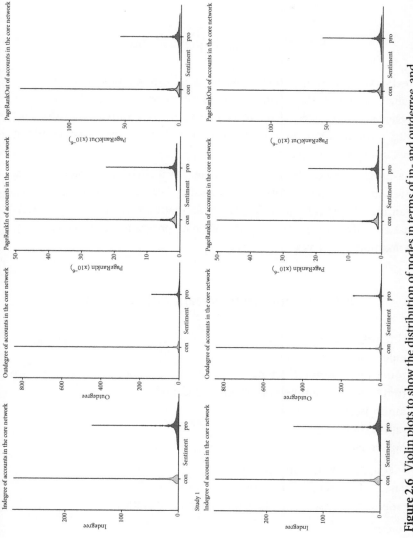

Figure 2.6 Violin plots to show the distribution of nodes in terms of in- and outdegree, and PageRankIn and -Out for both studies.

Gert_van_Dijk, @nvkp_nl, @VaccinatieRaad, @AnthonySc6, @LotusOak, @jelani9

exclude: @realdonaldtrump, @RandPaul

6.2 Twitter search query for Study 2

text: vax, vaxxed, vaccine, vaccination, vaccinations, vaxsafety, vax saftey, vaccineswork, vaccines work, vaccinesaftey, vaccine saftey, vaccines revealed, vaccinesrevealed, novax, no vax, no-vax, antivax, anti-vax, anti vax, immunisation, Vaccin, Vaccinaties, vaccinatiezorg, vaccine injury, vax injury, vaccinatieschade

hashtags: #vax, #vaxxed, #vaccine, #vaccination, #vaccinations, #vaxsafety, #vaccineswork, #vaccinesaftey, #vaccinesrevealed, #novax, #antivax, #immunisation, #Vaccin, #Vaccinaties, #vaccinatiezorg, #vaccinatieschade, #nvkp, #rvp, #rijksvaccinatieprogramma, #vaccineinjury, #vaxinjury, #anti-vax

6.3 Code for Twitter stream API in Python 3

```
# import libraries
import tweepy            .
from tweepy import Stream
from tweepy.streaming import StreamListener
import json
import time
import datetime
# Set up the Twitter Stream
class MyListener(StreamListener):
    def __init__(self, api, file_name_base, file_length):
        self.tweet_list = []
        self.count = 1
        self.file_name_base = file_name_base
        self.file_length = file_length
```

```
def on_data(self, data):
    try:
        j = json.loads(data)
        self.tweet_list.append(j)
        n = len(self.tweet_list)
        if (n % self.file_length == 0):
            ts = time.time()
            stamp = datetime.datetime.fromtimestamp(ts).
            strftime('%m%d%H%M%S')
            file_name = self.file_name_base + stamp + '.json'
            #writes the file of tweets to your computer
            with open(file_name, 'w') as f:
                json.dump(self.tweet_list, f)
            print("Output File", self.count)
            self.count = self.count + 1
            self.tweet_list = []
        return True
    except BaseException as e:
        print("Error on_data:", str(e))
    return True
def on_error(self, status):
    print("Error",status)
    return False
class Credentials:
    def __init__(self, access_token, access_token_secret, consumer_key,
        consumer_secret):
        self.access_token = access_token
        self.access_token_secret = access_token_secret
        self.consumer_key = consumer_key
        self.consumer_secret = consumer_secret
def mine_tweets(credentials, search_terms, file_name, file_length):
    auth = tweepy.OAuthHandler(credentials.consumer_key, credentials.
consumer_secret)
    auth.set_access_token(credentials.access_token, credentials.access_
token_secret)
```

```
api = tweepy.API(auth)
twitter_stream = Stream(auth, MyListener(auth, file_name, file_length))
print("Starting up!")
while(True):
    try:
        twitter_stream.filter(track=search_terms)
    except:
        time.sleep(30)
        print("program restart")
# Input your personal Twitter-keys and Path
ACCESS_TOKEN = "** input access token"
ACCESS_TOKEN_SECRET = "** input access token secret"
CONSUMER_KEY = "** input consumer key"
CONSUMER_SECRET = "** input consumer_secret"

file_name_base = "** input personal path"

#sets how many tweets you want per file.
file_length = 100

#Customize your twitter search query
text_list = []
hashtag_list = []
mentions_list = []
from_list = []
to_list = []
exclude_list = []

full_list = text_list
full_list.extend(hashtag_list)
full_list.extend(mentions_list)
full_list.extend(from_list)
full_list.extend(to_list)
full_list.extend(exclude_list)

# Start the stream
credentials = Credentials(ACCESS_TOKEN, ACCESS_TOKEN_SECRET,
    CONSUMER_KEY, CONSUMER_SECRET)

mine_tweets(credentials, full_list, file_name_base, file_length)
```

Acknowledgments

This publication was supported by a subaward agreement from the University of Connecticut with funds provided by Grant No. 58942 from John Templeton Foundation. Its contents are solely the responsibility of the authors and do not necessarily represent the official views of UConn or John Templeton Foundation.

References

Alfano, M. (2016). The topology of communities of trust. *Russian Sociological Review*, 15(4): 30–56.

Alfano, M. and Higgins, A. (2019). Natural language processing and network visualization for philosophers. In E. Fischer and M. Curtis (eds.), *Methodological Advances in Experimental Philosophy*, 265–94. Bloomsbury.

Alfano, M. and Huijts, N. (forthcoming). Trust and distrust in institutions and governance. In J. Simon (ed.), *Handbook of Trust and Philosophy*. Routledge.

Blei, D., Ng, A., and Jordan, M. (2003). Latent dirichlet allocation. *Journal of Machine Learning Research*, 3(4–5): 993–1022.

Brin, S. and L. (1998). The anatomy of a large-scale hypertextual Web search engine. *Computer Networks and ISDN Systems*, 30: 107–17.

Coady, C. A. J. (1992). *Testimony: A Philosophical Study*. Oxford University Press.

Dubois, E. and Blank, G. (2018). The echo chamber is overstated: The moderating effect of political interest and diverse media. *Information, Communication & Society*, 21(5): 729–45.

Easley, D. and Kleinberg, J. (2010). *Networks, Crowds and Markets: Reasoning About a Highly Connected World*. Cambridge University Press.

Fricker, M. (2007). *Epistemic Injustice: Power and the Ethics of Knowing*. Oxford University Press.

Hedden, B. (2017). Should juries deliberate? *Social Epistemology*, 31(4): 368–86.

Holman, B. and Bruner, J. P. (2015). The problem of intransigently biased agents. *Philosophy of Science*, 82(5), 956–68.

Lackey, J. (2014). A deflationary account of group testimony. In *Essays in Collective Epistemology*, 64–94. Oxford University Press.

Lackey, J. (2018). Group assertion. *Erkenntnis*, 83(1): 21–42.

Levy, N. (2017). The bad news about fake news. *Social Epistemology Review and Reply Collective*, 6(8): 20–36.

List, C. and Goodin, R. E. (2001). Epistemic democracy: Generalizing the Condorcet Jury Theorem. *Journal of Political Philosophy*, 9(3): 277–306.

Lurquin, J. and Miyake, A. (2017). Challenges to ego-depletion research go beyond the replication crisis: A need for tackling the conceptual crisis. *Frontiers in Psychology*, 8: 586.

Masterton, G. and Olsson, E. J. (2017). From impact to importance: The current state of the wisdom-of-crowds justification of link-based ranking algorithms. *Philosophy and Technology*, 31(4): 593–609.

Masterton, G., Olsson, E. J., and Angere, S. (2016). Linking as voting: How the Condorcet Jury Theorem in political science is relevant to webometrics. *Scientometrics*, 106(3): 945–66.

Medina, J. (2013). *The Epistemology of Resistance: Gender and Racial Oppression, Epistemic Injustice, and the Social Imagination*. Oxford University Press.

Meulemans, W. and Schulz, A. (2015). A tale of two communities: Assessing homophily in node-link diagrams. Revised selected papers of the 23rd International Symposium on Graph Drawing and Network Visualization, LNCS volume 9411, 489–501, doi: 10.1007/978-3-319-27261-0_40.

Mill, J. S. (1859/1989). *On Liberty*. Edited by S. Collinni. Cambridge University Press.

Munzner, T. (2014). *Visualization Analysis and Design*. AK Peters.

Pariser, E. (2011). *The Filter Bubble: What the Internet is Hiding from You*. Penguin.

Poland, B. (2016). *Haters: Harassment, Abuse, and Violence Online*. University of Nebraska Press.

Radzikowski, J., Stefanidis, A., Jacobsen, K. H., Croitoru, A., Crooks, A., and Delamater, P. L. (2016). The measles vaccination narrative in Twitter: A quantitative analysis. *JMIR Public Health and Surveillance*, 2(1): 50–9.

Rosenstock, S., Bruner, J., and O'Connor, C. (2017). In epistemic networks, is less really more? *Philosophy of Science*, 84(2): 234–52.

Senturk, R. (2005). *Narrative Social Structure: Anatomy of the Hadith Transmission Network, 610–1505*. Stanford University Press.

Surowiecki, J. (2004). *The Wisdom of Crowds*. Anchor.

Tafuri, S., Gallone, M. S., Cappelli, M. G., Martinelli, D., Prato, R., and Germinario, C. (2014). Addressing the anti-vaccination movement and the role of HCWs. *Vaccine*, 32(38): 4860–5.

Tollefsen, D. (2007). Group testimony. *Social Epistemology*, 21(3): 299–311.

Townsend, L. and Wallace, C. (2016). *Social Media Research: A Guide to Ethics*. University of Aberdeen.

Zollman, K. J. (2007). The communication structure of epistemic communities. *Philosophy of Science*, 74(5): 574–87.

Zollman, K. J. (2010). The epistemic benefit of transient diversity. *Erkenntnis*, 72(1), 17–35.

3

Maggots Are Delicious, Sunsets Hideous

False, or Do You Just Disagree? Data on Truth Relativism about Judgments of Personal Taste and Aesthetics

Dylan Murray
Universidad de los Andes

1. Disagreement in Natural Language Semantics

People disagree about matters of taste and aesthetics—about what's delicious and who's beautiful. For example:

(1) *A*: That sandwich was delicious.
(2) *B*: No, it was not delicious. That sandwich was disgusting.

This much, but only this much, is relatively uncontested. Intuitively, *A* and *B* disagree, as when they respectively say:

(3) *A*: The sun orbits the earth.
(4) *B*: It does not. The earth orbits the sun.

Indeed, most theorists take this fact to have extreme importance for the semantics of taste and aesthetic predicates. In particular, many theorists start from the supposed datum that *because* we disagree in making utterances like (1) and (2), these judgments must be capable of *contradicting* one another (like (3) and (4)), such that we need to build a semantic theory of taste and aesthetic predicates that is able to capture this fact.

It is widely agreed that disagreement lies at the heart of (formal) semantics, and that debates between the major theories of evaluative and

Dylan Murray, *Maggots Are Delicious, Sunsets Hideous: False, or Do You Just Disagree? Data on Truth Relativism about Judgments of Personal Taste and Aesthetics* In: *Oxford Studies in Experimental Philosophy*. Edited by: Tania Lombrozo, Joshua Knobe, and Shaun Nichols, Oxford University Press (2020). © Dylan Murray.
DOI: 10.1093/oso/9780198852407.003.0004

normative predicates—contextualism, relativism, and non-cognitivism—largely turn on the presence and nature of disagreement.[1] Recently, truth relativists have proposed a theory they claim captures disagreement in the sense of contradiction while also being more subjective than factual disagreement. Whether people do disagree in any particular linguistic domain, and if so in what sense, however, is an empirical question. Here, I present the results of three new experiments exploring the nature of disagreement in the domain of taste and aesthetics.

These results suggest that, for taste and aesthetic predicates, the supposed contradiction datum likely is no datum. Most ordinary English speakers think they disagree in virtue of making conflicting taste and aesthetic judgments, but not because they think these judgments are contradictory. A slight majority of speakers think these judgments are not truth-apt at all. Speakers' actual intuitions not only fail to motivate most semantic theories in this domain, especially truth relativism—they in fact provide evidence against them. I go on to discuss the broader relevance of these results for taste and aesthetic predicates and the nature of disagreement involving judgments that embed them.

1.1 Evaluative semantics

In evaluative and normative domains, like those of morality, humor, epistemic matters, etiquette, and other conventions, as well as taste and aesthetics, the most fundamental division is between semantic theories that take judgments to be truth-apt—capable of being true or false, like descriptive judgments, and theories that take them to be non-truth apt—some other kind of judgment with different "content" entirely. The general consensus has been that non-cognitivism has little hope of success precisely because there are disagreements in the sense of contradiction in these domains. Contradiction may be the most recognizable form of

[1] See, for example, Gibbard (1990, 2003), DeRose (2004), Kölbel (2004), Lasersohn (2005), Dreier (2006, 2009), Egan (2007), MacFarlane (2007, 2014), Stephenson (2007), Richard (2008), Schroeder (2008), Plunkett and Sundell (2013), Knobe and Yalcin (2014), and Khoo and Knobe (2018).

disagreement. This is the sense in which *A* and *B* disagree in virtue of (3) and (4)—what they respectively say and think can't both be *true*; each judgment *precludes* the truth of the other. Because it is widely thought that the same applies to (1) and (2), a semantics according to which such judgments are not even truth-apt is a non-starter. Hence, most semantic theories of evaluative and normative predicates have been cognitivist, and are motivated in part precisely to capture disagreement in the sense of contradiction. In other words, most semantic theorists take it as a datum that we intuitively *disagree* in a given linguistic domain and then argue that this datum requires a formal semantic theory that explains this fact. Call this the *disagreement-to-contradiction inference.*[2] (Of course, if there are other forms of disagreement, this inference is unwarranted, as I return to in Section 5.)

In many evaluative domains, it is typically thought that any semantic theory must also capture another datum. Many claim that *A* and *B*'s disagreement about what is delicious in virtue of (1) and (2) is somehow more *subjective* than their disagreement about whether the sun orbits the earth (in virtue of (3) and (4))—to be more, as it's often said, "a matter of taste." A semantics for taste and aesthetic predicates, in particular, ought to meet both desiderata: it ought to account for genuine aesthetic and taste *disagreement* (not just *difference* in attitude), but also account for how such disagreement is somehow more *subjective* than disagreement about matters of descriptive fact.

Most cognitivists attempt to capture both desiderata—they posit semantic theories that allow for contents that preclude one another's truth, and then attempt to capture subjectivity in different ways depending on how those contents and their truth conditions are understood. The exception is "objectivism" or invariantism, which essentially claims that evaluative discourse is no different from descriptive discourse. According to *invariantism*, the fact that *A* and *B* genuinely disagree in virtue of (1) and (2) suggests that judgments of taste and aesthetics describe objective facts about the world, perhaps relative to the One True evaluative standard for the aesthetic and taste domains—a standard that remains

---

[2] See also Khoo and Knobe (2018). What is at issue throughout is disagreement in the *state* ("being in disagreement") rather than *activity* ("having a disagreement") sense (MacFarlane 2014: 156–8).

invariant across all contexts. There are familiar worries about what metaphysical status such objective aesthetic and taste facts would need to have, and about what our epistemic and motivational connection to them could be. Even more worrisome in the domain of taste and aesthetics, however, is the fact that invariantism simply refuses to capture any sense in which these judgments are more subjective than those about, for example, astronomy. Other cognitivist theories promise more hope of capturing both disagreement as contradiction and the comparative subjectivity of evaluative discourse.

1.2 Contextualism

According to contextualists (and relativists), the truth of sentences in a given domain is relativized to more than just a world (and time). Contextualists hold that sentences about taste and beauty are only true or false relative to a (variable) taste and aesthetic standard, which assigns an intension (extension in each possible world) to each predicate in the domain—e.g., 'tasty,' 'delicious,' 'beautiful,' and 'hideous'. For instance, one version holds that the relevant standard is that of the speaker at the context of use or utterance. According to *speaker indexical contextualism*, a sentence is true at a context of use C_U iff the proposition that sentence expresses in C_U is true at the world of C_U and the aesthetic/taste standard of the speaker at C_U. 'Delicious,' for example, is an indexical (like 'I,' 'here,' and 'now'), but which property 'delicious' picks out (and hence which proposition is expressed by judgments and sentences containing it) depends on the aesthetic/taste standard of the person making the judgment or uttering the sentence. In turn, the contextual variability of these standards seems to account for why aesthetic and taste discourse is more subjective than discourse about matters of descriptive fact.

But there's a glaring problem: by capturing subjectivity in this way, contextualism apparently makes genuine disagreement (the other desideratum) impossible. Consider again A and B's judgments (1) and (2). According to speaker indexical contextualism, A and B's standards may be different, so 'delicious' may pick out different properties in each speaker's mouth. A may express the proposition that the sandwich is delicious-according-to-A's-taste-standard, and B may assert that it is not delicious-according-to-B's-taste-standard. But if neither asserts anything inconsistent with what the other asserts, the two just talk past each other, they do not disagree (as when A in China says over the phone "It's raining here" and B, in Mexico, retorts: "No. It's not raining here").

One attempted fix is to switch to some salient *group standard*, typically shared by the speaker, her interlocutor, and perhaps others. According to *single-scoreboard indexical contextualism*, a sentence is true at a context of use C_U iff the proposition that sentence expresses in C_U is true at the world of C_U and the shared aesthetic/taste standard of C_U.[3] In that case, if A and B met or communicated via other means, such that they came to occupy a shared context, their disagreement would be secured. A would assert that the sandwich falls in the extension of 'delicious'— that it is delicious-according-to-the-shared-aesthetic/taste-standard of their scoreboard or common ground—and B would deny this very same proposition. Note that this still secures a type of subjectivity—a sort of folk "cultural relativism" (distinct from truth relativism, discussed in Section 1.4). On this version of contextualism, the same aesthetic/taste judgments may be true for one *group* but false for another depending on their standards. Similarly, Egan (2010) predicts that disagreement wanes the more dissimilar the prospective parties' standards (or the standards they can reasonably hope to have by changing the other's mind). Thus, conviction that two parties disagree decreases the less similar are their cultures.[4]

On the stipulation that A and B never meet nor otherwise come to occupy the same conversational context, however, single-scoreboard contextualism still mistakenly predicts that they do *not* disagree. Since A and B occupy different conversational contexts, there is no single scoreboard for both to attempt to update (or resist updates to).[5]

---

[3] DeRose (2004) develops such an account for 'knows' by appealing to Lewis' (1979) metaphor of a shared "scoreboard," which is updated through speakers' conversational moves (by *accommodation*).

[4] Moral "relativism" in its traditional sense (e.g., Harman 1975) is best understood as a species of contextualism. Egan (2010) appeals to centered worlds, though, and so is a truth relativist.

[5] Another complication lies in specifying the relevant shared standard. Surely there can be disagreements between people in different conversations (if one overhears the other, say), but also between more disparate individuals—those from long ago or in far away places, for instance. Intuitively, your view does not merely *differ* from spatiotemporally separated others

1.3 Relativism

Recently, several theorists have argued that truth relativism succeeds in capturing subjectivity *and* disagreement as contradiction.[6] Relativism builds subjectivity not into the content or very *meaning* of a sentence (as does contextualism), but into its *assessment*. The variable standard is not supplied by the context at which a sentence is used or uttered, but instead by the context at which it is evaluated for truth or falsity—the context of assessment, C_A. According to *assessor truth relativism*, a sentence is true at a context of use C_U when assessed from C_A iff the proposition that sentence expresses in C_U is true at the world of C_U and the aesthetic/taste standard of the assessor at C_A. Thus, aesthetic and taste predicates have fixed contents or *meanings* and pick out the same property across all contexts of use from the perspective of any single C_A—i.e., regardless of who is speaking. But the *truth* of judgments containing such predicates depends on who is evaluating or assessing them. This allows the relativist to claim that A's assertion can be true (and B's false) when assessed from A's standard, whereas B's can be true (and A's false) when assessed from B's standard, capturing subjectivity. However, A's and B's assertions cannot both be true—they preclude one another's truth—when assessed from any one context of assessment, and so in this sense A and B disagree. Whether we use A's C_A, or B's C_A, or anyone else's, at most one of A's and B's judgments is true—they have different truth values. The contextualist loses disagreement by building subjective variability into propositions' very content or meaning; the relativist hopes to regain it by moving variability into assessment instead.

who judge, e.g., that rotten maggots are delicious. You genuinely *disagree* with them. However, contextualists are apparently forced to claim that each two people who disagree are part of the *same* C_U; otherwise, they only talk past each other. So to account for the full range of intuitive aesthetic and taste disagreement, single-scoreboard contextualists seem forced to say that *everyone*, at *every* time and place, counts as a member of the relevant group. But if there's just one group or common ground, it seems there's just One True standard according to which all aesthetic and taste claims are assessed. And in that case, it's not clear that the theory is substantively different from invariantism.

[6] Following MacFarlane (2014), we should distinguish relativism from *nonindexical contextualism* (which also holds that the *content* of a sentence does not vary across contexts of use, but unlike relativism does not relativize truth to a *context of assessment*). In the interest of space, I'll leave nonindexical contextualism to one side. Many relativists (e.g., Richard and Egan) do not clearly distinguish their positions from nonindexical contextualism, but the presentation of relativism here follows MacFarlane in doing so.

Qua cognitivists, truth relativists hope to preserve the supposed datum that disagreements about beauty and taste require contradictory contents, and they build their semantic framework precisely to capture what they take to be the right balance between this and the other desideratum for a semantics of taste and aesthetic predicates. Truth relativism accounts for a recognizable form of subjectivity: variability in aesthetic/taste standard. And relativism captures disagreement, but not as strong a type of disagreement as that involved in discourse about matters of descriptive fact (where, if there is any "standard," there's presumably just One, invariant across contexts of assessment). Specifically, the truth relativist's version of disagreement as contradiction is *preclusion of joint accuracy*: "[t]he accuracy of my attitudes (as assessed from any context) precludes the accuracy of your attitude or speech act (as assessed from that same context)" (MacFarlane 2007: 26; 2014: 129).[7] Hence, *only* the occurrence of disagreement in the *preclusion of joint accuracy* sense can motivate truth relativism in any given linguistic domain.

Nonetheless, truth relativists have inferred that because people intuitively disagree over certain properties in various domains, judgments predicating those properties must have contents that preclude one another's accuracy. For instance:

To really disagree with John, Mary would have to negate a sentence that expresses the same content as his utterance.   (Lasersohn 2005: 647)[8]

Lasersohn and I both assume that two speakers disagree only if the content of the sentence asserted by one is the negation of the one asserted by the other... By assumption, disagreement can only occur with contradictory contents.   (Stephenson 2007: 521; cf. 496)

Kölbel (2004: 54) goes on to claim that there is "a healthy pre-theoretical intuition" that there are "faultless disagreements" in the truth relativist's sense (cf. Lasersohn 2005: 658; see also Richard 2004, 2008 and Egan 2007).

---

[7] See also MacFarlane (2003, 2004). According to invariantism, both parenthetical clauses would read "as assessed from any context." According to invariantism, contexts of assessment do no real work.

[8] Lasersohn notes this is "an obvious simplification," but the argument depends on it.

Thus, many relativists jump from the intuition that people disagree in a given domain to the claim that it contains judgments with contents that preclude one another's truth.[9] In other words, like other cognitivists (and most semantic theorists), relativists endorse the disagreement-to-contradiction inference, at least in some domains. The domain that relativists themselves profess to be their deepest stronghold is that of taste and aesthetics. Hume (1757/1965) and Kant (1790/1987) both note that the tension between genuine disagreement and subjectivity—the combination that relativism is tailor-made to explain—is at its most acute in this corner of language. And both Lasersohn (2005: 682) and Kölbel (2004: 53) explicitly claim that predicates of personal taste are the most hospitable linguistic domain for truth relativism (though many of Kölbel's examples involve aesthetic predicates). There is a stronger sense here than in most domains that people both genuinely disagree *and* neither need be incorrect.

1.4 Experimental precedents

Given that the disagreement-to-contradiction inference is a domain-by-domain affair, we can ask whether it holds in any given linguistic domain. More generally, whether any particular domain involves disagreement at all, and if so in what sense, is largely an empirical question. Experimental work has been done in several domains.[10]

Knobe and Yalcin (2014) investigate *eavesdropper cases,* involving epistemic modals like 'might.' A crime scene expert says "Fat Tony might be dead," but the experimental participants have been informed that Fat Tony is in fact still alive. The truth relativist about epistemic modals

---

[9] MacFarlane (2007, 2014) is more cautious, noting that there are other forms of disagreement.

[10] This research and the experiments I present below assume that data on lay intuitions can bear on philosophical debates about semantics. This is a somewhat controversial assumption and is questioned, for example, by semantic externalism. This assumption is perhaps safest, however, in the present context. People can be radically wrong about the referent of WATER, but it would seem more incredible that people could (under conditions of ideal reflection and controlling for possible performance errors) radically mistaken about whether they disagree in any given instance. Indeed, it's unclear what else could more ultimately bear on the question of what counts as disagreement.

predicts that participants will say the expert's statement is false, since Fat Tony's being dead is ruled out by the evidence at participants' contexts of assessment. Relativists also predict that if the crime scene expert gains new evidence that Fat Tony is alive, the expert should retract her previous statement, since it will no longer be compatible with the evidence at her C_A.[11] However, while Knobe and Yalcin (2014) find that most participants do think it would be appropriate to retract the modal statement, most also judge that the expert's statement is *true*, not false. This suggests that what ordinary intuitions about disagreement involving epistemic modals are tracking is not contradictory content, contra truth relativism.[12]

Khoo and Knobe (2018) investigate moral judgments. They use a vignette where two individuals are discussing a third party who "bought an expensive new knife and tested its sharpness by randomly stabbing a passerby on the street." One individual says this action was morally wrong. The other says it was not morally wrong. Khoo and Knobe find that participants are significantly more likely to say that these interlocutors 'disagree' than they are willing to accept that at least one of their judgments must be 'incorrect.' Thus, there is evidence that moral disagreement is not disagreement in the sense of preclusion of joint accuracy. If participants think the interlocutors disagree in the sense that their judgments are contradictory, they should be just as willing to say that at least one must be 'incorrect' as they are to say that they 'disagree.'[13]

In contrast, some results in the moral domain do seem favorable to contextualism. Khoo and Knobe (2018) and Sarkissian et al. (2011) find that incorrectness attributions decrease with increased cultural distance, as single-scoreboard contextualism would predict. They use three vignettes: one in which the agent is from the same culture as participants, one in which the agent is from a different culture on Earth—the Mamilons (a tribe from the Amazonian rainforest), and a third in which

---

[11] "I was wrong that Fat Tony might be dead. I take it back. He's alive."

[12] Other work on epistemic modals includes Khoo (2015), Yu (2016), and Katz and Salerno (2017).

[13] More cautiously, relativists should not expect any *large* discrepancies between attributions of disagreement and incorrectness, all else being equal. Relativists (and contextualists) can skirt some of the problem cases by allowing flexibility ("promiscuity") in the C_A (or C_U), not requiring these to be the assessor's (speaker's). However, this move will not help to explain away participants' denial that at least one of two seemingly contradictory judgments must be incorrect, since that is a denial made from one and the same C_A.

the agent is from an extraterrestrial culture—the Pentars (whose sole goal in life is to rearrange everything in the universe into pentagrams). Participants are more likely to say that members of their own culture are incorrect than members of the other cultures, and more likely to say the Mamilons are incorrect than the Pentars.

Thus, experimental evidence does not support relativism in other domains. However, even if relativism is not true of moral and epistemic modal discourse, it might be elsewhere. Little empirical work has been done specifically in the domains of taste and aesthetics. Cova and Pain (2012) find evidence against invariantism about aesthetic predicates, but while their experiments are designed in a way that would allow them to distinguish between different versions of non-invariantism, they do not report these results, nor do they discuss disagreement directly. So the relativist's inner sanctum remains untested.

In the next three sections, I present the results of three new experiments that investigate whether truth relativism can be motivated with the disagreement-to-contradiction inference in what its proponents claim is the most probable domain for it to be true in. These experiments test whether people think that disagreements about what is tasty and beautiful are disagreements in the truth relativist's sense—preclusion of joint accuracy. In addition, Experiment 2 tests the prediction of single-scoreboard contextualism that people should be more willing to say that members of their own culture are incorrect compared to members of other cultures, and Experiment 3 tests whether people take judgments of taste and aesthetics to be truth-apt.

2. Experiment 1

Experiment 1 asks: If people say they 'disagree' with an aesthetic or taste judgment, do they mean that this judgment is precluded from being 'correct' by the correctness of their own judgment, as required by relativism? If the disagreement-to-contradiction inference holds in this domain—if it is true that if someone disagrees with an aesthetic/taste judgment, then she thinks it is incorrect—then there should be no significant difference between 'disagree' and 'incorrect' ascriptions.

Experiment 1 also asks: does cultural distance affect ascriptions of disagreement or incorrectness?

Methods: Experiment 1 (and all subsequent experiments) adapt the materials of Sarkissian et al. (2011) and Khoo and Knobe (2018) to the aesthetic/taste domain. In Experiment 1, 272 participants (59% male, mean age 33) were recruited through Amazon's Mechanical Turk. Each participant read a vignette about a member of some **culture**: their own culture (Sam, a college student), another culture (Awa, a Mamilon from the Amazon), or an extraterrestrial (Zog, a member of the pentagram-obsessed Pentars). Each participant was then given one scenario in which this actor makes a judgment in the **domain** of taste *and* another in which the actor makes a judgment in the domain of beauty, in randomized order. After each scenario, participants were asked a **question**: *either* whether they '**disagreed**' with this person's judgment *or* whether they thought it was '**incorrect**' (each participant was given the same question in the taste and beauty conditions). Thus, Experiment 1 has a 3 (culture: same, other, extraterrestrial) × 2 (question: disagree, incorrect) × 2 (domain: beauty, taste) mixed design, with domain a within-subjects factor and culture and question between-subjects factors.

Participants first read a short description of the actor, and then a scenario in which this actor makes a judgment. The *same culture beauty* scenario, for example, read:

Sam is having a discussion with one of his classmates. Eventually, the conversation turns to a recent event. As the sun went down that night, there was a brilliant purple, orange, red and yellow sunset.

Sam says, about this case, "That sunset was hideously ugly."

Suppose you are listening in on the conversation, and believe the sunset was beautiful.

The other culture conditions were identical, except Sam and his interlocutor were replaced with Awa or Zog and another Mamilon or Pentar, respectively. The *extraterrestrial culture taste* scenario, for example, read:

Two Pentars, Zog and Zar, are having a discussion. Eventually, the conversation turns to a recent event. Earlier that day, a person named Daryl bought and ate a sandwich that happened to contain rotten maggots.

Zog says, about this case, "That rotten maggot-filled sandwich was delicious."

Suppose you are listening in on the conversation, and believe the sandwich was disgusting.

The other beauty and taste conditions were identical save for changes to the respective actors. After reading the scenario, participants were given the question—i.e., asked to indicate how accurate they found *one* of two randomly assigned statements about their reaction to the actor's judgment (on a scale from 1, "Definitely not" to 7, "Definitely"):

I disagree with [Sam/Awa/Zog].
[Sam/Awa/Zog] is incorrect.

Assuming that participants do not think that brilliant sunsets are hideously ugly and that rotten maggots are delicious (or that they at least follow the instructions to suppose as much), attributions of 'incorrect' will be attributions of preclusion of joint accuracy. Thus, any *higher* ratings for the 'disagree' question (compared to the 'incorrect' question) will be attributions of some *other* type of disagreement, which cannot be used to motivate relativism with the disagreement-to-contradiction inference.

Results: Complete results can be found in the Appendix. As can be seen in Figure 3.1, there were significantly higher ascriptions of disagreement than incorrectness. There were also significantly higher ratings of disagreement and incorrectness in the same culture condition than in the other culture and extraterrestrial culture conditions.

Discussion: Experiment 1 asked: If people say they 'disagree' with an aesthetic or taste judgment, do they mean that this judgment is precluded from being 'correct' by the correctness of their own judgment? The results of Experiment 1 suggest not. Contra relativists' prediction that there should be no large difference between 'disagree' and 'incorrect' ascriptions (because disagreement just is a matter of preclusion of joint correctness), the results reveal significantly higher average

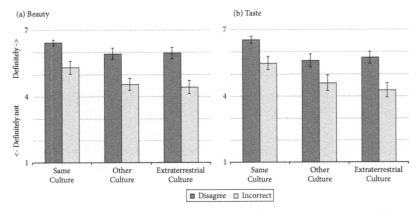

Figure 3.1 Mean ratings for the 'disagree' and 'incorrect' questions in the (a) Beauty and (b) Taste conditions of Exp. 1.

Note: Ratings given on a 7-point scale, from 1, "Definitely not" to 7, "Definitely." Error bars represent one SEM in each direction.

attribution of disagreement than incorrectness, as seen in Figure 3.1. These ascriptions of disagreement over-and-above ascriptions of incorrectness cannot be ascriptions of disagreement in the sense of preclusion of joint accuracy. This suggests, contra the disagreement-to-contradiction inference, that it is *not* necessarily the case that when people think they disagree with a judgment about tastiness (what is delicious) or beauty (what is hideous), this is because they think that judgment is incorrect. The datum with which relativists would motivate their semantics seems not to be a datum in the domain of aesthetics and taste.[14]

Experiment 1 also asked: Does cultural distance affect ascriptions of disagreement or incorrectness? The results of Experiment 1 suggest that it does, compatible with single-scoreboard contextualism's prediction that incorrectness is attributed to members of other cultures less than to members of one's own. Participants gave higher ratings of both disagreement and incorrectness in the same culture condition compared

---

[14] It is worth acknowledging that the ecological validity of the Sarkissian et al. (2011) materials is somewhat suspect, as they may amuse or bewilder participants. And to ensure that what's being measured are attributions of disagreement in the state, rather than activity, sense, it might be preferable to describe Sam, Awa, and Zog as "thinking" rather than "saying" what they do about maggots and sunsets. However, because these issues apply to all experimental conditions, they cannot explain the differences observed between conditions—most importantly, the divergence in ascriptions of disagreement and incorrectness.

to both the other and the extraterrestrial culture conditions (ratings for which did not differ significantly from each other). Experiment 2, however, casts this effect of culture into doubt.

3. Experiment 2

It could be that previous studies (including Experiment 1) have found divergent disagreement and incorrectness ascriptions only because calling a judgment incorrect seems disrespectful or harsh in a way that merely disagreeing with it need not. No extant studies have controlled for this possibility, so it stands as one alternative (deflationary) explanation of the findings. Experiment 2 asks: Does the asymmetry between 'disagree' and 'incorrect' ascriptions remain after controlling for the potential pragmatic confound with (dis)respect? Additionally, does the effect of cultural distance persist?

Methods: In Experiment 2, 270 participants (65% male, mean age 40) were recruited using the same procedure and methods as Experiment 1. The only departure from Experiment 1 was that questions in Experiment 2 were explicitly designed to allow participants to disentangle 'incorrect'/ 'disagree' responses from showing disrespect. Thus, Experiment 2 has a 3 (culture: same, other, extraterrestrial) × 2 (question: disagree, incorrect) × 2 (domain: beauty, taste) mixed design, with domain a within-subjects factor and culture and question between-subjects factors.

Each participant was randomly assigned to one of the six between-subjects conditions, and after reading the taste (beauty) scenario, each participant was asked which of the following statements most accurately represented his or her response to Sam's (Awa's/Zog's) judgment, with choices presented in randomized order:

(i) I can't respect Sam's judgment, and [I disagree with it/strictly speaking it's incorrect].

(ii) I respect Sam's judgment, but [I disagree with it/strictly speaking it's incorrect].

(iii) I can't respect Sam's judgment, but [I don't disagree with it/ strictly speaking it's not incorrect].

(iv) I respect Sam's judgment, and [I don't disagree with it/strictly speaking it's not incorrect].

Results: Complete results can be found in the Appendix. As can be seen in Figure 3.2, which "collapses" across (dis)respect in order to accentuate the variables of interest, there were significantly higher ascriptions of disagreement than incorrectness. 91.8% of participants disagree with the actor's judgment, but only 53.7% judge that it is incorrect. There were no significant differences in disagreement or incorrectness ratings between the same culture condition and either the other culture or extraterrestrial culture condition.

Discussion: Experiment 2 asked: Does the asymmetry between 'disagree' and 'incorrect' ascriptions remain after controlling for the potential pragmatic confound with (dis)respect? The results of Experiment 2 suggest that it does. If anything, controlling for the potential confound actually strengthens this asymmetry.

However, the opposite is true for the finding from Experiment 1 that seemed congenial to single-scoreboard contextualism: the observation of differences between the same culture and other culture (Mamilon and Pentar) conditions. After controlling for (dis)respect in Experiment 2, there is no effect of culture on 'disagree' or 'incorrect' ratings. Thus, these ratings may have been lower in the other culture conditions of Experiment 1 only because saying another person's judgment is incorrect

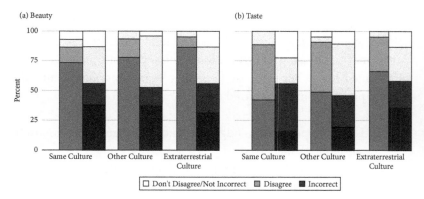

Figure 3.2 Percentage of participants giving each response to the 'disagree' and 'incorrect' questions in the (a) Beauty and (b) Taste conditions of Exp. 2.

(or that one disagrees with it) carries more risk of expressing disrespect when that person is a member of another culture compared to a member of one's own—a purely pragmatic effect that has nothing to do with the meaning or semantics of taste and aesthetic predicates.

While most participants in Experiment 2 say they 'disagree' with the other actor's judgment, 'incorrect' ratings are at midpoint, as can be seen in Figure 3.2, which may indicate participants' uncertainty about incorrectness ascriptions. Presumably, ratings are not at midpoint because participants think the actor's judgment is correct or incorrect, but are unsure which. Nearly half of participants in Experiment 2 positively say that the actor's judgment is 'not incorrect'. Experiment 3 attempts to determine why participants say this.

4. Experiment 3

Experiment 3 asks: Why do participants say that others' conflicting taste and aesthetic judgments are 'not incorrect'—because they think these judgments are also correct, or because they think taste and aesthetic judgments are neither true nor false?

Methods: In Experiment 3, 180 participants (61% male, mean age 35) were recruited using the same procedure and methods as Experiments 1 and 2. Experiment 3 used only the Mamilon vignette, and included two **descriptive** conditions as contrasts for the **evaluative** (taste and beauty) conditions (cf. Sarkissian et al. 2011, Study 6). Instead of Awa judging "That sunset was hideously ugly," as in the evaluative (beauty) condition of **sunset**, the end of the descriptive version of the sunset scenario read:

Awa says, about this case, "That sunset occurred because the sun stopped emitting light."

Suppose you are listening in on the conversation, and believe the sunset occurred because the sun fell below the Earth's horizon.

And instead of Awa judging "That rotten maggot-filled sandwich was delicious," the end of the descriptive version of **maggots** read:

Awa says, about this case, "Those maggots are reptiles."

Suppose you are listening in on the conversation, and believe the maggots are insects.

Thus, Experiment 3 has a 2 (realm: descriptive, evaluative) × 2 (domain: sunset, maggots) fully between-subjects design. Each participant was randomly assigned to one of these four conditions. After reading the scenario, participants were asked which of the following statements most accurately represented their reaction to Awa's judgment, with choices presented in randomized order:

(i) Strictly speaking, neither Awa's judgment nor my judgment is true and neither is false.
(ii) Strictly speaking, both Awa's judgment and my judgment are true.
(iii) Strictly speaking, only my judgment is true, Awa's is false.
(iv) Strictly speaking, both Awa's judgment and my judgment are false.

Results: Complete results can be found in the Appendix. As can be seen in Figure 3.3, the dominant response in the descriptive realm is (iii) "my judgment is true, Awa's is false." In contrast, the most popular response in the evaluative realm is (i) "neither is true, neither is false."

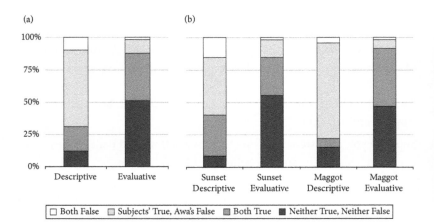

Figure 3.3 Percent of participants giving each response, (i)–(iv), in Exp. 3, collapsing across domain (a), and separated by domain (b).

There were significantly fewer (iii) responses in the evaluative than in the descriptive realm, but significantly more (i) responses. There were also significantly more (ii) "both are true" responses in the evaluative compared to the descriptive realm (though only in the taste, and not in the beauty, domain).

Discussion: Experiment 3 asked: Why do participants say that others' conflicting taste and aesthetic judgments are 'not incorrect'—because they think these judgments are also correct, or because they think taste and aesthetic judgments are neither true nor false? The results of Experiment 3 suggest a role for both explanations. There were more "both true" responses in the evaluative than in the descriptive realm, but an even larger asymmetry in "neither true, neither false" responses, as seen in Figure 3.3.

These results are consistent with and corroborate those of Experiments 1 and 2: the disagreement-to-contradiction inference does not seem to hold in the domain of taste and aesthetics. The most natural prediction for the relativist to make about Experiment 3 is that participants should be equally likely to say that Awa's judgment is false in the evaluative (taste and beauty) realm as they are in the descriptive realm (but see note 13). For the relativist, to disagree with someone's judgment just is for that judgment to be false according to one's own C_A (and participants' own C_A is presumably the most natural perspective for them to take when answering all questions in Experiments 1–3).[15]

The results of Experiment 3 also suggest that a slight majority of people think that beauty and (perhaps to a lesser extent) taste judgments are *not* truth-apt at all. In that case, truth relativism may go wrong not so much in taking judgments in this domain to have contents that preclude one another's truth, but more fundamentally, in taking them to be truth-apt in the first place. Relativism is at least no worse off in making this more fundamental assumption than cognitivism more generally.

---

[15] As mentioned in note 13, relativists might allow some flexibility in which C_A is used for any given assessment, but this flexibility is unlikely to explain away the present results, since participants should use the same C_A to evaluate both their own judgments and the actors'. Compare also the experimental methods used here to those of Knobe and Yalcin (2014) and Khoo and Knobe (2018), which invite participants to take a more third-personal stance by asking them to evaluate whether two (other) actors' judgments preclude one anothers' accuracy and whether these actors disagree in virtue of making them, rather than asking participants directly about the relation between their own judgment and an actor's.

5. General Discussion

The results of Experiments 1–3 bear on several facets of the semantics of taste and aesthetic predicates. Most directly, the results pose a challenge for truth relativism, but they may also cast doubt on more fundamental assumptions. I first discuss these negative upshots before addressing what can be positively gleaned from the results about the type of disagreement that *is* present in the domain of taste and aesthetics.

5.1 Relativism and the disagreement-to-contradiction inference

The results of Experiments 1–3 do not refute truth relativism, but they do call into question the main argument that's been given *for* it: the disagreement-to-contradiction inference—and in what seemed, by relativists' own lights, to be the theory's most hospitable domain, using two of its most extreme judgments. If *any* judgments of taste and aesthetics were incorrect, presumably "maggots are delicious" and "sunsets are hideous" would be. The results of Experiments 1–3 suggest that people do not think disagreement with even these taste and aesthetic judgments involves contradiction.

As mentioned at the outset, many relativists take it as a datum that taste and aesthetic disagreement is preclusion of joint accuracy, a claim they appeal to ordinary speakers' intuitions to support. They then propose a semantic theory that can explain this datum, and claim to have tailor-made one to do so. Most fundamentally, the results of Experiments 1–3 suggest this project may be misguided: the datum the whole project is built to explain may not be a datum. Most people think taste and aesthetic disagreements are genuine, but not because they think conflicting taste and aesthetic judgments are contradictory.

These findings also surprisingly suggest that linguistic competence in this domain tracks disagreement more closely than incorrectness. Participants are clear about disagreement—91.8% say they disagree with the judgments that rotten maggots are delicious and that sunsets are hideous (in Experiment 2), but they are divided about incorrectness—only 53.7% say such judgments are incorrect, perhaps reflecting a high degree of uncertainty. The basic project of explaining aesthetic and taste disagreement (something that clearly obtains) in terms of contents that preclude one another's truth or that contradict (something that ordinary English speakers are much more divided on) seems unpromising.

Only preclusion of joint accuracy could ground the inference to truth relativism (MacFarlane 2014). Thus, the results of Experiments 1–3 suggest that the type of disagreement actually exhibited in this domain does not motivate the theory. This casts doubt on the primary argument that's been advanced in support of truth relativism. But the results may also call relativism as such into question, if the theory proves unable to capture the sense of disagreement that *does* obtain in the domain of taste and aesthetics, as discussed below.[16]

5.2 Non-cognitivism and the nature of aesthetic and taste disagreement

Experiments 1 and 2 render the main argument for relativism unprom-ising, but Experiment 3 raises the possibility that a more fundamental assumption may be at fault. Relativists and other cognitivists are typically led to the disagreement-to-contradiction inference because of the con-jecture that taste and aesthetic judgments have truth-apt contents. But the results of Experiment 3 reveal that people's views on truth-aptness vary considerably in this domain, with slightly more than half reporting that they do *not* think taste and aesthetic judgments are true or false at all. Thus, it may be that disagreement in this domain is not only *not* to be explained in terms of contradictory content, but not in terms of truth-apt content period. Relativism does not face this obstacle alone. That 51% of people in the evaluative condition of Experiment 3 claim

---

[16] Another challenge to relativism concerns whether it can account for *why* we would dis-agree in relativistic domains. MacFarlane (2007: 30) writes that "[i]f you say 'skiing is fun' and I contradict you, it is not because I think that the proposition you asserted is false as assessed by you in your current situation, with the affective attitudes you now have, but because I hope to change these attitudes. Perhaps, then, the point of using controversy inducing assessment-sen-sitive vocabulary is to foster coordination of contexts." As several authors have noted, though, this still leaves somewhat mysterious why people would change their attitudes, and so contexts, in the face of such controversy (Haslanger 2007; Dreier 2009). After all, doing so would induce precisely what are, according to one's *current* standard and context, false beliefs.

that "neither Awa's judgment nor my judgment is true and neither is false" is a hurdle for all versions of cognitivism—relativism, contextualism, and invariantism alike.

This hypothesis is importantly less direct and more speculative than the main line of argument against the disagreement-to-contradiction inference. In using that inference to motivate their theory, relativists themselves appeal to ordinary intuitions about the presence of disagreement in the domain in question. In contrast, semantic theorists typically do not directly appeal to speakers' intuitions in order to justify the choice of a semantic theory with truth-apt content. Instead, truth-apt content is usually a theoretical postulate meant to explain the presence of various linguistic phenomena (such as the potential for negation), so it may be more plausible to maintain that ordinary speakers are simply mistaken about this latter, "meta-linguistic" question.[17]

Cognitivists might also attempt to accommodate the results of Experiment 3. Khoo and Knobe (2018), for instance, argue for a version of contextualism that allows judgments to be neither true nor false, though this occurs when they lack a determinate evaluative standard, which seems inapplicable to the extreme judgments used in the experiments here.[18] And relativists might hope that some of the 37% of participants responding that "both Awa's judgment and my judgment are true" in the evaluative condition of Experiment 3 are attempting to ascribe "faultless disagreement" (Kölbel 2004).

But the results of Experiment 3 may instead suggest looking elsewhere: to theories that do not posit truth-apt content in the first place. Classical non-cognitivists like Ayer (1936), Stevenson (1937, 1963), Carnap (1947), and Hare (1952, 1970) deny that evaluative judgments are truth-apt, full stop.[19] Modern expressivists like Gibbard (1990) and Blackburn (1993, 1998), in contrast, try to capture (minimal) notions of truth and correctness, and so somewhat paradoxically may seem no better poised

---

[17] There are pros and cons to asking ordinary English speakers both about 'correctness' and about 'truth.' The best solution may be to use both terms, as in the experiments here.

[18] See also DeRose (2004) on the "exploding scoreboard."

[19] Many of these theories are versions of *moral* non-cognitivism, specifically, though Kant (1790/1987) and Wittgenstein are non-cognitivists about aesthetics. On Kant, see Ginsborg (1990).

to explain the results of Experiment 3 than are cognitivists. Even on these modern non-cognitivist theories, though, evaluative judgments are not true or false "in the first instance." Gibbard and Blackburn propose semantics that are more structurally similar to cognitivist theories than early versions of non-cognitivism, but they reverse their order of explanation: truth and falsity are to be analyzed in terms of a type of disagreement other than contradiction, taken as basic, rather than the other way around. However, once this non-cognitivist analysis has been given, we secure the right to talk of taste and aesthetic judgments' truth and falsity, in at least a minimal sense.[20] Gibbard and Blackburn, then, might take the results of Experiment 3 to reflect participants' (implicit) recognition of this "pre-(in)correctness," non-cognitivist level of analysis.

Experiments 1–3 impugn disagreement as contradiction in the domain of taste and aesthetics. But they leave open the precise nature of the disagreement that does occur in this domain. There are several other (not necessarily exclusive or exhaustive) types of disagreement consistent with these results, and compatible with non-cognitivism.

First, people may disagree in virtue of holding conflicting psychological attitudes—attitudes that do not necessarily have contradictory contents. Stevenson (1937, 1963) argues that A and B can disagree in virtue of having plans that cannot both be realized—for example, conflicting plans about where to go to dinner (together)—even though plans, or intentions, are not truth-apt. Gibbard (2003) and Dreier (2009) note that disagreement in attitude is not always Stevensonian disagreement. If I think that people should take painkillers when they have headaches but you think they ought to tough it out, then we disagree, even though our respective plans to take and not take the one remaining aspirin if we both have a headache do not conflict in Stevenson's sense, since these plans can be jointly realized. Gibbard goes on to offer a

---

[20] "My basic claim about normative thought and talk, though, I now realize, is not about aptness for truth. Rather, mine is a claim about how best to *explain* normative language. An expressivist for a term like 'wrong' starts by explaining the state of mind that calling something 'wrong' expresses. He does not, in the first instance, explain it just as the belief that such-and-such, but in some other, psychological way" (Gibbard 2003: 62–3). On minimal truth, see Horwich (1990) and Dreier (1996).

similar account of disagreement in attitude that appeals to a different type of planning state.

Gibbard's (2003) theory begins with more basic normative attitudes that address the question of "how to live," and he then defines moral judgments derivatively: moral sentences express plans about what moral sentiments to have in different (hypothetical) circumstances. Translating into the domain in question: taste and aesthetic judgments might express plans about what *taste and aesthetic sentiments* to have in different circumstances (Gibbard 1990: 51–2). Thus, people might disagree about matters of taste and aesthetics in virtue of having plans (or preferences) about what taste and aesthetic sentiments to have in one and the same circumstance (in some particular person's "shoes") that cannot be jointly satisfied. This is one type of disagreement that appears to be consistent with the results of Experiments 1–3.[21]

In a second sense, I disagree with someone's attitude about a subject just in case I could not coherently adopt it without changing my current attitude(s) about that subject—that is, if our attitudes or utterances are *non-cotenable* (MacFarlane 2014). This is the sense in which the agnostic disagrees with the theist, and the forecaster who thinks there is a 0.7 chance of snow disagrees with one who thinks it is 0.6. However, non-cotenability is too weak to capture disagreement in many domains and is over-inclusive in others. For instance, it threatens to count as disagreement the exchange in which *A* says, in China, "It's raining here" and *B* says, in Mexico, "No, it's not raining here." Intuitively, these judgments merely *differ*: *A* and *B* do not disagree, even though in one sense, neither could adopt the other's attitude without changing her own (so long as these attitudes do not have indexical or relativized contents).

A related, third type of disagreement is making *incompatible updates to the common ground*—roughly, to the content taken for granted as shared in a given conversational context. Assertions of descriptive matters of fact constitute one way of updating the common ground—they are proposals to narrow down the space of possible worlds to those where

---

[21] Of course, non-cognitivism is thought to have serious problems with embedding (Geach 1960, 1965), which most now take to depend on a solution to the negation problem (Unwin 2001, Schroeder 2008). If Gibbard is right that the negation problem can be solved by taking a type of disagreement in plan as primitive, however, then the embedding problem more generally can be solved by non-cognitivists.

the asserted proposition is true, removing all worlds in which it is not. Thus, assertions with contradictory contents propose to update the common ground in incompatible ways. But there are also other ways to update the common ground—for example, using statements containing epistemic modals, which propose to *leave* certain worlds in play (Yalcin 2007, 2012). These and other types of proposal to update the common ground can be incompatible without being assertions of descriptive matters of fact with contradictory contents. *A* and *B* cannot update the shared scoreboard such that there both might be and might not be a chance of snow, for instance. If the common ground also contains non-informational components like shared plans or preferences, people will not be able to change these in incompatible ways, either—for example, both planning to join the Free French and planning to aid one's ailing mother (together) when the group cannot do both—and attempts to do so will amount to disagreement in this sense.[22]

Thus, non-cognitivism is able to capture (varieties of) the types of disagreement that the present experiments leave open as those that taste and aesthetic disagreement might still be: disagreement in attitude (for example, using Gibbard's framework) and incompatible updates to the common ground (for example, using Yalcin's framework).[23] But some cognitivist theories may be able to capture varieties of these types of disagreement, as well. For instance, Khoo and Knobe's (2018) version of contextualism also allows for disagreement in the sense of incompatible updates to the common ground. Pluralism is another possibility—it may be that the results of Experiment 3 indicate that some people are non-cognitivists about taste and aesthetic disagreement, while others understand it in a way that can be captured by cognitivism (on pluralism, see esp. Wright et al. 2013, 2014). The results of Experiments 1–3 suggest that taste and aesthetic disagreement is not disagreement in the sense of contradiction, but further experimental work is needed to determine which remaining type of disagreement it is, and so which semantic theory accurately describes judgments of taste and aesthetics.

---

[22] Stalnaker's (1973) original formulation of common ground does not include non-informational components like plans or preferences, but these are familiar additions in evaluative domains.

[23] Another possibility is that taste and aesthetic disagreement is "meta-linguistic" (Sundell 2011 and Plunkett and Sundell 2013; cf. Björnsson and Finlay 2010).

5.3 Cultural effects

Finally, previous studies have found evidence consistent with single-scoreboard contextualism in the moral domain (Sarkissian et al. 2011 and Khoo and Knobe 2018), but the present experiments suggest that any apparent cultural differences in the domain of taste and aesthetics are mere pragmatic artifacts. Experiment 1 found that incorrectness and disagreement ratings were higher for judgments of a member of one's own culture compared to judgments made by members of Amazonian and extraterrestrial cultures, but this difference disappeared in Experiment 2 after controlling for the confound with disrespect. This suggests that the effect in Experiment 1 was driven by participants' (stronger) desire to avoid implying disrespect toward members of other cultures compared to members of their own. It is possible that similar effects of disrespect are driving observed cultural differences in moral incorrectness ascriptions, as well, which would call into question the purported evidence for folk (cultural) moral relativism.[24]

6. Conclusion

Truth relativism and other versions of cognitivism are often mobilized to explain the supposed datum that people disagree over matters of taste and aesthetics in virtue of making judgments with contradictory contents. The results of the three experiments presented here suggest that no such explanation is needed because there is no such datum. Nearly all participants in these experiments clearly 'disagree' with conflicting taste and aesthetic judgments, but they are extremely divided about whether these judgments are incorrect. Many explicitly deny that they are 'incorrect.' This makes it doubtful that contradictory content could explain the intuition of disagreement, and discredits the central disagreement-to-contradiction inference, in the domain of taste and

---

[24] See, for example, Harman (1975). For other empirical studies on this ("your Grandpa's") type of relativism, see Nichols (2004), Goodwin and Darley (2008, 2012), Wright et al. (2013, 2014), and Beebee (2015). For concerns about the methodologies used in these experiments, see Pölzler (2018).

aesthetics—where proponents of relativism most expected to find relative truth.

This conclusion assumes that participants' intuitive responses are a reliable guide to their underlying linguistic competence, but ascriptions of incorrectness (and so preclusion of joint accuracy) are still significantly lower than ascriptions of disagreement even after controlling for perhaps the most likely performance error in this context—disrespect.

More radically—and tentatively—these results put pressure on an assumption made by most semantic theories: that taste and aesthetic judgments are truth-apt. Slightly over half of participants in Experiment 3 claim that neither their own taste and aesthetic judgments nor those they disagree with are true *or* false.[25] Non-cognitivism preserves many truth relativist aspirations, capturing comparative subjectivity and preserving the claim that neither of two conflicting taste and aesthetic judgments need be false.[26] Further work is needed on just what type of disagreement is exhibited in the domain of taste and aesthetics. But most ordinary English speakers apparently do not think it is disagreement in the sense of contradiction.

7. Appendix

7.1 Experiment 1

In Experiment 1, a 3 × 2 × 2 ANOVA was performed on ratings with domain (taste vs. beauty) as a within-subjects factor and question (disagree vs. incorrect) and culture (same vs. other vs. extraterrestrial) as between-subjects factors. This analysis revealed significant main effects of question, $F(1, 266) = 43.20$, $\eta_p^2 = 0.14$, $p < 0.001$, with higher ascriptions of disagreement ($M = 6.04$, $SD = 1.41$) than incorrectness ($M = 4.78$, $SD = 1.80$), and of culture, $F(1, 266) = 7.95$, $\eta_p^2 = 0.06$, $p < 0.001$ (see Figure 3.1). Post-hoc tests correcting for multiple comparisons revealed significantly higher ratings in the same culture condition ($M = 5.95$,

---

[25] *Pace* many-valued logics, which Experiment 3 is too coarse-grained to test.
[26] This is not because these judgments have relativized truth values, according to non-cognitivism, but because they are not truth-apt in the first place—at least not "in the first instance."

$SD = 1.42$) than both the other culture condition ($M = 5.18$, $SD = 1.82$) and the extraterrestrial culture condition ($M = 5.12$, $SD = 1.83$). There was no significant main effect of domain, nor any significant interactions.

7.2 Experiment 2

In Experiment 2, a Generalized Estimating Equation was employed on the multinomial response (i)–(iv), with domain (beauty vs. taste) as a within-subjects predictor and question (disagree vs. incorrect) and culture (same vs. other vs. extraterrestrial) as between-subjects predictors. Answer (iii) was used as the reference class. This analysis revealed significant main effects of domain and question, but not of culture. There was also a significant interaction between domain and question (Table 3.1).

To further analyze results, responses were dichotomized in two different ways (rendering the multinomial variable binomial). For the parameter of interest—**incorrect/disagree** ratings—(i) and (ii) were treated as the same response, and (iii) and (iv) as the other. The resulting variable provides a measure of 'disagree' and 'incorrect' ratings that effectively collapses across and so removes any influence of (dis)respect; hence, it can be used to test whether these ratings significantly differ by condition after controlling for (dis)respect. (In addition, for **disrespect** ratings, (i) and (iii) were treated as the same response, (ii) and (iv) as the other, providing a measure of 'disrespect' ratings that collapses across and so removes any influence of (in)correctness/(dis)agreement.)

Table 3.1 Generalized Estimating Equation for responses (i)–(iv) in all conditions of Exp. 2. Question: Incorrect = 0, Disagree = 1. Culture: Same = 1, Other = 2, Extraterrestrial = 3. Domain: Beauty = 0, Taste = 1.

Parameter	β	SE	95% CI	Generalized Score $\chi2$
Question	1.62	0.42	0.80 – 2.44	71.89**
Culture			−0.821 – 0.618	4.36
Domain	−1.07	0.54	−2.14 – −0.01	22.05**
Question x Domain	1.21	0.66	−0.08 – 2.51	6.61*

Note: * $p = 0.01$, ** $p < 0.001$. No other interactions significant.

Table 3.2 Generalized Estimating Equation for dichotomized incorrect/disagree ratings ((i) and (ii) vs. (iii) and (iv)) in all conditions of Exp. 2.

Parameter	β	SE	95% CI	Generalized Score $\chi2$
Intercept	3.05	0.72	1.63 – 4.46	84.46**
Question	−2.73	0.78	−4.27 – −1.19	64.70**
Culture			−0.821 – 0.618	2.30
Domain	0.00	1.02	−2.01 – 2.01	0.04
Question x Domain	−0.09	1.11	−2.26 – 2.08	0.00

Note: ** $p < 0.001$. No interactions significant.

A Generalized Estimating Equation with equivalent parameters to those above was employed on binomial incorrect/disagree ratings. This analysis revealed a significant intercept and a significant main effect of question, but no significant effects of culture, domain, nor any significant interactions (Table 3.2). A chi-square test of independence on question type and incorrect/disagree ratings was significant, $\chi^2(1, N=540) = 98.57$, $p < 0.001$, with 91.8% of participants reporting that they disagree with the actor's judgment, but only 53.7% reporting that the actor's judgment is incorrect (see Figure 3.2).

A Generalized Estimating Equation with equivalent parameters to those above was also employed on binomial disrespect ratings. This analysis revealed a significant intercept and significant main effects of question and domain, but not of culture (Table 3.3). There was a significant interaction between question and domain, accounting for the interaction in the initial (multinomial) Generalized Estimating Equation. A chi-square test of independence on domain and disrespect ratings was significant,

Table 3.3 Generalized Estimating Equation for dichotomized disrespect ratings ((i) and (iii) vs. (ii) and (iv)) in all conditions of Exp. 2.

Parameter	β	SE	95% CI	Generalized Score $\chi2$
Intercept	−0.87	0.33	−1.52 – −0.22	48.46**
Question	0.27	0.45	−0.62 – 1.16	5.01*
Culture			−0.821 – 0.618	5.15
Domain	−1.43	0.62	−2.65 – −0.22	39.76**
Question x Domain	1.53	0.76	0.04 – 3.02	5.09*

Note: * $p < 0.05$, ** $p < 0.001$. No other interactions significant.

$\chi^2(1, N=540) = 26.43$, $p < 0.001$, with 43.0% of participants in the taste condition, but only 22.2% in the beauty condition, reporting that they could not respect the actor's judgment. This difference between domains was also larger for the incorrect question (41.0% vs. 14.9%) than for disagreement (44.9% vs. 29.4%), accounting for the interaction with domain in the Generalized Estimating Equation on disrespect ratings.

7.3 Experiment 3

In Experiment 3, a Generalized Linear Model (GLM) was conducted on the multinomial response (i)–(iv), using realm (descriptive vs. evaluative) and domain (sunset vs. maggots) as predictors (lack of any within-subjects variables obviates the need for a Generalized Estimating Equation, unlike in Experiment 2). Answer (iv) was used as the reference class. This analysis revealed significant main effects of realm and domain, as well as a marginally significant interaction between these variables (Table 3.4).

A set of pre-planned chi-square tests of independence revealed the details of the Generalized Linear Model (see Figure 3.3). Distribution of (i) "neither is true, neither is false" and (ii) "both are true" responses varied significantly by realm, with more (i) responses, $\chi^2(1, N=180) = 31.45$, $p < 0.001$, and more (ii) responses, $\chi^2(1, N=180) = 7.09$, $p < 0.01$, in the evaluative than in the descriptive realm. However, the distribution of (ii) responses only differed significantly by realm in the maggots

Table 3.4 Generalized Linear Model for responses (i)–(iv) in all conditions of Exp. 3. Realm: Descriptive = 0, Evaluative = 1. Domain: Maggots = 0, Sunset = 1.

Parameter	β	SE	95% CI	Likelihood Ratio χ^2
Realm	−1.24	0.44	−2.04 – −0.45	36.33**
Domain	−0.10	0.29	−0.82 – 0.62	5.05*
Realm x Domain	−1.09	0.60	−2.24 – 0.04	3.60†

Note: † $p < 0.06$, * $p < 0.05$, ** $p < 0.001$. Omnibus chi-square test of model: $\chi^2(3, N=180) = 41.67$, $p < 0.001$.

(taste) domain, $\chi^2(1, N=90) = 16.88$, $p < 0.001$; a chi-square test restricting to the sunset (beauty) domain was not significant. This difference likely explains the lion's share of the marginally significant interaction between realm and domain observed in the Generalized Linear Model. Distribution of (iii) "my judgment is true, Awa's is false" and (iv) "both are false" responses also differed significantly by realm, but with *fewer* (iii) responses, $\chi^2(1, N=180) = 47.63$, $p < 0.001$, and fewer (iv) responses, $\chi^2(1, N=180) = 4.74$, $p < 0.05$, in the evaluative than in the descriptive realm. However, the distribution of (iv) responses only differed significantly by realm in the sunset (beauty) domain, $\chi^2(1, N=90) = 4.94$, $p < 0.05$; a chi-square test restricting to the maggots (taste) domain was not significant.

Acknowledgments

This paper was presented at the *Society for Philosophy and Psychology* in 2018 and at the *Princeton Program in Cognitive Science* in 2018. In addition to the audiences there, I would also like to thank for their generous help and feedback Melissa Fusco, Tania Lombrozo, Eddy Nahmias, Shaun Nichols, Lauren Olin, Jonathan Phillips, Rachel Rudolph, Jordan Theriault, Mark van Roojen, Nadya Vasilyeva, Seth Yalcin, two anonymous reviewers for *Oxford Studies in Experimental Philosophy*, and especially Justin Khoo, Joshua Knobe, and John MacFarlane.

References

Ayer, A. 1936. *Language, Truth, and Logic*. New York: Dover.

Beebee, J. 2015. "The Empirical Study of Folk Metaethics." *Etyka*, 50: 11–28.

Björnsson, G. and Finlay, S. 2010. "Metaethical Contextualism Defended." *Ethics*, 121: 7–36.

Blackburn, S. 1993. *Essays in Quasi-Realism*. Oxford: Oxford University Press.

Blackburn, S. 1998. *Ruling Passions*. Oxford: Oxford University Press.

Carnap, R. 1947. *Meaning and Necessity*. Chicago: Chicago University Press.

Cova, F. and Pain, N. 2012. "Can Folk Aesthetics Ground Aesthetic Realism?" *The Monist*, 95: 241–63.

DeRose, K. 2004. "Single Scoreboard Semantics." *Philosophical Studies*, 119: 1–21.

Dreier, J. 1996. "Expressivist Embeddings and Minimalist Truth." *Philosophical Studies*, 83: 29–51.

Dreier, J. 2006. "Disagreeing (about) What to Do: Negation and Completeness in Gibbard's Norm-Expressivism." *Philosophy and Phenomenological Research*, 72: 714–21.

Dreier, J. 2009. "Relativism (and Expressivism) and the Problem of Disagreement." *Philosophical Perspectives*, 23: 79–110.

Egan, A. 2007. "Epistemic Modals, Relativism, and Assertion." *Philosophical Studies*, 133: 1–22.

Egan, A. 2010. "Disputing about Taste." In R. Feldman and T. Warfield (eds.), *Disagreement* (pp. 247–86). Oxford: Oxford University Press.

Geach, P. 1960. "Ascriptivism." *Philosophical Review*, 69: 221–5.

Geach, P. 1965. "Assertion." *Philosophical Review*, 74: 449–65.

Gibbard, A. 1990. *Wise Choices, Apt Feelings*. Cambridge, MA: Harvard University Press.

Gibbard, A. 2003. *Thinking How to Live*. Cambridge, MA: Harvard University Press.

Ginsborg, H. 1990. "Reflective Judgment and Taste." *Noûs*, 24: 63–78.

Goodwin, G. and Darley, J. 2008. "The Psychology of Meta-Ethics: Exploring Objectivism." *Cognition*, 106: 1339–66.

Goodwin, G. and Darley, J. 2012. "Why Are Some Moral Beliefs Perceived To Be More Objective Than Others?" *Journal of Experimental Social Psychology*, 48: 250–6.

Hare, R. 1952. *The Language of Morals*. Oxford: Oxford University Press.

Hare, R. 1970. "Meaning and Speech Acts." *Philosophical Review*, 79: 3–24.

Harman, G. 1975. "Moral Relativism Defended." *Philosophical Review*, 84: 3–22.

Haslanger, S. 2007. " 'But mom, crop-tops are cute!' Social Knowledge, Social Structure and Ideology Critique." *Philosophical Issues*, 17: 70–91.

Horwich, P. 1990. *Truth*. Oxford: Oxford University Press.

Hume, D. 1757/1965. "Of the Standard of Taste." In J. Lenz (ed.), *Of the Standard of Taste and Other Essays*. Indianapolis: Bobbs-Merrill.

Kant, I. 1790/1987. *Critique of Judgment*. Indianapolis: Hackett.

Katz, J. and Salerno, J. 2017. "Epistemic Modal Disagreement." *Topoi*, 36: 141–53.

Khoo, J. 2015. "Modal Disagreements." *Inquiry*, 58: 511–34.

Khoo, J. and Knobe, J. 2018. "Moral Disagreement and Moral Semantics." *Noûs*, 52: 109–43.

Knobe, J. and Yalcin, S. 2014. "Epistemic Modals and Context: Experimental Data." *Semantics and Pragmatics*, 7: 1–21.

Kölbel, M. 2004. "Faultless Disagreement." *Proceedings of the Aristotelian Society*, 104: 53–73.

Lasersohn, P. 2005. "Context Dependence, Disagreement, and Predicates of Personal Taste." *Linguistics and Philosophy*, 28: 643–86.

Lewis, D. 1979. "Scorekeeping in a Language Game." *Journal of Philosophical Logic*, 8: 339–59.

MacFarlane, J. 2003. "Future Contingents and Relative Truth." *Philosophical Quarterly*, 53: 321–36.

MacFarlane, J. 2004. "Making Sense of Relative Truth." *Proceedings of the Aristotelian Society*, 105: 321–39.

MacFarlane, J. 2007. "Relativism and Disagreement." *Philosophical Studies*, 132: 17–31.

MacFarlane, J. 2014. *Assessment Sensitivity: Relative Truth and its Applications*. Oxford: Oxford University Press.

Nichols, S. 2004. "After Objectivity: An Empirical Study of Moral Judgment." *Philosophical Psychology*, 17: 3–26.

Plunkett, D. and Sundell, T. 2013. "Disagreement and the Semantics of Normative and Evaluative Terms." *Philosophers' Imprint*, 13: 1–37.

Pölzler, Thomas. 2018. *Moral Reality and the Empirical Sciences*. New York: Routledge.

Richard, M. 2004. "Contextualism and Relativism." *Philosophical Studies*, 119: 215–42.

Richard, M. 2008. *When Truth Gives Out*. Oxford: Oxford University Press.

Sarkissian, H., Park, J., Tien, D., Wright, J., and Knobe, J. 2011. "Folk Moral Relativism." *Mind and Language*, 26: 482–505.

Schroeder, M. 2008. "How Expressivists Can and Should Solve Their Problem With Negation." *Noûs*, 42: 573–99.

Stalnaker, R. 1973. "Presuppositions." *Journal of Philosophical Logic*, 2: 447–57.

Stephenson, T. 2007. "Judge Dependence, Epistemic Modals, and Predicates of Personal Taste." *Linguistics and Philosophy*, 30: 487–525.

Stevenson, C. L. 1937. "The Emotive Meaning of Ethical Terms." *Mind*, 46: 14–31.

Stevenson, C. L. 1963. *Facts and Values*. New Haven: Yale University Press.

Sundell, T. 2011. "Disagreements about Taste." *Philosophical Studies*, 155: 267–88.

Unwin, N. 2001. "Norms and Negation: A Problem for Gibbard's Logic." *Philosophical Quarterly*, 51: 60–75.

Wright, J., Grandjean, P., and McWhite, C. 2013. "The Meta-Ethical Grounding of our Moral Beliefs: Evidence for Meta-Ethical Pluralism." *Philosophical Psychology*, 26: 336–61.

Wright, J., McWhite, C., and Grandjean, P. 2014. "The Cognitive Mechanisms of Intolerance: Do our Meta-Ethical Commitments Matter?" In K. Knobe, T. Lombrozo, and S. Nichols (eds.), *Oxford Studies in Experimental Philosophy*, Vol. 1 (pp. 28–61). Oxford: Oxford University Press.

Yalcin, S. 2007. "Epistemic Modals." *Mind*, 116: 983–1026.

Yalcin, S. 2012. "Bayesian Expressivism." *Proceedings of the Aristotelian Society*, 112: 123–60.

Yu, A. 2016. "Epistemic Modals and Sensitivity to Contextually-Salient Partitions." *Thought*, 5: 134–46.

4

Does Skepticism Lead to Tranquility?
Exploring a Pyrrhonian Theme

Mario Attie-Picker
Yale University

Pyrrhonian Skepticism, as described by the writings of Sextus Empiricus, presents itself, like most philosophical schools from the Hellenistic period, as offering advice on everyday life. That is, Sextus presents Skepticism as a philosophy with important practical consequences. The main claim is that the Skeptic, unlike the Dogmatist, is able to achieve *ataraxia* (tranquility).

Sextus argues that belief brings disturbance to our lives. The Skeptic, who holds no beliefs, is the only person capable of living a tranquil existence (*M* 11.140).[1] At the core of Sextus's project is the thesis that belief itself, independently of any action resulting from it, creates anxiety. As we shall see, the plausibility and success of Pyrrhonism depend on the veracity of this claim. The crucial point to note is that Sextus's thesis is an empirical claim about human psychology. In other words, Sextus's assertion that belief causes anxiety is a claim about our affective reaction to a specific mental state, namely the state of believing a proposition to be true or false. As an empirical hypothesis it is in principle falsifiable, and so it is subject to empirical investigation.

The chapter is organized as follows. In Section 1, I discuss Sextus's writings, focusing on his ethics and practical claims, specifically the relationship between belief and anxiety. My aim here is to show the central role of Sextus's empirical predictions in the rest of his philosophy.

---

[1] The texts of Sextus to which I refer are *The Outlines of Scepticism*, trans. Julia Annas and Jonathan Barnes (Cambridge University Press, 2000), referred to as *PH*; *Against the Ethicists*, trans. Richard Bett (Oxford University Press, 1997), referred to as *M*.

Mario Attie-Picker, *Does Skepticism Lead to Tranquility? Exploring a Pyrrhonian Theme* In: *Oxford Studies in Experimental Philosophy*. Edited by: Tania Lombrozo, Joshua Knobe, and Shaun Nichols, Oxford University Press (2020).
© Mario Attie-Picker.
DOI: 10.1093/oso/9780198852407.003.0005

In Section 2, I review modern research on dogmatism and anxiety, and the implication of their findings for Sextus's philosophy. In Section 3, I use experimental methods to examine Sextus's claim that skepticism is conducive to tranquility. In Section 4, I consider some objections to the conclusions drawn from the experimental results.

1. Belief and Anxiety in Sextus Empiricus

Sextus tells us that the Skeptic's end is "tranquility in matters of opinion and moderation of feeling in matters forced upon us" (*PH* 1.25). It is important to note that Sextus does not aim to relieve us from all anxiety. It is only in matters of opinion (*dogmata*), i.e., belief, which the Skeptic purports to remove disturbance. Sextus also recognizes that, being the creatures we are, there are instances where *ataraxia* is unattainable. Physical pain, hunger, fatigue, and the like naturally produce distress, "for he is not born from an oak of ancient legend, nor from a rock / But was of the race of men" (*M* 11.161). However, Sextus claims that the Skeptic would be better equipped to deal with these feelings than the Dogmatist. Why is this so?

Sextus writes that any belief about something being good or bad is a permanent source of anxiety (*M* 11.110–40; *PH* 1.27, 3.235–7). If one has what one believes to be good, one fears the prospect of losing it, and this creates distress. Conversely, lacking what one believes is good is a bad state of affairs, and so this produces anxiety as well. The claim is that any belief concerning what is good or bad is subject to the same logic: "those who hold the opinion that things are good or bad by nature are perpetually troubled" (*PH* 1.27). Now, there is an enormous literature devoted to the question of the *scope* of Pyrrhonism.[2] One common (though by no means uncontroversial) interpretation is that the Skeptic has no beliefs about the way things are, but accepts[3] the way things appear to him to be (see *PH* 1.13, 1.24–5).[4] If this is right, Sextus's

---

[2] See, e.g., Burnyeat (1980), Barnes (1982), Frede (1987), and Perin (2010).

[3] The issue of what 'accepting' an appearance involves and how it relates to belief is also the subject of great controversy. For one influential proposal, see Burnyeat (1980).

[4] Here is the key passage in full: "When we say that Skeptics do not hold beliefs, we do not take 'belief' in the sense in which some say, quite generally, that belief is acquiescing in

argument applies to beliefs, in contrast to appearances, about what is good or bad. Indeed, Sextus says that "from an everyday point of view," that is, from the point of view of ordinary appearances, Skeptics "accept...that piety is good and impiety bad" (*PH* 1.24). The Skeptic, at the time of action, follows what appears to be good and avoids what appears to be bad. It is only when belief is involved that anxiety ensues.

Sextus also points to the rashness and intensity by which Dogmatists pursue their "goods." Sextus gives money and glory as examples of putative goods which make people obsessive and self-destructive: "For each person, in pursuing intensely and with excessive confidence what he thinks is good and to be chosen, falls without realizing it into the neighboring vice" (*M* 11.121). Nussbaum emphasizes that such intensity obtains independently of the truth-value of one's beliefs: "The disease is not one of *false* belief," she writes, "belief itself is the illness—belief as a commitment, a source of concern, care, and vulnerability" (Nussbaum, 1994: 284).

How are we supposed to escape the "disease" of belief? Sextus's answer is simple: by suspending judgment about what is good or bad by nature and thereby losing the relevant beliefs. Suspension of judgment, however, cannot be reached simply by noticing that tranquility would come of it. The claim that belief about the good has unwanted affective consequences tells the Skeptic nothing about whether or not he ought to assent to such beliefs. Sextus's remarks merely show the positive effects of suspending judgment, and correspondingly, the negative implications of belief. Sextus makes this point explicitly: "But when *reason* has established that none of these things is by nature good or by nature bad, there will be release from disturbance and a peaceful life will await us" (*M* 11.130, emphasis mine).

Suspension of judgment, Sextus explains, comes about by the opposition of equally potent arguments (what he calls "equipollence") (*PH* 1.31). The Skeptic, seeing conflicting arguments for a given proposition, is unable to decide for one over the other, and so suspends judgment

---

something; for Skeptics assent to the feelings forced upon them by appearances—for example, they would not say, when heated or chilled, 'I think I am not heated (or: chilled).' Rather, we say that they do not hold beliefs in the sense in which some say that belief is assent to some unclear object of investigation in the sciences; for Pyrrhonists do not assent to anything unclear" (*PH* 1.13).

about the topic at hand. This works for any proposition p. The Skeptic reflects that it appears to her that there is no reason to believe either p or its negation. This consideration causes her to experience a new psychological state—suspension of judgment. A belief drops out when the Skeptic is able to produce a state of equipollence, as she comes to realize that there is no adequate justification for it. If some beliefs bring disturbance to our life, the solution is to lose these beliefs. And for this to happen, Sextus needs to produce equipollence.

A sizable portion of *Against the Ethicists* is devoted precisely to this end (e.g., *M* 11.68–71; see also *PH* 1.145–63). Sextus goes to considerable lengths to argue against the existence of objective values.[5] Whether these arguments are sound is beside the point.[6] What is important is that Sextus's arguments lead him to suspend judgment on whether something is by nature good (or bad), and as a result he finds himself tranquil.

The fortuitous manner in which the Skeptic first attains *ataraxia* illustrates an important point in Sextus's Skepticism. The classic passage is the Apelles story (*PH* 1.28–9). Apelles, a painter, is unable to draw the lather of the horse's mouth. In desperation he throws his sponge at the picture, but it just so happens that the impact "produced a representation of the horse's lather." Similarly, the Skeptic, like everyone else annoyed by the "anomalies" in things, embarked on the search of truth with the hope that knowing the truth would relieve her of distress. The Skeptic, like Apelles, failed to find the truth, and instead suspended judgment. But then the Skeptic made an important discovery—his original disturbance was gone: "When they suspended judgment, tranquility followed as it were fortuitously, as a shadow follows a body" (*PH* 1.29).

The Pyrrhonian project is thus built upon the empirical observation that suspension of judgment regularly—in fact invariably ("as a shadow follows a body")—brings about tranquility. The Apelles story (*PH* 1.28–9) is presented as the accidental discovery of this fact about human

---

[5] There is an ongoing debate in the literature concerning Sextus's use of seemingly dogmatic arguments in *Against the Ethicists*. The details of the debate fall outside the scope of the present chapter. It suffices to say that there is a cogent interpretation claiming that Sextus does not offer these arguments to convince the reader of their truth—rather, the point is to counteract the arguments given by the Dogmatists, and so take the reader to suspension of judgment. See, e.g., Hankinson (1994).

[6] For a thorough discussion of these arguments, see McPherran (1990), Annas (1993), and Bett's commentary in Sextus Empiricus (1997).

psychology. Once the Skeptic experiences this process and its result (*ataraxia*), he devises a system that enables him to consistently reach the desired mental state. Sextus defines his philosophy as the continual reenactment of this procedure—the creation of opposing arguments of equal force—with the explicit end of becoming tranquil (*PH* 1.8–10). Furthermore, he claims that Skepticism is the only way to achieve *ataraxia*; since the problem is with belief itself, and not with any particular beliefs, any philosophy consisting of beliefs would fail (*M* 11.140).

But what if we disagree? How can Sextus convince us? Annas writes, "if we disagree with Sextus...about the claim that scepticism is the best way to happiness, there seems to be a standoff....Sextus can only say that if we disagree, it is because we have dogmatic beliefs; if we became sceptical we would lose those beliefs and then, he predicts, we would have appearances like his." She concludes: "There is nothing to be done but try and see" (Annas, 1993: 362). To this end, precisely, we turn next.

2. The Empirical Study of Dogmatism

There is a tradition in psychology that investigates, just as Sextus did, the relationship between our affective states and our cognitive processes. In this context, research on dogmatism has had an important place. Psychologists have followed Sextus in seeing a connection between affective responses to the world and the way we form and maintain our beliefs. In particular, dogmatism as a stable trait, and dogmatic behavior more generally, have often been understood as *reactions* to unpleasant states such as anxiety and fear. This line of research has obtained important findings that bear on Sextus's claim that dogmatism leads to anxiety.

Nevertheless, a worry arises about whether the Pyrrhonian concept of 'dogmatism' has any relation to the psychological phenomenon referred to by the same word. The worry can be put as an objection: one should not draw from psychology to illuminate Sextus's claims, as each employs a different concept of dogmatism. For the Pyrrhonians, dogmatism is the holding of *belief*, especially those (associated with the philosophical schools) about the way the world really is. In contrast, psychologists often conceptualize dogmatism as a kind of *epistemic profile*, that is, a manner of forming and revising beliefs. Different researchers vary in how they characterize such profile. Some emphasize excessive subjective confidence and how open one is to the possibility of being wrong (e.g., Altemeyer, 1996); others focus on how dependent one's beliefs are on an external authority (e.g., Rokeach, 1960). At its core, however, researchers agree that the dogmatic profile is characterized by a reluctance to change one's beliefs in light of contradictory evidence; the dogmatist's beliefs are fixed, and as such they are not sensitive to new information.

Now, Sextus does not distinguish between different kinds of epistemic profiles (and so between dogmatic and non-dogmatic beliefs). Psychologists, however, make this distinction explicit. This is, of course, a fundamental difference, and to that extent it complicates the relation between contemporary research and Sextus's claims. But it would be a mistake to conclude from this that existing research has nothing to say about the Pyrrhonian hypothesis.

Sextus regards as a dogmatist anyone who holds beliefs, and he does not differentiate beliefs that are the product of adequate epistemic profiles from those that are not, but this is because he thinks that no epistemic profile can be adequate if it leads to the formation of beliefs (i.e., he takes skepticism as the only adequate epistemic profile). Or to put it differently, Sextus takes all belief to be epistemically flawed. Importantly for our purposes, Sextus argues against the adequacy of the Dogmatists' beliefs in a specific manner. Not only does Sextus argue that the Dogmatists' beliefs are unjustified, but also that they are so in a way resembling the dogmatic profile as defined by psychologists.[7] Sextus often portrays the Dogmatists as overconfident and unwilling to revise, let alone question, their beliefs. What is crucial to notice is that this characterization plays an important role in Sextus's claims about anxiety. Recall that Sextus points to the "excessive confidence" of the Dogmatists, and the behaviour that results from it, as causes of anxiety (M 11.121). In other words, Sextus locates anxiety not only in beliefs of certain kind, but also in a manner of holding them, i.e., in an epistemic profile. If this is right, then research on what psychologists call 'dogmatism' is relevant in assessing the Pyrrhonian hypothesis. For the epistemic profile tied to

---

[7] As Burnyeat puts it, "to the extent that it is justified to read in [that is, to read in Sextus] the modern connotation of 'dogmatism', viz. person with an obstinate and unreasonable attachment to his opinions, this belongs not to the core meaning of the Greek term but to the sceptic's argued claim…that all belief is unreasonable" (Burnyeat, 1980: 26, emphasis original).

anxiety in Sextus's writings has much in common with that at play in psychological research.

Consider how Sextus first presents his brand of skepticism. He opens the *Outlines* by arguing that "the most fundamental difference among philosophies" is that the Dogmatists, convinced that they have arrived at the truth, have stopped investigation, whereas "the Sceptics are still investigating" (*PH* 1.1–3). For Sextus, the refusal to terminate inquiry is what fundamentally sets Skepticism apart from other epistemic profiles.[8] Correspondingly, premature termination of inquiry is usually thought to be constitutive of the dogmatic manner of belief-formation. The dogmatist is said to end inquiry not after a proper consideration of opposing viewpoints, but rather at the point that best suits what he already believes (Altemeyer, 1996).[9]

Another important point of contact concerns the believer's reaction to contradictory evidence. As mentioned above, it is a platitude in psychology to take dogmatism as a persistence of belief in spite of contradictory evidence. Sextus, of course, charges the Dogmatists with precisely this fault. A central component of the Pyrrhonian project is to present the Dogmatists with arguments against their views. From the Skeptic's perspective, their refusal to suspend judgment in light of such arguments is partly what defines them *as* Dogmatists.

There is, therefore, substantive overlap between how psychologists understand dogmatism and Sextus's characterization of the epistemic profile that is said to bring about anxiety. My hope is that the overlap is enough to justify studying the former to draw inferences about the latter.

2.1 Empirical results and interpretations

Dogmatism and anxiety, and the relationship between them, have been studied empirically by a variety of psychologists and social scientists.

---

[8] Sextus's insistence that the Skeptics "are still investigating" raises interesting questions vis-à-vis the Pyrrhonist's end of achieving tranquility. For what if the investigation yields belief, and thus, according to Sextus, anxiety? In other words, if tranquility is the end, why keep investigating? See Perin (2010) for an insightful discussion of this question.

[9] As we shall see, the tendency to prematurely settle on an answer is a key component of cognitive closure, a psychological construct resembling dogmatism in many respects (Kruglanski and Webster, 1996).

In the present section, I review the existing research and discuss its relevance for Sextus's theory. Most of the empirical work assessing the relationship between dogmatism and anxiety has focused on the impact of anxiety on the content and structure of belief systems. The emphasis on one side of the relation—the effects of anxiety on dogmatism—tends to ignore the possibility that the causal relation could go in the other direction. This is what Sextus claims. According to Sextus, it is dogmatism that leads to anxiety. For this reason, the existing research cannot properly test the Pyrrhonian hypothesis. As we shall see, however, the findings are relevant and seem to tell against Sextus. This is because psychologists, in direct opposition to Sextus, have theorized that dogmatism tends to allay anxiety.

The empirical evidence describing the relationship between dogmatism and anxiety is far from conclusive. A large body of correlational findings suggests that they are positively correlated (Fruchter et al., 1958; Plant et al., 1965; Rebhun, 1966; Sticht and Fox, 1966; Vacchiano et al., 1968). But the Dogmatism Scale (D scale), used in all of the above studies, has been extensively criticized for its lack of construct validity (Altemeyer, 1996) and for its semantic overlap with anxiety (Gaensslen et al., 1973). A review of the literature on dogmatism and anxiety showed that eleven items of the D scale have a semantic connection to anxiety and similar manifestations of it (e.g., helplessness, worry). The thought was simple enough: remove these eleven items and see if the resulting score still correlates with anxiety. If the relationship disappears, it means that what correlated with anxiety in the previous findings was not dogmatism—but other manifestations of anxiety. And this is exactly what was found (Gaensslen et al., 1973).

As far as I know, there has been no direct experimental work manipulating anxiety to measure dogmatism—but there has been research related to both anxiety and dogmatism. Manipulations often involve feelings of threat and uncertainty rather than anxiety, while the measures often involve cognitive closure, system-justification, and conservatism, instead of dogmatism. Unfortunately, this is the closest the existing data gets to our original question.

Especially relevant to dogmatism is people's inclination, under situational constraints, to desire definite knowledge on a given issue. This desire, known as need for cognitive closure, has been demonstrated to heighten under time pressure and ambient noise (Kruglanski and Webster, 1996), variables that could conceivably elicit anxiety levels. People under high need for cognitive closure exhibit many of the characteristic epistemic markers of dogmatism. Under the urgency tendency (a desire to achieve closure as soon as possible), information processing is reduced, both in time and in depth, and hypothesis generation decreases while subjective confidence increases. Similarly, the permanence tendency (a desire to maintain closure for as long as possible) pushes against the possibility of disconfirmation, leading people to seek consensus by punishing deviates and fostering confirmation bias (Mayseless and Kruglanski, 1987; Kruglanski and Webster, 1991, 1996). It is not clear that need for cognitive closure increases as a result of anxiety, but if this were the case (as seems plausible given the situational variables that have been shown to do so), it would suggest that similar mechanisms are in place regarding dogmatism.[10]

Nevertheless, the effect of anxiety on dogmatism is far from clear. On the one hand, some studies have directly manipulated anxiety and have found an increase in epistemic profiles that overlap with dogmatism. For example, research in compensatory control underscores the extent to which anxiety arising from perceptions of randomness and uncertainty increase belief in controlling authorities like God and the government (Kay et al., 2008; Kay et al., 2009; Kay et al., 2010). Participants who were asked to think of a memory where they lacked control over a specific situation later expressed stronger beliefs in God and higher support of the sociopolitical system (Kay et al., 2008). While dogmatism does not necessarily imply any sort of belief about God or the government, it is closely tied to epistemic reliance on an external authority (Rokeach, 1960). To the degree that anxiety causes people to strengthen their belief in such authorities, it is again plausible that it could increase dogmatism in a general manner. On the other hand, recent research in political psychology suggests that anxiety fosters open-mindedness and reflective deliberation (Valentino et al., 2008; MacKuen et al., 2010). In one study,

---

[10] The Need for Closure Scale (NFC), a scale designed to measure individual differences in need for cognitive closure, correlated positively with the D scale (0.28) (Webster and Kruglanski, 1994).

a manipulation designed to induce anxiety regarding one's political beliefs (in contrast to one designed to induce aversion) made participants more willing to seek more information, take others' perspective, and reach for compromise (MacKuen et al., 2010; see Kurth (2016, 2018) for a discussion of these findings and of the epistemic benefits of anxiety more generally). Therefore, the causal impact of anxiety on the formation of dogmatic epistemic profiles remains largely an open question.

As we have seen, however, it is the other side of the relationship that is the focus of Pyrrhonian ethics, for Sextus's claim is that dogmatism leads to anxiety. On this score, psychologists have been less equivocal, as they have theorized that dogmatism enables the individual to successfully cope with anxiety (Rokeach, 1960). If this were the case, Sextus would be in great trouble. The Pyrrhonian claim that dogmatism causes anxiety is in direct conflict with the modern claim that dogmatism reduces anxiety.

In light of the data reviewed above, many researchers have argued that dogmatism, and related systems of beliefs, serve an anxiety-reducing function (Rokeach, 1960; Jost and Hunyady, 2003; Jost et al., 2003; Kay et al., 2009). The idea is that all belief systems serve certain psychological and epistemic needs. Specifically, belief systems perform two fundamental (and sometimes conflicting) functions: (1) the need to know and understand the world, and (2) the need to protect against anxiety, worry, and a variety of negative affective states. Thus, by closing our belief system (i.e., becoming more dogmatic) people can preserve the illusion of knowledge and consistency while defending against external and internal anxiety. Dogmatism, conceptualized as a belief system dependent on external authority and exhibiting isolation among its individual beliefs,[11] prevents people from experiencing the anxiety involved in having contradictory beliefs (internal anxiety) and from new information threatening the validity of the system (external anxiety) (Rokeach, 1954, 1960). More generally, research on system-justification explains people's overall propensity to justify, legitimatize, and rationalize the status quo of existing sociopolitical systems by positing that it helps disadvantaged groups and minorities to eliminate anxiety arising from

---

[11] A belief is isolated when its rejection or acceptance does not affect other beliefs that are objectively related to it.

perceiving their position as unjust and unfair (Jost and Hunyady, 2003; Jost et al., 2004).

To sum up, there seems to be a consensus among psychologists that dogmatism, and overlapping phenomena like system-justification, serves the psychological need to cope with anxiety by protecting the person against perceptions of uncertainty and threat. The theory is offered as an explanation for the empirical data showing a positive correlation between anxiety and dogmatism, as well as some experimental manipulations suggesting that anxiety makes people more likely to adhere to dogmatic epistemic profiles. Note that the empirical results, by themselves, do not pose a problem for Sextus, for even if it is true that anxiety leads to dogmatism, it may still be the case that the latter could, in turn, exacerbate the former. The problem for Sextus, however, is the following: dogmatism is thought to be in part motivated by a psychological need to reduce anxiety. This putative function stands in stark contrast with Sextus's claim. Sextus presents his Skepticism as a therapeutic practice capable of alleviating the anxiety resulting from the beliefs of the Dogmatists. But existing research proposes that it is dogmatism, as opposed to open-mindedness, that has an anxiety-reducing effect. Thus, the palliative function that Sextus ascribes to Skepticism, modern psychologists attribute to dogmatism. In order to adjudicate between them it is necessary to experimentally manipulate dogmatism (or certain aspects of it) and test for its effect on anxiety. This is the goal of the present research.

3. An Experimental Approach to Pyrrhonian Skepticism

3.1 Study 1

To my knowledge, no one has tested for a correlation between anxiety and dogmatism using Altemeyer's DOG scale.[12] This was the first step taken in the present study.

---

[12] The DOG scale is a twenty-item scale designed to measure dogmatism understood as "unchangeable, unjustified certainty" (Altemeyer, 1996: 201). Recent studies have shown its construct validity, arguing that the DOG scale accurately reflects Altemeyer's conceptualization (Altemeyer, 2002; Crowson et al., 2008; Crowson, 2009).

3.1.1 Method

One hundred participants were recruited from Amazon's Mechanical Turk pool. The participants' ages ranged from 19 to 74 years with a mean of 33.5 years. Forty-one percent were females, 66% identified themselves as white, 13% as Asians, 11% African American, 6% Hispanic, and the rest answered "other." Eight participants were excluded due to failing basic attention checks and three more were excluded due to failure to complete the entirety of the study.

Participants were instructed to complete a series of surveys as part of an ongoing "investigation of general public opinion concerning a variety of social issues." Altemeyer's DOG scale and a religious fundamentalism scale (Altemeyer and Hunsberger, 2004) were then administered.[13] In addition, participants filled out a survey, call it the 'Sextan scale,' (see Appendix) comprising eight items designed to measure agreement with the type of moral beliefs that Sextus describes as leading to anxiety (e.g., 'some things are good or bad by nature') (Cronbach's $\alpha = 0.73$). Participants responded using a nine-point scale ranging from "very strongly disagree" to "very strongly agree." Finally, participants completed the State-Trait Anxiety Inventory for Adults (STAI) developed by Spielberger and Gorsuch (1983). The STAI was used for its proven validity and for its ability to measure, and differentiate between, state and trait anxiety (Oei et al., 1990).

3.1.2 Results

There was a significant correlation between DOG score and trait anxiety. Contrary to Sextus's claim, however, it went in the opposite direction ($r = -0.31$, $p < 0.01$). There was also a significant negative correlation between Sextan score and trait anxiety ($r = -0.33$, $p < 0.001$). Religiosity also correlated negatively with trait anxiety, but not as strongly as dogmatism did ($r = -0.26$, $p < 0.05$).

A multiple linear regression was run with trait anxiety as the dependent variable and DOG score, Sextan score, and religiosity as the independent variables. Sextan score significantly predicted anxiety ($\beta = -0.27$, $p = 0.01$),

---

[13] The religiosity scale was administered because it seemed reasonable to suppose that religiosity could influence the relationship between dogmatism and anxiety.

DOG score was marginally significant ($\beta = -0.24$, $p = 0.07$), and religiosity did not predict anxiety ($\beta = 0$, $p = 0.98$).[14]

3.1.3 Discussion

The findings show a significant relationship between anxiety and dogmatism: they are inversely correlated. That is, higher levels of dogmatism predict lower levels of trait anxiety. Further, higher scores in Dogmatic moral statements (Sextan score) are also inversely correlated with anxiety. The results are the exact opposite of Sextus's claims.

It is crucial to remember that the measure of interest was *trait anxiety*. Trait anxiety is defined, contrary to state anxiety, as a personality trait; it does not describe a temporary affective state but a relatively stable characteristic in an individual (Spielberger, 2010). People with high trait anxiety scores tend to be more anxious generally in their everyday life. What this correlation shows is that dogmatic people are less likely to be anxious individuals. This runs contrary to Sextus's claim. Pyrrhonian ethics is motivated by the claim that the Dogmatists live with greater levels of anxiety than they otherwise would. The correlation shows that people high in dogmatism are *less*, as opposed to *more*, anxious.

3.2 Study 2

The results of Study 1, however, are merely correlational—no claim about causality can be made based on them. In fact, most research done so far has been correlational.

These studies are thus limited in their reach. A design is needed where dogmatism is manipulated and anxiety measured; such a design would make it possible to study the causal relation between the two variables. Study 2 was designed with this in mind.

3.2.1 Method

Two hundred and one participants were recruited from Amazon's Mechanical Turk pool. The participants' ages ranged from 18 to 67 years

---

[14] Test for multicollinearity indicated that a low level of multicollinearity was present (*VIF* = 1.13 for Sextan score, 1.97 for DOG score, and 2.08 for religiosity).

with a mean of 35.2 years. Fifty three percent were females, 77% identified themselves as white, 4% as Asians, 9% African American, 5% Hispanic, and the rest answered "other." Two participants were excluded due to failing basic attention checks.

Participants were informed that their assignment was to read a science article for high school students and rate its grade-level appropriateness. Participants were randomly assigned to three different conditions. In the 'certain' condition, participants read a fictitious scientific article claiming that science has discovered what determines happiness. The article cites (fake) experts and experiments arguing that we now possess actual knowledge about the causes of happiness. It argues that happiness is a predictable phenomenon arising specifically from a positive attitude and a rich social life. It emphasizes that the road to happiness may be a hard one, but that if followed correctly it will succeed. In the 'skeptic' condition, the article claims the opposite. It argues that science has failed in its attempt to arrive at any plausible theory of happiness. Experts communicate the unpredictable nature of happiness and the need to suspend judgment about its causes. The article does not claim that happiness is random or outside of one's control; it simply argues that, as of now, we have little knowledge about what determines happiness. Finally, the third condition was a 'control', where participants read an article about the Earth's core. Geology was selected for being an emotionally neutral subject matter. To make the cover story believable participants answered questions regarding the appropriateness and length of the material. Participants were then asked to answer based on their own opinion whether we possess knowledge about what determines happiness. Six different statements, three worded positively (e.g., 'we know what determines happiness') and three negatively (e.g., 'as of now, we lack knowledge about the factors determining happiness') were answered using a seven-point scale ranging from "strongly disagree" to "strongly agree." This was done to test if the manipulation influenced the participants' own views. Participants then filled out the STAI and the DOG scale, and were debriefed.

3.2.2 Results

The first step was to check if the manipulation was effective. A one-way ANOVA showed that the manipulation had a significant effect on

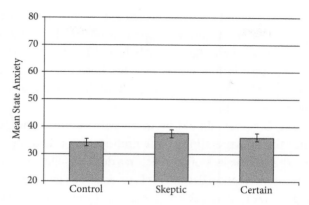

Figure 4.1 Mean state anxiety by condition. Error bars indicate standard error of the mean.

participants' own opinions, $F(2, 196) = 33.21$, p <0.001. Tukey's post-hoc tests showed that participants reported having less knowledge about what determines happiness in the "skeptic" condition ($M = 3.66$, $SD = 1.18$) than both in the 'certain' condition ($M = 5.06$, $SD = 1.02$), p <0.001 and in the 'control' condition ($M = 4.46$, $SD = 0.70$), p <0.001. Participants reported less knowledge in the 'control' condition than in the 'certain' condition, $p = 0.002$.

However, a one-way ANOVA showed no significant effect between the conditions in terms of state anxiety, $F(2, 196) = 1.13$, $p = 0.30$ (Figure 4.1). Finally, since the manipulation had no effect on anxiety, we collapsed across conditions to correlate DOG score and trait anxiety. Once again, a significant negative correlation was found ($r = -0.26$, p <0.001).

3.2.3 Discussion

The manipulation was designed with Sextus in mind. It aimed to mirror Sextus's theory on the relationship between anxiety and belief. According to Sextus, belief that something is good would cause anxiety. Thus, the idea was to test if people who were told "by science" that we *know* the factors that determine happiness (e.g., positive attitude and social relations) would exhibit higher levels of state anxiety than people who, like the Pyrrhonian, hear that "science" is in a state of suspension—that we do not know about such factors. The success of the design hinged on whether participants believed, and internalized, what the article claimed.

That is, we manipulated scientific claims about our current knowledge regarding what is good, but we hoped to indirectly manipulate the subjects' certainty about their own beliefs. The manipulation check suggested that this was indeed the case. This, however, had absolutely no effect on state anxiety score. The results thus failed to find any evidence supporting Sextus's claims.

The results, however, should be taken with caution. The null effect complicates the interpretation of the findings, for it is not possible to determine whether the lack of an effect was due to a failure to manipulate dogmatism (or measure anxiety). This is especially so given the possibility of demand characteristics. Even though we took special care in concealing the goal of the study, it is nevertheless possible that participants responded in the way they thought the experimenter wanted them to (and so that dogmatism was not successfully manipulated).

It is also important to note that, unlike the correlational study, here the measure of interest was state anxiety. Trait anxiety is a personality characteristic, indicating how people generally feel. By manipulating certainty we were only able to capture how anxious people were *at that time*, i.e., state anxiety. One might object that Sextus's theory is better understood as the claim that people with beliefs about what is good or bad by nature are generally disturbed, and thus that the appropriate measure should be trait anxiety. The point is well taken. It is possible that the effects of belief on anxiety manifest in the long run and not immediately after assenting to a given belief. However, the inverse correlation between trait anxiety and dogmatism was again significant, replicating the findings from the correlational study.

3.3   Study 3

Sextus's main claim is that belief in objective moral values invariably leads to anxiety. For Sextus, to say that a moral value is objective is to claim that it is good (or bad) by nature. Ancient Greek ethics is primarily concerned with good and bad character: each ethical school presents a specific vision of 'the good life.' In this sense, Greek ethics is very different from much of contemporary moral theory, which focuses on rightness and wrongness of action.

The goal of the present experiment is to adapt Sextus's claim to our times. That is, unlike the previous experiment which focused on the modern conception of the good, i.e., happiness, here the focus is on moral belief. The questions remain the same: What is the relationship between moral belief and anxiety? Is moral belief, in general, conducive to anxiety? Or rather, in line with our previous results, are people with stronger moral views less anxious than people who express less certainty in their beliefs? Study 3 is a first attempt to answer these questions.

3.3.1 Method

Two hundred participants were recruited from Amazon's Mechanical Turk pool. The participants' ages ranged from 18 to 72 years with a mean of 37 years. Fifty four percent were females, 81% identified themselves as white, 3% as Asians, 9% African American, 3% Hispanic, and the rest answered "other." Two participants were excluded due to failing basic attention checks.

Participants were informed their assignment was to read an article for high school students and rate its grade-level appropriateness. Participants were randomly assigned to four different conditions. In the 'objectivist' condition, participants read a short article arguing that moral values are objective. The article compares a disagreement in matter of taste (a discussion between two friends on whether *The Godfather* is better than *The Terminator*) with a moral disagreement (where one of the friends expresses his desire to burn a cat alive for fun) and argues that in the latter case there *is* a fact of the matter. The comparison between the two cases was designed to elicit strong objectivist intuitions. The last section of the article uses the example of the eradication of slavery in the United States to appeal to a notion of moral progress. It concludes by arguing that a commitment to moral progress implies belief in objective values. In the 'relativist' condition, participants read a short article arguing that moral values are relative. The article introduces two characters, a vegetarian from New York and a hunter-gatherer from the Sentinelese tribe of the Andaman Islands. The American believes that killing animals for food is morally wrong whereas the Andamanese, who bases his life on this practice, thinks it is morally permissible. The article argues that it is evident that none of them is mistaken, but rather that moral values are a product of culture and societal customs. The particular case was designed to elicit strong relativist intuitions. In the 'skeptic' condition participants read both of the articles. The order was counterbalanced: half of the participants read the 'objectivist' article first and half read the 'relativist' article first. Finally, in the 'control' condition participants read a shortened version of the geology article used in Study 2.

To make the cover story believable participants answered questions regarding the appropriateness and length of the material. They were then presented with three statements and were asked to respond based on their own opinion. The statements were (1) 'When two people disagree about a moral case, at least one of them must be wrong,'[15] (2) 'Moral values are culturally relative; they are based on cultural practices and customs,' and (3) 'Moral values are objective; they are timeless and do not depend on our personal opinions.' Participants responded using a seven-point scale ranging from "strongly disagree" to "strongly agree." This was done to test if the manipulation influenced the subject's own views. Participants filled out the STAI and an additional 'moral anxiety' scale (Cronbach's α = 0.75).[16] Finally, they completed the DOG scale, and were debriefed.

3.3.2 Results

Scores from the three statements of the manipulation check did not form a single reliable scale (Cronbach's α = 0.59).[17] For this reason, each question was analyzed separately. We decided to focus on statement 1 ('when two people disagree about a moral case, at least one of them must be wrong'), since it has been widely used in previous research.

Before analyzing the effect of our manipulation on state anxiety, we checked to make sure the manipulation worked correctly. A one-way ANOVA showed that the manipulation had a significant effect on the participants' own opinions, $F(3, 193)$ = 2.60, p = 0.05. Tukey's post-hoc

---

[15] This is the standard question used in the literature to assess moral objectivism in people's ordinary understanding of morality. See Nichols (2004), Goodwin and Darley (2008), Sarkissian et al. (2011), and Beebe et al., (2015).

[16] The moral anxiety scale was constructed by making some of the items in the state-form of the STAI specific to moral matters. For example, item 5 of the state form, 'I feel at ease,' was adapted to read 'I feel at ease regarding my present moral commitments.' Item 12, 'I am nervous,' read 'I am nervous to share my moral values with other people.' This was done with eight items.

[17] Responses for statement 2 were coded inversely.

Table 4.1 Means and standard deviations for all conditions.

	Control	Objectivist	Relativist	Skeptic
At least one must be wrong	3.41 (1.53)	3.76 (1.43)	2.96 (1.49)	3.15 (1.57)
Moral values are culturally relative	3.45 (1.67)	3.20 (1.61)	2.54 (1.47)	2.67 (1.26)
Moral values are objective	3.84 (1.68)	4.10 (1.89)	3.52 (1.70)	3.71 (1.42)

Note: Higher values indicate stronger agreement with moral objectivism. Note that responses for Statement 2 were coded inversely.

tests showed that participants reported more objectivist views in the 'objectivist' condition ($M = 3.76$, $SD = 1.43$) than in the "relativist" one ($M = 2.96$, $SD = 1.49$), $p = 0.04$. No other pairwise comparison was significant, all p's >0.20.[18] See Table 4.1 for the means and standard deviations of Statements 2 and 3, and note 18 for the complete analyses.

A one-way between-subjects ANOVA showed no significant effect between the groups in terms of state anxiety, $F(3, 193) = 0.4$, $p = 0.75$ (Figure 4.2). Likewise, a one-way ANOVA revealed no significant differences in moral anxiety, $F(3, 193) = 0.32$, $p = 0.80$.

Finally, since the manipulation had no effect on anxiety, we collapsed across conditions to correlate DOG score and trait anxiety. Once again, a significant negative correlation was found ($r = -0.24$, p <0.001).

3.3.3 Discussion

A few remarks about the method are in order. One of the goals of this experiment was to have the 'skeptic' group undergo a genuine skeptical exercise. Instead of having one article expressing a general standoff in our knowledge (as in Study 2), here participants in the 'skeptic' condition were confronted with two articles arguing for contrary positions. The idea was to force participants to evaluate the arguments from both sides,

---

[18] Statement 2 ('moral values are culturally relative; they are based on cultural practices and customs'): A one-way ANOVA showed a significant effect on participant's views, $F(3, 193)$ = 3.98, $p = 0.008$. Tukey's post-hoc tests showed that participants reported more objectivist views in the 'control' condition ($M = 3.45$, $SD = 1.67$) than in the 'relativist' one ($M = 2.54$, $SD = 1.47$), $p = 0.01$. No other pairwise comparison was significant, all p's >0.06. **Statement 3** ('moral values are objective; they are timeless and do not depend on our personal opinions'): A one-way ANOVA did not show a significant effect on participant's scores, $F(3, 193) = 1.02$, $p = 0.38$. No pairwise comparison reached significance, all p's >0.31.

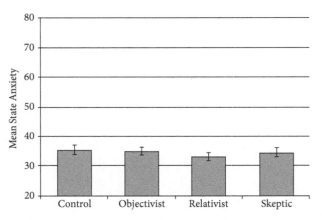

Figure 4.2 Mean state anxiety by condition. Error bars indicate standard error of the mean.

pitting one against the other in their minds. The hope was that uncertainty (and perhaps suspension) would arise as a result of this individual evaluation, rather than by merely telling them that suspension is the most reasonable position (as in Study 2).

We expected the 'skeptic' condition to fall between the 'objectivist' and the 'relativist' in our measures of moral objectivism. This was indeed the case for all three measures, but the difference failed to reach significance. The manipulation worked in influencing strength of opinion with respect to the two extremes conditions ('objectivist' and 'relativist') but not with the conditions in between ('control' and 'skeptic'). It is worth noting, however, that most participants regardless of condition expressed relativist intuitions. This appears to support the view that people are, if anything, meta-ethical pluralists (Wright et al., 2013). Early studies appeared to support the notion that most people reject moral relativism and favor a version of objectivism (Goodwin and Darley, 2008). In an important study, Sarkissian et al. (2011) showed that this is the case only when participants are thinking about people in their own culture; when primed to think of individuals in other cultures, people expressed relativist intuitions. Judging from our sample, it is only reasonable to assume that most people have some sort of relativist intuitions whether or not they are thinking about other cultures. Participants in the 'control' and 'objectivist' conditions expressed somewhat relativist intuitions even though they were not primed to think about other cultures.[19]

Coming back to Sextus, the results again failed to support the hypothesis that moral belief causes anxiety. There were no differences between the groups in state anxiety scores. At this point someone may advance the following objection. The experiment shows that changes in confidence (or strength) regarding moral belief do not affect state anxiety. But state anxiety is not the appropriate measure. State anxiety captures general feelings of anxiety at a particular moment, but has no specific object, i.e., it is a measure of one's overall mood. What the experiment should be measuring are changes in anxiety regarding moral matters. That is, the purported anxiety may be specific to the domain of the stimulus producing it. To address this concern, we introduced a 'moral anxiety scale' designed to capture changes in anxiety specific to morality (see note 16 for details). The results failed to support this further hypothesis: there were no differences in moral anxiety between the groups. It is worth keeping in mind, however, the concerns regarding null effects discussed above (see p. 112). That is, the null effect could be the result of a failure to manipulate moral objectivism/relativism or to adequately measure state anxiety.

Importantly, the negative correlation between trait anxiety and dogmatism was again significant, replicating the findings from the previous two studies.

3.4 General Discussion

Sextus claims that dogmatism increases anxiety, while theories coming out of psychology suggest that, first, it is anxiety that leads to dogmatism (though this is by no means uncontroversial), and second, that dogmatism helps to alleviate such anxiety. We consistently found a correlation showing that increased levels of dogmatism predict lower anxiety. However, our manipulations of the former showed no effect on the latter.

---

[19] Contrary to Beebe et al.'s (2015) findings, there was no significant correlation between age and moral objectivism ($r = 0.11$, $p = 0.12$).

The results of the three studies did not provide any evidence for Sextus's anxiety claim. Making people more dogmatic did not help reduce anxiety, and people who scored higher in dogmatism were actually *less* anxious. While the results are far from conclusive, they strongly suggest that the relationship between dogmatism and anxiety is the opposite of what Sextus claimed.

It thus seems that Sextus's theory is unable to explain the results. However, it is not clear what the explanation is. The possibility that dogmatism functions as a coping mechanism against anxiety was not supported by the experimental results. We successfully manipulated different aspects of dogmatism and in both cases there were no effects on anxiety.

An obvious alternative is that it is anxiety that influences dogmatism. But note that to explain the correlational data, increasing anxiety would have to *decrease* dogmatism. This is indeed possible. As discussed in Section 2.1, one line of research suggests that anxiety tends to make people more reflective and open to considering different viewpoints (Valentino et al., 2008; MacKuen et al., 2010). Such a claim, however, stands in tension with the idea that anxiety-reducing motives incline people to adopt systems of beliefs that are correlated with dogmatism (e.g., authoritarianism and political conservatism) (Jost et al., 2003).

It is also possible that anxiety increases dogmatism which in turn helps to alleviate anxiety. That is, both variables may have a causal influence on each other. This hypothesis, however, does not seem to be compatible with the present data. The problem is that we failed to see any causal effect of dogmatism on anxiety. Perhaps this is a problem with the local nature of our manipulation. An open possibility is that a domain-specific manipulation (happiness in Study 2 and morality in Study 3) cannot influence overall levels of anxiety. It might be the case that a domain-general dogmatism is necessary to have a reducing effect on anxiety. Only a global kind of dogmatism, not one focused on happiness or morality, would prove beneficial. This hypothesis is hard to test, for no experimental manipulation would instantaneously increase a person's global dogmatism. Given the correlational results, it is not easy to elucidate what the causal relation, if any, might be.

4. Objections and Replies

One possible objection goes something like this: 'All of the participants in your studies retained some sort of ethical belief (belief about what is good) regardless of their score in the DOG scale or the experimental condition they were assigned to. To a lesser or greater extent they are all dogmatists in Sextus's sense and so of course they will not exhibit the type of tranquility the real Skeptic experiences. As long as people hold *some* beliefs they will be disturbed. In short, *ataraxia* follows from total suspension of judgment, which none of the participants underwent.'

The objection entails the view that tranquility cannot increase incrementally as the would-be Skeptic (or anyone else) loses the appropriate beliefs. But I do not think that Sextus is committed to such view. In fact, I think he explicitly endorses the idea that tranquility follows from gradual changes in belief. Consider the Skeptic's initial discovery that suspension brings tranquility, as illustrated by the Apelles story. Presumably, the first time the Skeptic suspends judgment, she does not suspend judgment about everything. Rather, just as Apelles was painting a particular painting (a horse), the Skeptic was investigating a particular problem. When she suspends judgment about that problem, Sextus tells us, she discovers that suspension is followed by tranquility. She then proceeds to apply the Pyrrhonian method to *all* problems. The whole project would not have been possible if the initial discovery had not produced tranquility. Thus, it is not necessary to suspend judgment about everything to obtain the benefit of abandoning *some* beliefs. This is especially clear in the last chapter of the *Outlines*. Sextus writes, "Sceptics are philanthropic and wish to cure by argument, *as far as they can*, the conceit and rashness of the Dogmatists" (*PH* 3.280, emphasis mine). Sextus's language makes it clear that any shift away from dogmatism, no matter how small, is an improvement.

Therefore, I conclude that the fact that the participants were not radical Skeptics does not represent an impediment to drawing conclusions from the experimental results. If Sextus were right, we should expect dogmatic people to be more anxious. The contrary was observed. Hence, the results are evidence against Sextus.

A second and more serious objection questions the suitability of the manipulation in its attempt to test Sextus's claim: 'The participants were not actually suspending judgment about whether anything is by nature good, bad, or indifferent the way a Skeptic would. Rather, they held the belief that happiness is good but that they do not know how to obtain it, which would seem to fit Sextus's description of the Dogmatist. In other words, the participants in the 'skeptic' condition did not become more skeptical with respect to the belief that really matters, i.e., that happiness is good. A Pyrrhonist, Sextus might say, becomes tranquil not merely by suspending judgment about what brings about happiness, but rather by suspending judgment about the value of happiness itself.'

I am sympathetic to this objection, and I take it as a genuine problem to consider when assessing Sextus's claims from these results. However, there is an important way in which the Skeptic's situation parallels that of the participants: just as the latter do not question the belief that happiness is good, the Skeptic never questions the claim that tranquility is the goal of human life. Consider what would happen if Sextus suspended judgment about whether tranquility is the end. What reason would he then have to keep devising a contrary account to every account? Questioning that "for the sake of which everything is done or considered" (*PH* 1.25) puts into question the very purpose of being a Skeptic. Nussbaum writes, "we notice that there is one major ethical thesis that is never put through the Skeptic's antithetical procedures... This is, of course, the belief that *ataraxia* is an important end (or even the end)" (Nussbaum, 1994: 304). Nussbaum may have gone too far in requiring *belief* for the procedure to work, but I think her point stands even if the epistemic status of the Skeptic's end falls short of belief. This is because, functionally, the end is for the Skeptic something very close to a belief, in that it organizes her life, guides her behavior, and gives purpose to her philosophizing.

The Pyrrhonian project is constructed around the claim—supposedly corroborated by experience—that *ataraxia* follows from suspension. If this interpretation is right, it follows that the Pyrrhonian method is justified and predicated by the original value placed on tranquility. Nussbaum again: "The structure of the whole is incomprehensible except on the supposition that the practitioner believes *ataraxia* is an end worth going for by some sort of deliberate effort, and believes that these procedures have a connection with *ataraxia* that other available procedures do not" (Nussbaum, 1994: 304).

Therefore, just like the participants, the Skeptic does not suspend judgment about the goal (happiness for the former, tranquility for the latter). In both cases, the goal is fixed. Thus, in an important sense, the fact (if it is a fact) that the participants do not suspend judgment about whether happiness is good is not enough to invalidate the results. Furthermore, at key passages Sextus seems to equate *ataraxia* with *eudaimonia* (happiness): "the person who suspends judgment about all matters of opinion enjoys the most complete happiness" (*M* 11.161); "it is scepticism's achievement, therefore, to procure the happy life" (*M* 11.140). In light of these passages, it is fair to conclude that the Skeptic, like the participants, does not question the value of happiness.

5. Conclusion

Taken together, Studies 1–3 are a modest attempt to start an empirical investigation of Pyrrhonian Skepticism. Much remains to be done. That said, the present results counsel us to treat Sextus's claims with skepticism.

6. Appendix

Sextan Scale

1. Some things are good or bad by nature.
2. I have doubts that my ideas about what constitutes a good life are correct.
3. Certain practices and actions are naturally bad.
4. Certain practices and actions are naturally good.
5. Life generally goes better for those who doubt their beliefs.
6. It is possible to know what constitutes a good life.
7. Doing what's naturally good is the basis of morality.
8. Moral people don't do what's naturally bad.

Acknowledgments

I want to thank Tina Butoiu, Brad Inwood, Don Rutherford, Anat Shor, Andrew Wong, two anonymous reviewers at *Oxford Studies in Experimental Philosophy* and the editors of the present volume for helpful comments on previous versions of this chapter. I am especially grateful to Monte Johnson, Josh Knobe, and Nico Christenfeld for invaluable help and encouragement throughout the writing of the chapter.

References

Altemeyer, Bob (1996). *The Authoritarian Specter*. Harvard University Press.

Altemeyer, Bob (2002). "Dogmatic behaviour among students: Testing a new measure of dogmatism." *The Journal of Social Psychology*, 142.6, 713–21.

Altemeyer, Bob and Bruce Hunsberger (2004). "Research: A revised religious fundamentalism scale: The short and sweet of it." *The International Journal for the Psychology of Religion*, 14.1, 47–54.

Annas, Julia (1993). *The Morality of Happiness*. Oxford University Press.

Barnes, Jonathan (1982). "The beliefs of a Pyrrhonist." *The Cambridge Classical Journal*, 28, 1–29.

Beebe, James, Runya Qiaoan, Tomasz Wysocki, and Miguel A. Endara (2015). "Moral objectivism in cross-cultural perspective." *Journal of Cognition and Culture*, 15.3–4, 386–401.

Burnyeat, Myles (1980). "Can the sceptic live his scepticism?" in *Doubt and Dogmatism*, ed. M Schofield, M. Burnyeat, and J. Barnes. Clarendon Press, 20–53.

Crowson, H. Michael (2009). "Does the DOG Scale measure dogmatism? Another look at construct validity." *The Journal of Social Psychology*, 149.3, 365–83.

Crowson, H. Michael, Teresa K. DeBacker, and Kendrick A. Davis (2008). "The DOG Scale: A valid measure of dogmatism?" *Journal of Individual Differences*, 29.1, 17–24.

Frede, Michael (1987). "The Skeptic's beliefs," in *Essays in Ancient Philosophy*. University of Minnesota Press.

Fruchter, Benjamin, Milton Rokeach, and Edwin G. Novak (1958). "A factorial study of dogmatism, opinionation, and related scales." *Psychological Reports*, 4.1, 19–22.

Gaensslen, Hermann, Friedrich May, and Friedrich Wolpert (1973). "Relation between dogmatism and anxiety." *Psychological Reports*, 33.3, 955–8.

Goodwin, Geoffrey P. and John M. Darley (2008). "The psychology of meta-ethics: Exploring objectivism." *Cognition*, 106.3, 1339–66.

Hankinson, Robert J. (1994). "Values, objectivity and dialectic: The sceptical attack on ethics: Its methods, aims, and success." *Phronesis*, 39.1, 45–68.

Jost, John, Jack Glaser, Arie W. Kruglanski, and Frank J. Sulloway (2003). "Political conservatism as motivated social cognition." *Psychological Bulletin*, 129.3, 339–75.

Jost, John, Mahzarin R. Banaji, and Brian A. Nosek (2004). "A decade of system justification theory: Accumulated evidence of conscious and unconscious bolstering of the status quo." *Political Psychology*, 25.6, 881–919.

Jost, John and Orsolya Hunyady (2003). "The psychology of system justification and the palliative function of ideology." *European Review of Social Psychology*, 13.1, 111–53.

Kay, Aaron C., Danielle Gaucher, Jamie L. Napier, Mitchell J. Callan, and Kristin Laurin (2008). "God and the government: Testing a compensatory control mechanism for the support of external systems." *Journal of Personality and Social Psychology*, 95.1, 18–35.

Kay, Aaron C., David A. Moscovitch, and Kristin Laurin (2010). "Randomness, attributions of arousal, and belief in God." *Psychological Science*, 21.2, 216–18.

Kay, Aaron C., Jennifer A. Whitson, Danielle Gaucher, and Adam D. Galinsky (2009). "Compensatory control: Achieving order through the mind, our institutions, and the heavens." *Current Directions in Psychological Science*, 18.5, 264–8.

Kruglanski, Arie W. and Donna M. Webster (1991). "Group members' reactions to opinion deviates and conformists at varying degrees of proximity to decision deadline and of environmental noise." *Journal of Personality and Social Psychology*, 61.2, 212–25.

Kruglanski, Arie W. and Donna M. Webster (1996). "Motivated closing of the mind: 'Seizing' and 'freezing.'" *Psychological Review*, 103.2, 263–83.

Kurth, Charlie (2016). "Anxiety, normative uncertainty, and social regulation." *Biology & Philosophy*, 31.1, 1–21.

Kurth, Charlie (2018). *The Anxious Mind: An Investigation into the Varieties and Virtues of Anxiety*. The MIT Press.

MacKuen, Michael, Jennifer Wolak, Luke Keele, and George E. Marcus (2010). "Civic engagements: Resolute partisanship or reflective deliberation." *American Journal of Political Science*, 54.2, 440–58.

McPherran, Mark L. (1990). "Pyrrhonism's arguments against value." *Philosophical Studies*, 60.1, 127–42.

Mayseless, Ofra and Arie W. Kruglanski (1987). "What makes you so sure? Effects of epistemic motivations on judgmental confidence." *Organizational Behavior and Human Decision Processes*, 39.2, 162–83.

Nichols, Shaun (2004). "After objectivity: An empirical study of moral judgment." *Philosophical Psychology*, 17.1, 3–26.

Nussbaum, Martha C. (1994). *The Therapy of Desire: Theory and Ppractice in Hellenistic Ethics*. Princeton University Press.

Oei, Tian P. S., Larry Evans, and Gabrielle M. Crook (1990). "Utility and validity of the STAI with anxiety disorder patients." *British Journal of Clinical Psychology*, 29.4, 429–32.

Perin, Casey (2010). *The Demands of Reason: An Essay on Pyrrhonian Scepticism*. Oxford University Press.

Plant, Walter T., Charles W. Telford, and Joseph A. Thomas (1965). "Some personality differences between dogmatic and nondogmatic groups." *The Journal of Social Psychology*, 67.1, 67–75.

Rebhun, Martin T. (1966). "Dogmatism and test anxiety." *The Journal of Psychology*, 62.1, 39–40.

Rokeach, Milton (1954). "The nature and meaning of dogmatism." *Psychological Review*, 61.3, 194–204.

Rokeach, Milton (1960). *The Open and Closed Mind*. Basic Books.

Sarkissian, Hagop, John Park, David Tien, Jennifer Cole Wright, and Joshua Knobe (2011). "Folk moral relativism." *Mind & Language*, 26.4, 482–505.

Sextus Empiricus (1997). *Against the Ethicists*, translation, commentary, and introduction by Richard Bett. Oxford University Press.

Sextus Empiricus (2000). *Outlines of Scepticism*, translated and edited by Julia Annas and Jonathan Barnes. Cambridge University Press.

Spielberger, Charles D. (2010). *State Trait Anxiety Inventory*. John Wiley & Sons.

Spielberger, Charles D. and R. L. Gorsuch (1983). *State-Trait Anxiety Inventory for Adults: Manual and Sample: Manual, Instrument and Scoring Guide*. Consulting Psychologists Press.

Sticht, Thomas G. and Wayne Fox (1966). "Geographical mobility and dogmatism, anxiety, and age." *The Journal of Social Psychology*, 68.1, 171–4.

Vacchiano, Ralph B., Paul S. Strauss, and David C. Schiffman (1968). "Personality correlates of dogmatism." *Journal of Consulting and Clinical Psychology*, 32.1, 83–5.

Valentino, Nicholas A., Vincent L. Hutchings, Antoine J. Banks, and Anne K. Davis (2008). "Is a worried citizen a good citizen? Emotions, political information seeking, and learning via the Internet." *Political Psychology*, 29.2, 247–73.

Webster, Donna M. and Arie W. Kruglanski (1994). "Individual differences in need for cognitive closure." *Journal of Personality and Social Psychology*, 67.6, 1049–62.

Wright, Jennifer C., Piper T. Grandjean, and Cullen B. McWhite (2013). "The meta-ethical grounding of our moral beliefs: Evidence for meta-ethical pluralism." *Philosophical Psychology*, 26.3, 336–61.

5

The Subscript View

A Distinct View of Distinct Selves

Hannah Tierney
University of Sydney

1. Introduction

Frank O'Hara's gravestone reads "Grace to be born and live as variously as possible." This epitaph nicely captures the sentiment that we strive to be a great many things. We take on the roles of parent and child, friend and spouse, mentor and mentee, often all at the same time. Thus, the question "What am I?" seems to rightly admit of a multitude of answers—most of us would object to the idea that we are only one kind of person. Yet, when philosophers answer the question "What am I?" they typically provide a single response. This is perhaps because philosophers are interested in, among other things, what kind of beings we are *fundamentally* and what is required for beings like us to persist through time. These are two distinct concerns but they can get run together, often explicitly. John Locke (1975), for example, argues that consciousness is what distinguishes persons from other creatures and sameness of consciousness is what makes a person the same person over time. Lynne Rudder Baker (2000, 2007), herself a neo-Lockean, argues that what it means to be a person is to have a first-person perspective and diachronic persistence requires sameness of first-person perspective. And Eric Olson (1997) contends that creatures like us are fundamentally biological organisms and biological continuity is the relation that determines persistence. Though these philosophers defend very different views, they all take both synchronic and diachronic features of personal identity and

Hannah Tierney, *The Subscript View: A Distinct View of Distinct Selves* In: *Oxford Studies in Experimental Philosophy.*
Edited by: Tania Lombrozo, Joshua Knobe, and Shaun Nichols, Oxford University Press (2020). © Hannah Tierney.
DOI: 10.1093/oso/9780198852407.003.0006

persistence to be grounded in a single relation. The assumption of monism is a useful theoretical desideratum, usually generating the simplest explanations with the most minimal ontologies. And when it comes to personal identity and persistence, there is something deeply appealing about the notion that a single feature grounds both our personhood (or humanity) and our ability to survive.

However, this traditional monistic picture has recently been called into doubt. Work by philosophers and psychologists illuminates the great number of our evaluative practices and experiences that presuppose personal identity. It is unlikely that traditional monistic approaches can ground *all* of them. In order to accommodate these practices, philosophers have begun to eschew the monistic persistence relations of traditional accounts in favor of more complex and novel approaches. For example, Marya Schechtman (2014) incorporates a plurality of persistence-relevant properties into her account of personal identity, while David Shoemaker (2016) rejects traditional persistence relations in favor of another relation altogether in order to ground our seemingly identity-related practical concerns.

These accounts go a long way in accommodating the wide variety of our cares and concerns, but I argue that they do not go far enough. Both accounts fail to question the assumption that we are only one thing fundamentally. But just as we have multiple identities in our personal and professional lives, I argue that our identity-related practical concerns indicate that we also identify as more than one kind of entity at the most fundamental level. In this chapter, I propose an account of personal identity that reflects this ontological pluralism—the Subscript View. On this view, there typically exist (at least) two individuals whenever we once thought there was only one, a psychological individual ($self_p$) and a biological individual ($self_b$). Distinct survival relations obtain between these distinct individuals: $self_p$ survives psychologically—surviving$_p$—and $self_b$ survives biologically—surviving$_b$. According to the Subscript View, there is no singular, more basic persistence relation beyond survival$_p$ or survival$_b$, and there is no singular, more basic being beyond $self_p$ and $self_b$. Rather, we make judgments about both $self_p$ and $self_b$ persisting through time and we refer to both $self_p$ and $self_b$ by using pronouns like 'I,' 'me,' and 'you.'

In Section 2, I review the empirical work on persistence-judgments and practical concerns, focusing specifically on a complex pattern of care and concern, known as ambiguous loss (Boss 1999, 2004) that characterizes the advanced stages of dementia. In Section 3, I present the Subscript View and argue that it can better account for our many identity-related practical concerns and ambiguous loss than traditional monistic approaches to persistence. In Section 4, I discuss both Schechtman's and Shoemaker's approaches to accommodating these same concerns and argue that they ultimately fall short. Finally, in Section 5, I explore three objections to the Subscript View with the aim of developing and clarifying the view.

2. Our Many Practical Concerns

Before reviewing the empirical work on judgments about persistence, it will be useful to briefly introduce two of the most popular approaches to identity over time in the philosophical literature:

Psychological Approach: X at t_1 is the same person as Y at t_2 if and only if X is uniquely psychologically continuous with Y, where psychological continuity consists in overlapping chains of strong psychological connectedness, itself consisting in significant numbers of direct psychological connections like memories, intentions, beliefs/goals/ desires, and similarity of character.   (Parfit 1984: 207)

Biological Approach: What it takes for us to persist through time is ... biological continuity: one survives just in case one's purely animal functions—metabolism, the capacity to breathe and circulate one's blood, and the like—continue.   (Olson 1997: 16)

These views are popular, in part, because each is able to capture a set of intuitions about persistence that the other view cannot. The biological approach can ground the intuition that we were once fetuses and can enter a persistent vegetative state (PVS). And the psychological approach can make sense of "the transplant intuition": the idea that if all of our relevant psychological properties were to become associated with a new body, *we* would persist in the new body.

Though pluralism about personal identity is underrepresented in the literature, the complex nature of our intuitions about personal identity is well charted. Bernard Williams (1970) famously illustrates how malleable our intuitions can be through a series of thought experiments. In some of Williams's cases, our self-concern can be understood in biological, or physical, terms.[1] We fear torture that will be inflicted in the future, even if all of our psychological characteristics will be destroyed prior to the torture.

> Someone in whose power I am tells me that I am going to be tortured tomorrow. I am frightened, and look forward to tomorrow in great apprehension...He then adds...when the moment of torture comes, I shall not remember any of the things I am now in a position to remember. This does not cheer me up either...Fear, surely, would still be the proper reaction: and not because one did not know what was going to happen, but because in one vital respect at least one did know what was going to happen—torture, which one can indeed expect to happen to oneself...   (Williams 1970: 167–8)

Despite radical psychological discontinuity, it still seems appropriate, and even inevitable, to fear what will happen to *you* in the future.

However, if the case is described differently, it looks as though psychological continuity can ground our intuitions about survival. Williams (1970) describes the case by first explaining that two individuals, person A and person B, will switch psychologies,[2] such that person B's psychology will be associated with person A's body and person A's

---

[1] Peter Unger (1990) and Jeff McMahan (2002) each defend physical, as opposed to biological, views of persistence. According to McMahan, identity over time consists in "...the continued existence and functioning, in nonbranching form, of enough of the same brain to be capable of generating consciousness or mental activity" (2002: 68). Unger argues that we survive so long as "there is a sufficiently continuous physical realization of...core psychology..." (1990: 109), where core psychology includes the capacity for consciousness, reasoning, and the formation of simple intentions (1990: 68). These views, though distinct from the biological approach in a variety of ways, are able to capture many of the same intuitions.

[2] I will stipulate that this swap is done through a non-physical process to avoid complications with physical views.

psychology will be associated with person B's body. If the A-body-person were tortured, the B-body-person may feel a sense of relief that the torture wasn't happening to *her*, despite the fact that her psychological features were, until recently, associated with the tortured body. This attitude, which is also natural and inevitable, indicates that psychological continuity can ground survival judgments as well.[3]

Williams's reflection on these hypothetical scenarios is paradigmatic of how philosophers tend to theorize about persistence. Traditionally, philosophers generate cases that disentangle the different relations commonly thought to ground persistence. Then, to determine which relation actually grounds persistence, they reflect on the practical implications the loss of a particular relation will have compared to the loss of another relation. But rarely will this approach prove conclusive, because our judgments conform to different approaches to persistence in different cases. But why do we make such drastically different judgments about persistence in different contexts?

2.1 Empirical work on persistence and practical concerns

Recently, both philosophers and psychologists have begun to delve deeper into the nature of our judgments about persistence. Daniel Bartels and Oleg Urminsky have developed a manipulation that allows researchers to alter individuals' beliefs about psychological connectedness:

> Day-to-day life events change appreciably after college graduation, but what changes the most [least] between graduation and life after college is the person's core identity... The characteristics that make you the person you are... are likely to change radically around the time of graduation [are established early in life and fixed by the end of adolescence]...

---

[3] Williams's prediction has been born out in research. In a survey study, participants were presented with the statement: "In order for some person in the future to be *you*, that person doesn't need to have any of your memories" (Nichols and Bruno 2010). Over 80% of the participants disagreed with this claim (Nichols and Bruno 2010). However, when presented with a version of Williams's thought experiment, a majority of the participants agreed that it would be *them* who would feel the pain of shocks administered even after their characteristic psychological traits were destroyed (Nichols and Bruno 2010).

Several studies conducted with young adults before and after college graduation found large fluctuations in these important characteristics [have shown that the traits that make up your personal identity remain remarkably stable].   (Bartels and Urminsky 2011: 185)

When asked to rate on a scale from 0 to 100, where 0 indicates that "I will be completely different in the future" and 100 indicates that "I will be exactly the same in the future," participants in the low-connectedness condition give significantly lower ratings than the baseline and those in the high-connectedness condition give significantly higher ratings than the baseline (Bartles and Rips 2010; Bartles and Urminsky 2011; Bartels et al. 2013).

Using this manipulation, one study found that participants' judgments about how much blame they deserve for a wrong committed a year ago are largely affected by whether they believed that there was high psychological connectedness between their past and present self (Tierney et al. 2014). Participants in the low-connectedness condition, who were made to believe that they are psychologically very different than their past selves, believe that they deserved significantly less blame for cheating on a test a year ago than the participants in the high-connectedness condition, who believed that their past selves and current selves are psychologically very similar (Tierney et al. 2014).

However, Tierney et al. (2014) also found that participants' anxiety about future pain (from a root canal) was not significantly different in the high- and low-connectedness conditions. This finding indicates that our judgments regarding self-concern cannot be explained entirely in terms of the psychological approach to identity over time. Rather, a relation like biological connectedness may best ground such judgments. Thus, in some contexts, like those involving issues of punishment and moral responsibility, our survival judgments are in-line with a psychological approach to survival,[4] while in other contexts our judgments are in-line with a completely different approach.

---

[4] In a series of studies, Christian Mott (2018) found that our intuitions about the statute of limitations on legal punishment and moral criticism are also affected by our judgments about psychological connectedness over time, further indicating that judgments of moral responsibility are grounded in the psychological approach.

2.2   When we come apart: ambiguous loss

The above discussion suggests that we make judgments that track different persistence relations in response to different cases. But there is also evidence that we make judgments that track distinct persistence relations in response to the very same case. An intuitive, though painful, belief is that we, and our loved ones, can one day persist in the late stages of Alzheimer's and other forms of dementia. When we visit our loved ones who are suffering from these illnesses, we do so, in part, because we believe them to still be our loved ones. But there is also a sense in which we do not think we, or those we love, will survive such radical psychological discontinuity. We often mourn the loss of our loved ones in these states and grief is ubiquitous in the narratives of their caregivers. Pauline Boss (2004: 554) refers to the loss one experiences when a loved one is "physically present, but psychology absent" as ambiguous loss and it is a distinctive feature of caring for an individual who has dementia. In this section, I will discuss some empirical work that bears on ambiguous loss and the seemingly paradoxical aspects of grieving and caring for a loved one in the advanced stages of dementia.

Nina Strohminger and Shaun Nichols (2015) conducted a study in which they surveyed the family members of people suffering from Alzheimer's disease, frontotemporal dementia, and amyotrophic lateral sclerosis (ALS), also known as Lou Gehrig's disease.[5] The participants were asked questions about the persistence of their family members, such as "Regardless of the severity of the illness, how much do you sense the patient is still the same person underneath?" and "Does the patient ever seem like a stranger to you?" Participants reported significantly greater identity disruption in family members with Alzheimer's disease and frontotemporal dementia than family members with ALS, $t(112) = 6.50, p < 0.0001, d = 1.05$ and $t(115) = 8.75, p < 0.0001, d = 1.54$, respectively (Strohminger and Nichols 2015). This study suggests that certain forms of dementia can threaten our persistence-judgments.

Interestingly, even those critical of Strohminger and Nichols's analysis agree that dementia can undermine persistence. Christina Starmans and

---

[5] ALS is a neurodegenerative disease that primarily affects motor function and was used as the control in this study (Strohminger and Nichols 2015).

Paul Bloom (2018a) recently argued that Strohminger and Nichols's study tracked judgments about similarity and not personal identity. Yet, they too grant that "There are cases…where it may be thought that a person ceases to exist while their body survives, as in severe dementia" (2018a: 567). In short, while there is debate over how to differentiate persistence-judgments from similarity-judgments and *which features* destroyed by neurodegeneration threaten identity over time, most agree that dementia can threaten persistence.

This consensus is also found in the growing literature on the grief experienced by caretakers of those with dementia (e.g., Noyes et al. 2010; Lindauer and Harvath 2014; Blandin and Pepin 2017). Much of this research indicates that the relatives of those in the advanced stages of dementia perceive their family members to be dead (Doka 2004; Lindauer and Harvath 2014), gone (Marwit and Meuser 2002, 2005), or lost (Blandin and Pepin 2017).

Allison Lindauer and Theresa Harvath's analysis of pre-death grief makes explicit reference to the "psychological death" of those with advanced dementia:

> Pre-death grief in the context of dementia family caregiving is the car-egiver's emotional and physical response to the perceived losses in a valued care recipient…This pre-death grief is due to (a) *care recipient psychological death*, which is asynchronous with physical death…
>
> (Lindauer and Harvath 2014: 2203, emphasis added)

And Kenneth Doka argues that, in the advanced stages of dementia, "the sense of individual identity is so changed now that family members experience the death of the person who once was" (Doka 2004: 142). Additionally, one of the only measures of caregiver grief, the Marwit and Meuser Caregiver Grief Inventory (MM-CGI), along with its short form (MM-CGI-SF), include two items that measure the extent to which caregivers think of their loved ones as "gone" (Marwit and Meuser 2002, 2005):

> 9. I have this empty, sick feeling knowing that my loved one is "gone."
>
> 30. It hurts to put her/him to bed at night and realize that she/he is "gone." (Marwit and Meuser 2002: 762)

And in their model of dementia grief, Kesstan Blandin and Renee Pepin isolate several features unique to the grief experienced by those caring for patients with dementia, one of which is the "receding of the known self":

> A common experience among family members is that eventually the person with dementia will express themselves as though they are someone else, someone new, or otherwise not who they used to be...Family members experience profound pre-death grief akin to post-death bereavement as they experience *the loss of the person they know*...   (Blandin and Pepin 2017: 70, emphasis added)

This research indicates that caretakers of those in the advanced stages of dementia often experience the literal loss of their loved one.

However, a sense of loss is not the *only* feature that characterizes the experiences of the loved ones of those in the late stages of dementia. Another important feature of this experience is the sense that one continues to love and care for their family member, who is very much alive. More than sixteen million individuals in the United States care for people with Alzheimer's disease and other dementias without pay (Alzheimer's Association 2018). These caregivers provide significantly more care (in terms of the quantity of time they dedicate to caregiving and the range of activities they provide help with) than caregivers of people without dementia (Alzheimer's Association 2018: 387–8). These caregivers also experience more emotional and physical stress, higher rates of depression, and more difficulty with cognitive tasks than caregivers of people without dementia and non-caregivers (Alzheimer's Association 2018: 388–90).

Those who work on caregiver grief are alive to the tension between grieving a loved one and simultaneously caring for them. After the passage quoted above, Blandin and Pepin continue:

> Yet their loved one is still alive...This creates a paradoxical disconnection between the physical and psychological losses, capturing the crux of ambiguity in the receding of the known self in dementia grief.
> (2017: 70)

Lindauer and Harvath also note the disconnect between psychological and physical loss when they contend that pre-death grief in cases of dementia is caused by "... the care recipient's psychological death, *which is asynchronous with physical death...*" (2014: 2203, emphasis added). And Noyes et al. (2010: 12) argue that the discrepancy between psychological and physical loss makes the grief experienced by caregivers of those with dementia unique. Finally, Pat Sikes and Mell Hall completed a study in which they interviewed several children and young adults who have parents with dementia. Many of the excerpts from their interviews nicely capture the ambiguity surrounding individuals who are psychologically gone but physically present. For example:

> ... it's like there's two Mums and in your head you never quite let go of, but you're constantly grieving for the old Mum because she's sort of there but not... people... just think actually you should be grateful that your Mum is still here and she's not dead and it's like well, it's really not that simple... (Elizabeth, 28).   (Sikes and Hall 2018: 190)

Cases of ambiguous loss are heartbreaking. They also illuminate a fascinating feature of our judgments about persistence. In these cases, the pattern of care and concern seems to track distinct persistence relations. The loss of psychological continuity (or certain psychological features) in the advanced stages of dementia causes many individuals to judge that their loved one is gone. Yet, the loved one's physical presence and the continuation of their "purely animal functions" (Olson 1997) gives rise to the sense that they persist. In Section 2.1, I reviewed evidence that indicates that our judgments about persistence track different persistence relations in cases that feature different practical concerns. In this section, I have presented evidence that we also make seemingly contradictory persistence-judgments in response to single cases—namely those that feature ambiguous loss. Given these two sets of research, it is unlikely that a monistic view will be able to fully accommodate the folk conception of persistence.

2.3 What to do about our practical concerns

In Section 3, I will present a view—the Subscript View—that can accommodate these findings. Before proceeding, however, I would like to note two worries about constructing a view of identity over time with the aim of capturing our practical concerns.

First, it should be noted that the research discussed above, though illuminating, is preliminary. While the empirical work indicates that our persistence-judgments are informed by more than one relation, more work needs to be done to determine the exact nature of these relations. It could be that the relations that actually inform our persistence-judgments are very different from traditional persistence relations like psychological and biological continuity. In fact, though memory plays an important role in many psychological accounts of persistence, research indicates that *moral* properties are more central to our judgments about persistence than other psychological properties (Prinz and Nichols 2016; Strohminger and Nichols 2014, 2015).[6] Strohminger and Nichols (2015) found that when it comes to certain neurodegenerative diseases, the loss of our moral faculties, as opposed to our memories, desires, and preferences, exerts the strongest influence on perceived identity over time.[7] Kevin Tobia (2015, 2016) also found that moral deterioration affects our judgments about persistence, though, interestingly moral improvement does not. And Sarah Molouki and Daniel Bartels (2017) argue that this asymmetry between improvement and deterioration in other types of change (personality, preferences, etc.) affects judgments about persistence as well, though the effect was strongest in cases of moral change.

These are all interesting and important findings, and work needs to be done to modify or replace traditional persistence relations to reflect this research. Thus, when constructing a pluralist view of personal identity, it will be important to leave it flexible enough to accommodate these future modifications and/or new relations. In developing the Subscript View, I refer to psychological and biological continuity because these relations are the most developed in the philosophical literature, but the view is entirely compatible with more refined versions of these relations,

---

[6] Research also indicates that moral qualities are more central to the folk conception of the self than other psychological properties (Newman et al. 2014; De Freitas et al. 2017a, 2017b).

[7] As discussed above, Starmans and Bloom (2018a) argue that Strohminger and Nichols's study tracks judgments about similarity and not personal identity. They also register their skepticism that extreme moral change causes people to believe that others cease to exist (2018: 567). For a defense of Strohminger and Nichols's results and the centrality of morality for persistence, see De Freitas et al. (2018). And, for a response to De Freitas et al., see Starmans and Bloom (2018b).

entirely new relations, and/or additional relations that reflect this research.

Second, one might wonder, *should* we incorporate these identity-related practical concerns into our theories of persistence in the first place? Many argue that we should not. Olson (1997), for example, takes questions concerning practical matters to be under the purview of ethicists while questions concerning persistence to be purely metaphysical matters.[8] Others argue that it is just not possible to systematize these concerns. Williams (1970) notes that our equally strong commitment to contrary judgments of seemingly identical cases is baffling. And Ted Sider (2001: 197) argues that "[a] natural explanation is that ordinary thought contains two concepts of persisting persons, each responsible for a separate set of intuitions, neither of which is *our* canonical conception to the exclusion of the other." And perhaps Sider is right that no *traditional* monistic persistence relation can ground or explain all of these evaluative practices and concerns. But it does not follow from this that *no* view of persistence can accommodate them. Philosophers have already begun to eschew the monistic persistence relations of traditional accounts in favor of more complex and novel approaches precisely in order to accommodate these practices (e.g., Schechtman 2014; Shoemaker 2016). In the next section, I follow these philosophers' approaches and present a novel, pluralist view of personal identity.

3. The Subscript View

On the Subscript View, there typically exist (at least) two selves, one psychological (self_p) and another biological (self_b).[9] On this view,

---

[8] Susan Wolf (1986) and, as Schechtman (2014) discusses, Christine Korsgaard (1989) defend this view as well. Such a stance represents a fundamentally different methodology in dealing with issues of personal identity than the one that has been assumed up to this point. It is beyond the scope of this chapter to offer a full defense of treating our identity-related practical concerns and our theories of identity as in fact related, though others have mounted such arguments (e.g., West 2008; Schechtman 2014). The remainder of this chapter focuses only on views that attempt to capture our identity-related practical concerns, although some of these views do not focus on identity and persistence as such.

[9] While I use the locution 'self' in this chapter, I do not mean to invoke any particular view of the self. Rather, I use self_p and self_b to refer to individuals, understood as metaphysical entities, that persist psychologically and biologically, respectively. Though the Subscript View is a pluralist view of "selves," it is much different from pluralist views found in the philosophical

distinct survival relations obtain between these distinct selves: $self_p$ survives psychologically—surviving$_p$—while $self_b$ survives biologically—surviving$_b$. This is because these individuals are different kinds of entities and have distinct persistence conditions. According to the Subscript View, there is no singular, more basic persistence relation beyond surviving$_p$ or surviving$_b$, and there is no singular, more basic self beyond $self_p$ and $self_b$.

3.1 The prima facie case for the Subscript View

The Subscript View can better accommodate the folk conception of identity over time than traditional approaches to personal identity. While the biological and psychological approaches can each accommodate a set of problem cases, neither view is able to accommodate them both. However, like the biological approach, the Subscript View can capture the intuition that we were once fetuses and can also survive in a PVS. I_b was a fetus even if I_p was not and I_b can enter a PVS even if I_p cannot. And, like the psychological approach, the Subscript View can make sense of the intuition that we can survive psychology transplants—we$_p$ can, though we$_b$ cannot.

The Subscript View can also accommodate the empirical work on how we make judgments about persistence. These studies indicate that the folk form persistence-judgments in line with multiple relations. Given that the Subscript View is committed to there being multiple kinds of persistence, the view can easily make sense of these results. The view can also fully accommodate the complicated pattern of care and concern that is characteristic of ambiguous loss. According to the

literature on the self. For example, David Velleman defends an aspectual view of the self, according to which the "self" refers not to metaphysical entities but rather to multiple reflexive guises under which aspects of a person are presented to themselves (Velleman 2006: 1). And though one of these guises is self-sameness over time, in "Self to Self," Velleman argues extensively that this has nothing to do with identity over time (2006: 170–202). On Velleman's view: "If a person could retrieve experiential memories that were stored by Napoleon at Austerlitz, then Napoleon at Austerlitz would be genuinely related to him as a past self" (2006: 6). But this does not entail that the person is identical to, or the same person as, Napoleon. As Velleman argues: "A person's past and future selves are those past and future persons who present a particular aspect to him, but they need not be the same person" (2006: 359, fn. 73). Thus, though the Subscript View and Velleman's aspectual view are both pluralist views of the "self," the former is a metaphysical view of identity over time while the latter is a view about the many reflexive guises we use to present aspects of ourselves to ourselves.

Subscript View, individuals$_b$ can persist in such cases while individuals$_p$ cannot. This explains why we grieve the loss of a loved one while simultaneously caring for a loved one. On the Subscript View, we are grieving the loss of loved one$_p$ and caring for loved one$_b$. The Subscript View's traditional monistic competitors are unable to offer as natural an explanation of ambiguous loss.

Those in the advanced stages of dementia have lost the robust psychological capacities that the psychological approach to personal identity requires for persistence (Locke 1975; Baker 2000). So, on the psychological approach, we perish in the advanced stages of dementia. The psychological approach can then capture the sense of grief we experience when a loved one enters the late stages of such neurodegenerative diseases. However, the psychological approach cannot easily make sense of the belief that we continue to care for our loved ones in these cases. Defenders of the psychological approach can argue that we care for the individual in the late stages of dementia because we (falsely) believe that the *person* we love stills exists deep down or perhaps because we have formed a sentimental attachment to the body that was once associated with the *person* we loved. But both of these explanations are debunking— neither can make literal sense of the belief that we continue to care for a loved one. So, the psychological approach will struggle to accommodate the ambiguous loss that is wrought by dementia.

In contrast, the biological approach can easily ground the judgment that we can persist in the advanced stages of dementia. After all, the late stages of dementia are precisely the kind of circumstances in which human organisms can find themselves. However, the biological approach will have difficulty making sense of the kind of grief experienced by the loved ones of those with such neurodegenerative disorders.[10] On the biological approach, there is no relevant difference between these kinds of cases and paradigm cases of persistence—biological continuity obtains in exactly the same way in both.

---

[10] This is also true of physical views. Because individuals in the advanced stages of dementia continue to possess core psychological abilities, i.e. the capacity for consciousness, McMahan's (2002) and Unger's (1990) physical views are committed to individuals persisting in these cases. Though the physical and biological approaches point to different times at which we cease to persist—physical views draw the line at the loss of the capacity for consciousness and biological views draw the line at biological death—both views will struggle to make sense of ambiguous loss.

Defenders of the biological approach can try to account for ambiguous loss in a variety of ways. They could argue that we grieve the loss of certain features of our loved one—their memories, personality traits, moral character, etc.—or that we grieve the loss of our relationship with our loved one.[11] No doubt, we do grieve the loss of these things when caring for a loved one in the advanced stages of dementia. But it would be a mistake to conclude that these are the *only* losses we grieve or that our grief can be reduced to these losses. Strohminger and Nichols's (2015) work illustrates that certain kinds of dementia threaten our persistence-judgments. And, as discussed above, many caretakers experience the sense that their loved one is dead (Doka 2004; Lindauer and Harvath 2014), gone (Marwit and Meuser 2002, 2005), or lost (Blandin and Pepin 2017). The biological approach theorists cannot make literal sense of such beliefs.

Of course, they could argue that both the researchers on caregiver grief and the caretakers themselves are speaking metaphorically when they refer to losing those in the advanced stages of dementia. After all, Marwit and Meuser's two items that refer to those with advanced dementia as *gone* place quotation marks around the word (2002: 762). While some uses of "death," "gone," and "loss" in the caregiver grief literature may be metaphorical, it is difficult to believe that all, or even a majority of them, are. For example, Lindauer and Harvath claim that caregiver grief is caused by "care recipient psychological death" and explicitly contrast psychological death with physical death (2014: 2203). It is unclear how one could interpret their claims as metaphorical or why one would be motivated to do so. Even Starmans and Bloom (2018a), who think that some judgments we make about those with dementia do not actually track persistence, do not deny that we can make literal judgments about these individuals' failure to persist. In fact, as noted above, these authors make one such judgment (2018: 567).[12] Finally, to the extent that caregivers and researchers do speak metaphorically, this

---

[11] Thanks to an anonymous referee for raising this objection.

[12] Additionally, many of the materials in the empirical studies on persistence-judgments mirror the language used to describe caregiver grief. For example, the prompts in Tobia's study include the following wording: "...He thinks that after the accident, the original man named Phineas *does not exist anymore*; the man after the accident is *a different person*. To Bart, it seems like *one person died* (Phineas before the accident), and it is really a *different person entirely* that exists after the accident (the man after the accident)" (2015: 398, emphasis added).

could be due to background assumptions about the truth of monism. Perhaps the participant in Sikes and Hall's study who noted that "it's like there's two Mums..." didn't mean she literally thought she had two mothers (2018: 190). But this could be because she thinks that it is only possible for her to have one. We often use metaphors to express ourselves when literal language will not do. The Subscript View can provide the vocabulary to capture an experience that previously could not be understood without metaphor, for on the Subscript View, it is perfectly possible to have two mothers—mother$_p$ and mother$_b$.

While the psychological and biological approaches can each capture a subset of our practical concerns and some features of ambiguous loss, neither of these views can fully accommodate them. In contrast, the Subscript View can. The Subscript View's ability to make sense of these complex patterns of care and concern provides prima facie support for adopting the view.

3.2 Co-location and constitution

Even if the Subscript View best captures certain features of our commonsense conception of persistence, it faces a hurdle: The Subscript View entails that there typically exist two individuals where we once thought there was one. One might question how it can be that self$_p$ and self$_b$ occupy the same spatio-temporal region yet remain distinct objects. While it is a puzzle as to how two distinct objects can be co-located, it is a philosophically familiar puzzle. Normally, theorists address the problem of co-location by positing a credible relation between the two co-located objects. For example, Lynne Rudder Baker (2000, 2007) argues that human persons are constituted by, and not identical to, human animals. Since Baker proposes her analysis of constitution in the context of personal identity, it is well suited for the purposes of the subscript theorist as well.[13]

If we think that studies like Tobia's (2015) can tell us anything about the folk's literal judgments about persistence, we should think that the literature on caregiver grief can do so as well.

[13] The Subscript View is also compatible with other accounts of constitution that allow co-location.

According to Baker, human animals constitute human persons. Similarly, the subscript theorist can argue that $self_b$ constitutes, but is not identical to, $self_p$. On this view, there would be a close relationship between the biological and psychological individuals such that, though they are not identical, $self_p$ depends on $self_b$ in an intimate way. This view is entirely compatible with the basic tenets of the Subscript View. The subscript theorist could also argue that something more basic, a hunk of physical matter (Hunk), constitutes both $self_p$ and $self_b$. On this view, $self_b$ and $self_p$ are distinct entities that are often co-located. I will develop the Subscript View with this branching notion of constitution, but if one prefers a linear, or stacking, approach, it can easily be adopted.[14]

On Baker's analysis, constitution is not identity; it is a contingent, irreflexive, and asymmetric relation (Baker 2007). The existence of whatever does the constituting need not entail the existence of whatever is constituted. This seems right in the case of Hunk, $self_p$, and $self_b$. It is only in certain circumstances that a hunk of matter can constitute a living thing at all, let alone the complex biological and psychological creatures that we are. Constitution is also irreflexive; nothing can constitute itself, which again rings true of Hunk, $self_p$, and $self_b$. Constitution, according to Baker, is also asymmetric; if x constitutes y, then y cannot constitute x. Pretheoretically, it seems that $self_p$ and $self_b$ could not constitute Hunk, just as Baker thinks it is obvious that a statue cannot constitute a piece of marble (2007: 163).

Baker relies on the notion of primary-kind properties in her analysis of constitution. According to Baker, objects have their primary-kind properties essentially. An object cannot cease to have its primary-kind properties without ceasing to exist (2007: 159). On the Subscript View, $self_p$ and $self_b$ have different primary-kind properties. They are distinct kinds of entities and have different modal properties and persistence conditions. If certain essential psychological properties go out of existence, then $self_p$ will cease to exist and there will be one less object in the

---

[14] One might worry that branching constitution differs problematically from linear constitution. Though constitution is traditionally discussed as a one-to-one relation, there is nothing in the standard notion of constitution that precludes it from being a one-to-many relation. In fact, in her updated account of the Constitution View, Baker explicitly allows for branching constitution (2007: 164).

world. And if certain essential biological properties go out of existence, then self$_b$ will cease to exist and there will also be one less object in the world. The Subscript View is committed to the claim that creatures like us are more than one kind of thing at the most fundamental level. This is what allows the view to accommodate persistence-judgments that track distinct persistence relations and the complex pattern of concern characteristic of ambiguous loss. This ontological pluralism is also what sets the Subscript View apart from other views that seek to capture our practical cares and concerns.

4. Alternative Approaches to Persistence and our Practical Concerns

The Subscript View is not the only view to eschew monistic persistence relations nor is it unique in its attempt to accommodate the wide range of our identity-related cares and concerns. For example, Schechtman (2014) incorporates a variety of persistence-relevant properties and relations into the Person Life View, her account of personal identity. And Shoemaker (2016) argues that all of our seemingly identity-related practical concerns can actually be explained in terms of a relation that has nothing to do with identity. In this section, I will first present these alternative approaches to persistence and practical concerns. Then, I will argue that though these views go much further than the traditional approaches to persistence in accounting for our many practical concerns, they cannot fully accommodate the all too common experience of ambiguous loss.

4.1 The Person Life View

What it takes to be a person and to persist as such can be stated simply on Schechtman's Person Life View: "To be a person is to live a 'person life'; persons are individuated by individuating person lives; and the duration of a single person is determined by the duration of a single person life" (Schechtman 2014: 110). Persons, those that live person lives, are the target of our person-related questions and concerns. And for a person to persist, for their person life to continue, they must continue to be a single target of our practical concerns (2014: 152). Person lives are characterized by a host of biological, psychological, and social features, but no feature is either necessary or sufficient for a typical person life (2014: 147).

The inclusion of multiple kinds of identity-relevant features and relations, and the rejection of necessary and sufficient conditions on diachronic identity, makes the Person Life View exceedingly flexible. The view is able to ground a diverse set of practical concerns that are rooted in both the biological and psychological approaches to persistence. For example, it can easily make sense of our judgments about self-concern that track biological continuity and our judgments about moral responsibility that track psychological continuity. The Person Life View can also ground our intuitions in pairs of puzzle cases that the traditional views of personal identity cannot. Schechtman's view can accommodate the intuition that we could survive in a PVS *and* the intuition that we could survive a psychology transplant. Even though a host of psychological traits are lost when an individual enters a PVS, enough biological features are maintained such that the individual can remain a single locus of person-related concerns. And though biological continuity is lost when one's psychology becomes associated with a new body, psychological continuity is maintained and can allow the individual to continue to live a person life. In including a plurality of persistence-relevant properties in her account, Schechtman is able to advance beyond traditional monistic theorists in accommodating the folk conception of persistence.

4.2 Shoemaker on ownership

Like Schechtman, Shoemaker is sensitive to the diversity of our practical concerns and is adamant that they cannot all be grounded in a single persistence relation. But unlike Schechtman, Shoemaker is skeptical that *any* theory of personal identity could accommodate these concerns. Rather, he argues that all of our seemingly identity-related practical questions can actually be explained in terms of a relation that has nothing to do with identity—the ownership relation.

Shoemaker considers social treatment, responsibility, anticipation, self-concern, and compensation to illustrate how ownership grounds these concerns. While it is beyond the scope of this chapter to examine Shoemaker's careful analysis of each of these practical concerns, it will be helpful to list the set of platitudes that Shoemaker relies on to capture the role ownership plays in these practices: I can be responsible only for my *own* actions (2016: 318), I am justified in anticipating some set of future experiences only if they are *mine* (2016: 320), I have a special sort of concern only for *my*self (2016: 320), and I can truly be compensated with a benefit for a burden only if the burden underwent was my *own* (2016: 321). Shoemaker argues that traditional persistence relations are neither necessary nor sufficient for (or even relevant to) the role ownership plays in the context of these practical concerns. In this way, Shoemaker takes himself to defend the "Identity *Really* Doesn't Matter" view (2016: 325).

4.3 The Person Life View, ownership, and ambiguous loss

Both Schechtman's and Shoemaker's views go much further than traditional monistic accounts in accommodating our practical concerns. However, neither of these views can fully make sense of the pattern of care that surrounds cases of ambiguous loss. Because both views provide a single answer—either yes or no—to the question of whether we persist (or whether ownership obtains), they render the commonsense experience of both grieving the loss of a loved one and caring for a loved one incoherent.

Like the biological approach, the Person Life View can easily ground the intuition that we persist in the advanced stages of dementia. Because having certain psychological features is not necessary for persistence on the Person Life View, the view is not committed to those suffering from dementia not being persons or relevantly continuous with persons. In fact, Schechtman takes the Person Life View's ability to ground the intuition that we persist in the advanced stages of dementia to be one of the clear advantages of the view (2014: 150).

However, also like the biological approach, the Person Life View cannot easily accommodate the sense of loss that we experience when our loved ones enter the advanced stages of dementia. While the Person Life View can point to persistence-relevant features that are lost in these situations, the view is still committed to providing an exclusively affirmative answer to the question of whether we persist. Schechtman argues: "When someone looks at the Alzheimer's patient and claims 'Father is gone; that's not him,' she does not...truly see a brand new being, but rather the sad continuation of a once vigorous life—otherwise it would not be painful in just the way it is" (2014: 105). On the Person Life View, though it would be fitting to grieve many losses, it would not be fitting to grieve the actual loss of a loved one. But, as argued in Section 2.2, this runs contrary to Strohminger and Nichols's findings and much of the research on caregiver grief. Like the biological approach, the Person Life View cannot do justice to the intuition that there is a sense in which we fail to survive in the advanced stages of dementia.

Unlike the Person Life View, Shoemaker would not attempt to explain ambiguous loss in terms of persistence-relevant properties. Rather, Shoemaker analyzes third-person re-identification in terms of ownership, as he does all other seemingly identity-related practical concerns. On Shoemaker's view, perhaps the apt platitude regarding third-person re-identification would be "I care about *my* loved ones." As Shoemaker argues:

> To the extent I want to reidentify one of [my friends], then, this often involves establishing or ensuring that they have the same relation to me now that grounded my affective concern in the past. Depending on the nature of our friendship, then (i.e. what it is that warrants my affective concern), the relevant ownership relation may be delivered by (a) psychological continuity on their part, (b) one aspect of psychological continuity (perhaps just continuity of character or persistence of beliefs/desires/goals), (c) some combination of physical and psychological continuity, or (d) mere physical continuity (for those who are seriously shallow). (2016: 323–4, fn. 33)

So, in cases of dementia, the question will be whether these individuals continue to be *our* loved ones, which we can determine by establishing whether they continue to bear the same relation to us that grounded our care for them in the past.

Though Shoemaker is a pluralist about ownership and acknowledges that different relations ground different kinds of friendship and love, in asking us to determine "*the* relevant ownership relation" (2016: 324, fn. 33, emphasis added) that grounds our affective concern for a particular individual, he does not consider the possibility that we can re-identify, and continue to care for, a loved one in virtue of one relation, while simultaneously judging that our loved one no longer exists in virtue of another relation. But the sense of ambiguous loss that permeates cases of advanced dementia indicates that situations like this do occur. In assuming that there must be a univocal answer to the question of whether an individual continues to be *our* loved one, Shoemaker fails to consider the possibility that we can judge that our loved one no longer exists while continuing to care for our loved one.

One might wonder why Shoemaker does not argue that we can re-identify our loved one in virtue of one relation (or set of relations) and judge that our loved one fails to persist in virtue of another relation (or set of relations). Given that Shoemaker is a pluralist in many respects, why is he not a pluralist about loved ones, and individuals more generally? Shoemaker rejects this approach to third-person re-identification because he rejects pluralism about numerical identity:

> …we cannot be pluralists about numerical identity; we can only be pluralists about ownership. If the numerical identity we are talking about is numerical identity of individuals like us, then the proposal just given would require that I am both identical with, and not identical with, some past or future individual.   (2016: 322)

On Shoemaker's view, pluralism about identity over time is incoherent—it is contradictory to judge that one's loved one is gone and to judge that they continue to persist. But the Subscript View has a perfectly coherent take on such pairs of judgments. In cases where biological continuity obtains and psychological continuity is destroyed, rather than arguing that the individual both is and is not identical with a past individual, the subscript theorist would argue that $self_b$ survives$_b$ while $self_p$ does not survive$_p$. Not only is such a claim not contradictory, it is what allows the Subscript View to accommodate cases of ambiguous loss.

To conclude, Schechtman and Shoemaker expand on traditional approaches to identity over time by proposing views that provide a plurality of persistence and ownership-relevant properties. However, like traditional approaches to personal identity, these views also assume that the answer to questions about identity over time (or ownership) are binary—either we persist or perish (or, on Shoemaker's analysis, either a relevant ownership-relation obtains or it fails to). But the folk are not just pluralists about what matters when it comes to persistence (or ownership); they are also pluralists about the kinds of entities we are at the most fundamental level—questions about identity over time admit of more than one answer.

5. Objections and Replies

In this final section, I will explore three objections to the Subscript View with the aim of both developing and clarifying the view.

5.1 Are we unified?

The original motivation for the Subscript View was that pluralism, and pluralism alone, can accommodate our identity-related practical concerns. In order to accommodate these concerns, the subscript theorist argues that where we thought there was one, there are in fact many. There exist several distinct selves, all with different modal properties and persistence conditions. This fracturing of the individual, though it allows the Subscript View to ground our identity-related concerns in a single theory of persistence, may render the view unable to accommodate our experience of others as *unified* individuals. Schechtman puts this point forcefully: "The claim that we do not need to conceive of an ultimate locus to which the full range of our questions and concerns about a person are addressed, however, does not ring true to the experience of how we relate to the people who make up our social world" (2014: 83). The fact that we experience those around us as unified agents, not distinct biological and psychological beings, could count against the Subscript View.

First, one might grant that we experience one another as single individuals, but this does not entail that we *care* very much about unity.

Biological and psychological continuity usually obtain together and self$_p$ and self$_b$ are co-located most of the time. Though we tend to think of others as single individuals, this could be because it is simply convenient to do so. We rarely need to distinguish between self$_p$ and self$_b$. With the exception of very few claims, whatever we say of the one will be true of the other. It is true of both my brother$_p$ and brother$_b$ that he is taller than me, works in finance, and does not understand the value of philosophy for a life well-lived. But when discussing (or complaining about) him, it would be time-consuming and needless to specify that these things are true of *both* my brother$_p$ and my brother$_b$. Though we tend to treat one another as single targets of concern, more work needs to be done to argue that this illustrates that we *value* unity and should prioritize it when theorizing about persistence.[15]

Second, it is not clear that we always experience others as unified individuals. Schechtman herself reflects on the fractured experience of our many selves to motivate her view:

> In everyday life we use the word "person" in many different ways. Sometimes it means "human animal," sometimes "moral agent," sometimes "rational, self-conscious subject,"... Each of these conceptions of *person* has its own corresponding criterion of personal identity, and there is no reason to assume that we can find some single relation which underlies our judgments about the identity of a "person" in every context.   (2014: 2)

---

[15] Although, Shoemaker and Tobia (forthcoming: 27) recently argued that: "While some experimental studies suggest that our identity intuitions sometimes fracture and track multiple and differently-grounded relations (e.g. Tierney et al. 2014), in most cases we are indeed tracking a unified locus, albeit with different psychological features." However, Shoemaker and Tobia do not reference any particular study to support this claim and they do not address the work on caregiver grief and ambiguous loss in their essay. Additionally, it is not at all clear to me that the studies they do discuss (e.g., Strohminger & Nichols 2014; Tobia 2015; Molouki and Bartels 2017) illustrate that the folk's judgments about persistence track unified loci of concern. Much of this research indicates that psychological change, especially moral deterioration, threatens our persistence-judgments. But this is entirely consistent with the folk also valuing, and making judgments consistent with, other kinds of persistence relations in other contexts. Shoemaker and Tobia's reasoning reflects the traditional approach to theorizing about persistence, i.e., seeking to determine which relation actually grounds persistence by reflecting on the practical implications of the loss of a particular relation. But, as I argued in Section 2, this approach will rarely prove conclusive because our judgments conform to different approaches to persistence in different cases.

And, in cases where a single persistence relation fails to obtain while another is maintained, our treatment tracks distinct psychological and biological individuals, not unified loci of concern. Nowhere is this clearer than our treatment of those in the late stages of dementia. While we do not explicitly address those with dementia as individuals$_b$ and grieve their deaths$_p$, these beliefs are nevertheless reflected in our treatment of these individuals and the experience of ambiguous loss. Views that require unification, like the Person Life View, cannot provide a satisfying elucidation of these phenomena. Unification views require that there be a single answer to the question of whether we persist, but, as we have seen, this question admits of many answers.

5.2. Who am 'I'?

Schechtman's concerns about unification raise another problem for the Subscript View. What, if anything, is the referent of 'I,' 'me,' and 'you' on this view? If the subscript theorist revises our ontology to include two distinct selves, must she also revise how singular pronouns refer as well?

On the Subscript View, terms like 'I,' 'me,' and 'you' can refer to two distinct objects: self$_p$ and self$_b$. Despite appearances, this is not a particularly radical claim. Perhaps because words like 'I,' 'me,' and 'you' function as singular pronouns in English, it may seem that they refer unambiguously to single objects in the world. But, as Parfit argues, this is often not the case:

> But we can't usefully suppose either that we are the animal, or that we are the person, since we would then be supposing falsely that the words 'I' and 'we' must always refer to the same thing. Some uses of these words may refer to an animal, and others to a person. The names of nations have a similar ambiguity, since they may refer to a nation-state, as in the claim 'France declared war,' or to a part of the Earth's surface, as in the claim 'France is roughly hexagonal.' We shouldn't claim that France must be either a nation-state or a part of the Earth's surface, though we don't know which.   (2012: 21)

Additionally, the subscript theorist can explain why our pronouns refer ambiguously. Because $self_p$ and $self_b$ are often co-located, there is usually no need to specify what kind of individual one refers to when one utters the term 'I' or 'you.' But in many cases, we use 'I' or 'you' to refer to either $self_p$ or $self_b$ exclusively. For example, when visiting an individual in a PVS, one can ask 'how are her vitals?' and it is clear that 'her' refers to only $self_b$ (since $self_p$ no long exists and does not have any vitals). And, if we imagine a case in which an individual's body is completely replaced with inorganic material such that biological continuity is destroyed while psychological continuity is maintained, that individual can wonder 'Where am I?' where the referent of 'I' is clearly $self_p$.

On the Subscript View, terms like 'I,' 'me,' and 'you' can successfully refer in a wider range of cases than if monism were true. If monism were true, these terms would refer to either $self_p$ or $self_b$, but not both. So, these terms could not successfully refer both in cases where an individual is in a PVS and in cases where an individual's body is replaced with inorganic material. On the Subscript View, 'I,' 'me,' and 'you' refer to $self_p$, $self_b$, or both, given the context. Thus, these terms can successfully refer both in cases of PVS and in cases of inorganic matter body replacements. Though the Subscript View may be radical on many counts, there is nothing exceptionally radical about how our pronouns refer on the view. And, unlike monism, the Subscript View allows for terms like 'I' to refer successfully in a wide range of cases in which $self_p$ and $self_b$ are not co-located.

5.3 Will we proliferate?

When I introduced the Subscript View, I argued that there are typically (at least) two distinct individuals wherever we once thought there was one: $self_b$ and $self_p$. But one might wonder what is to stop selves from proliferating on the Subscript View. The primary motivation in developing the Subscript View was to construct a view that could ground the plurality of our identity-related practical concerns. But our practical concerns are varied—what if our practices recommend that there exist not only $self_p$ and $self_b$, but also parent and child selves, spouse and friend selves, boss and employee selves, etc.?

Though I take a view's ability to accommodate our many identity-related concerns to be an important desideratum when it comes to theorizing about persistence, it is far from the *only* desideratum. I proposed the existence of $self_p$ and $self_b$ not only because their existence can ground many of our practical concerns, but also because these particular kinds of entities have been studied extensively. Animalists like Olson have done a great deal of work exploring what it means to be a human animal and how such organisms can persist (1997, 2007). And neo-Lockeans like Baker have done the same with regard to persons and psychological continuity (Baker 2000, 2007). The fact that the theoretical puzzles surrounding the existence of biological and psychological individuals have received a great deal of attention counts in favor of including them in the Subscript View's ontology. As the empirical work on the folk conception of persistence develops, we may need to replace or modify the kinds of individuals and types of persistence relations included in the view. For example, adding the moral self ($self_m$), or modifying $self_p$ and $survival_p$ to capture the importance of moral features and the direction of moral change may soon be required. But modifying the Subscript View in response to a significant amount of empirical and philosophical work is not a harbinger for unlimited proliferation.

There are many grounds on which a subscript theorist can refuse to include a particular self in their ontology. While she can deny ontological entry to an entity whose existence does nothing to ground our practical concerns, she can also bar individuals whose inclusion would render the view incoherent or whose ontological status is extremely suspect. Even if it turns out that it will be impossible to capture *all* of our practical concerns by proposing the existence of a few distinct selves,[16] and there are great theoretical costs to proliferation beyond mere monistic bias, it does not follow that we should give up on the Subscript View. Rather, we should seek to include as many discrete selves that can ground as many of our practical concerns as theoretically desirable. Even if we will

---

[16] It is not clear to me that attempting to capture our identity-related concerns will lead to a proliferation. The folk are working with a view of personal identity that helps them navigate the world. If proliferation of individuals wreaks havoc on our philosophical theories, presumably it would wreak havoc on the folk's theory as well. Although, see Strohminger et al. (2017) for an argument that the folk concept of "true self" cannot properly be conceived of as a scientific concept.

ultimately be unable to accommodate all of our identity-related practical concerns in our theory of personal identity, it does not mean that we should not try.

6. Conclusion: A Distinct View

I will conclude by briefly highlighting the features of the Subscript View that distinguish it from other views. The subscript theorist argues that both $self_p$ and $self_b$ persist through time and are appropriate targets of judgments about personal identity. Though many are happy to accept co-location of objects like human animals and persons, no extant view accepts that both objects are relevant to personal identity and persistence. Olson, for example, grants that humans can also be persons, but he argues that being a person is irrelevant to persistence:

> Perhaps we cannot properly call that vegetating animal a *person* since it has none of those psychological features that distinguish people from non-people... If so, that simply shows that you can continue to exist without being a person, just as you could continue to exist without being a philosopher, or a student, or a fancier of fast cars.   (1997: 17)

For Olson, being a person (a $self_p$) is simply a phase—we are essentially animals and only accidently persons. Baker also accepts the existence of human animals and persons, though she argues that we are essentially persons, not animals: "On the Constitution View, I am an animal (in that I am wholly constituted by an animal), but I am not essentially an animal (in that I could be constituted by an inorganic body)" (2000: 226).

In contrast, on the Subscript View, we, at the most fundamental level, are more than one thing. Both $self_p$ and $self_b$ are able to persist, both $self_p$ and $self_b$ ground different identity-related practical concerns, and both $self_p$ and $self_b$ count as appropriate subjects in the study of personal identity. On the Subscript View, both Olson and Baker are partially correct—something essential is lost when either biological continuity or psychological continuity is lost. But to argue that either of these conditions is essential to identity over time is not quite right; psychological continuity is essential for the survival of $self_p$ and biological continuity is essential for the survival of self$_b$. To slightly modify Sider (2001), ordinary thought contains two concepts of persisting persons, each responsible for a separate set of intuitions, *both of which* are canonical conceptions and need not exclude the other.

Acknowledgments

I would like to thank Michael Gill, Terence Horgan, Michael McKenna, Shaun Nichols, Carolina Sartorio, Marya Schechtman, David Shoemaker, and three anonymous reviewers for helpful feedback on earlier drafts of this chapter.

References

Alzheimer's Association (2018). "2018 Alzheimer's Disease Facts and Figures," *Alzheimer's & Dementia* 14: 367–429.

Baker, L. R. (2000). *Persons and Bodies: A Constitution View*. Cambridge: Cambridge University Press.

Baker, L. R. (2007). *The Metaphysics of Everyday Life: An Essay in Practical Realism*. Cambridge: Cambridge University Press.

Bartels, D., Kvaran, T., and Nichols, S. (2013). "Selfless Giving," *Cognition* 129: 392–403.

Bartels, D. and Rips, L. (2010). "Psychological Connectedness and Intertemporal Choice," *Journal of Experimental Psychology: General* 139: 49–69.

Bartels, D. and Urminsky, O. (2011). "On Intertemporal Selfishness: The Perceived Instability of Identity Underlies Impatient Consumption," *Journal of Consumer Research* 38: 182–98.

Blandin, K. and Pepin, R. (2017). "Dementia Grief: A Theoretical Model of a Unique Grief Experience," *Dementia* 16: 67–78.

Boss, P. (1999). *Ambiguous Loss: Learning to Live with Unresolved Grief*. Cambridge, MA: Harvard University Press.

Boss, P. (2004). "Ambiguous Loss Research, Theory, and Practice: Reflections after 9/11," *Journal of Marriage and Family* 66: 551–66.

De Freitas, J., Tobia, K., Newman, G., and Knobe, J. (2017a). "Normative Judgments and Individual Essence," *Cognitive Science* 41: 382–402.

De Freitas, J., Cikara, M., Grossman, I., and Schlegel, R. (2017b). "Origins of the Belief in Good True Selves," *Trends in Cognitive Science* 21: 634–6.

De Freitas, J., Cikara, M., Grossmann, I., and Schlegel, R. (2018). "Moral Goodness Is the Essence of Personal Identity," *Trends in Cognitive Science* 22: 739–740.

Doka, K. (2004). "Grief and Dementia," in K. Doka (ed.), *Living with Grief: Alzheimer's Disease.* Washington, D.C.: Hospice Foundation of America.

Korsgaard, C. (1989). "Personal Identity and the Unity of Agency: A Kantian Response to Parfit," *Philosophy and Public Affairs* 18: 101–32.

Lindauer, A. and Harvath, T. A. (2014). "Pre-Death Grief in the Context of Dementia Caregiving: An Analysis," *Journal of Advanced Nursing* 70: 2196–207.

Locke, J. (1975). *An Essay Concerning Human Understanding,* ed. P. H. Nidditch. Oxford: Clarendon Press.

McMahan, J. (2002). *The Ethics of Killing: Problems at the Margins of Life.* New York: Oxford University Press.

Marwit, S. and Meuser, T. (2002). "Development and Initial Validation of an Inventory to Assess Grief in Caregivers of Persons with Alzheimer's Disease," *The Gerontologist* 42: 751–65.

Marwit, S. and Meuser, T. (2005). "Development of a Short Form Inventory to Assess Grief in Caregivers of Dementia Patients," *Death Studies* 29: 191–205.

Molouki, S. and Bartels, D. (2017). "Personal Change and the Continuity of the Self," Cognitive Psychology 93: 1–17.

Mott, C. (2018). "Statutes of Limitations and Personal Identity," in T. Lombrozo, J. Knobe, and S. Nichols (eds.), *Oxford Studies in Experimental Philosophy, Volume 2.* Oxford: Oxford University Press, 243–69.

Newman, G., Bloom, P., and Knobe, J. (2014). "Value Judgments and the True Self," *Personality and Social Psychology Bulletin* 40: 203–16.

Nichols, S. and Bruno, M. (2010). "Intuitions about Personal Identity: An Empirical Study," *Philosophical Psychology* 23: 293–312.

Noyes, B., Hill, R., Hicken, B., Luptak, M., Rupper, R., Dailey, N., and Bair, B. (2010). "The Role of Grief in Dementia Caregiving," *American Journal of Alzheimer's Disease & Other Dementias* 25: 9–17.

Olson, E. (1997). *The Human Animal: Personal Identity without Psychology.* New York: Oxford University Press.

Olson, E. (2007). *What Are We?* New York: Oxford University Press.

Parfit, D. (1984). *Reasons and Persons.* New York: Oxford University Press.

Parfit, D. (2012). "We are Not Human Beings," *Philosophy* 87: 5–28.

Prinz, J. and Nichols, S. (2016). "Diachronic Identity and the Moral Self," in J. Kiverstein (ed.), *The Routledge Handbook of the Philosophy of the Social Mind.* London: Routledge, 449–64.

Schechtman, M. (2014). *Staying Alive: Personal Identity, Practical Concerns, and the Unity of a Life.* New York: Oxford University Press.

Shoemaker, D. (2016). "The Stony Metaphysical Heart of Animalism," in S. Blatti and P. Snowdon (eds.) *Animalism.* Oxford: Oxford University Press, 303–28.

Shoemaker, D. and Tobia, K. (forthcoming). "Personal Identity," in J. Doris and The Moral Psychology Research Group (eds.) *The Moral Psychology Handbook.* Oxford: Oxford University Press.

Sider, T. (2001). "Criteria of Personal Identity and the Limits of Conceptual Analysis," *Philosophical Perspectives* 15: 189–209.

Sikes, P. and Hall, M. (2018). " 'It was then that I thought "whaat? This is not my Dad" ': The Implications of the 'Still the Same Person' Narrative for Children and Young People who Have a Parent with Dementia," *Dementia* 17: 180–98.

Starmans, C. and Bloom, P. (2018a). "Nothing Personal: What Psychologists Get Wrong about Identity," *Trends in Cognitive Science* 22: 566–8.

Starmans, C. and Bloom, P. (2018b). "If You Become Evil, Do You Die?" *Trends in Cognitive Science* 22: 740–1.

Strohminger, N., Knobe, J., and G. Newman (2017). "The True Self: A Psychological Concept Distinct from the Self," *Perspectives on Psychological Science* 12: 551–60.

Strohminger, N. and Nichols, S. (2014). "The Essential Moral Self," *Cognition* 131: 159–71.

Strohminger, N. and Nichols, S. (2015). "Neurodegeneration and Identity," *Psychological Science* 26: 1469–79.

Tierney, H., Howard, C., Kumar, V., Kvaran, T., and Nichols, S. (2014). "How Many of Us Are There?" in J. Sytsma (ed.), *Advances in Experimental Philosophy of Mind.* London: Bloomsbury Press, 181–202.

Tobia, K. (2015). "Personal Identity and the Phineas Gage Effect," *Analysis* 75: 396–405.

Tobia, K. (2016). "Personal Identity, Direction of Change, and Neuroethics," *Neuroethics* 9: 37–43.

Unger, P. (1990). *Identity, Consciousness, and Value*. New York: Oxford University Press.

West, C. (2008). "Personal Identity: Practical or Metaphysical?" in C. Mackenzie and K. Atkin (eds.), *Practical Identity and Narrative Agency*. New York: Routledge.

Williams, B. (1970). "The Self and the Future," *The Philosophical Review* 79: 161–80.

Wolf, S. (1986). "Self-Interest and Interest in Selves," *Ethics* 96: 704–20.

Velleman, D. (2006). *Self to Self: Selected Essays*. Cambridge: Cambridge University Press.

6

The Ship of Theseus Puzzle

David Rose

Florida State University, et al.[1]

Thought experiments play various roles in philosophy. Often, they have an *argumentative function*: The judgments they elicit bear on some philosophical debate. The Gettier case, the Gödel case, the Twin Earth case, the Frankfurt case, etc., illustrate the argumentative function of thought experiments. Much of recent metaphilosophy (e.g., Williamson, 2007; Machery, 2017) examines whether and how thought experiments can fulfill this argumentative function. But thought experiments also have less controversial functions. Sometimes they are just meant to *illustrate* a definition or a theory: Arguably, Davidson's swampman case

[1] Full list of contributors to this chapter: Edouard Machery (University of Pittsburgh), Stephen Stich (Rutgers University), Mario Alai (University of Urbino), Adriano Angelucci (University of Urbino), Renatas Berniūnas (Vilnius University, Lithuania), Emma E. Buchtel (The Education University of Hong Kong), Amita Chatterjee (Jadavpur University), Hyundeuk Cheon (Seoul National University), In-Rae Cho (Seoul National University), Daniel Cohnitz (Utrecht University), Florian Cova (University of Geneva), Vilius Dranseika (Vilnius University, Lithuania), Angeles Eraña Lagos (UNAM, Mexico), Laleh Ghadakpour (Independent Scholar), Maurice Grinberg (New Bulgarian University), Ivar Hannikainen (Pontifical Catholic University of Rio de Janeiro), Takaaki Hashimoto (The University of Tokyo), Amir Horowitz (Open University of Israel), Evgeniya Hristova (New Bulgarian University), Yasmina Jraissati (American University of Beirut), Veselina Kadreva (New Bulgarian University), Kaori Karasawa (University of Tokyo), Hackjin Kim (Korea University, Seoul), Yeonjeong Kim (Massachusetts Institute of Technology), Min-Woo Lee (Emory University), Carlos Mauro (CLOO Behavioral Insights Unit), Masaharu Mizumoto (Japan Advanced Institute of Science and Technology), Sebastiano Moruzzi (University of Bologna), Christopher Y. Olivola (Carnegie Mellon University), Jorge Ornelas (Universidad Autónoma de San Luis Potosí), Barbara Osimani (Università Politecnica delle Marche), Alejandro Rosas (National University of Colombia, Bogota), Carlos Romero (UNAM, Mexico), Massimo Sangoi (Independent Scholar), Andrea Sereni (Scuola Universitaria Superiore IUSS Pavia), Sarah Songhorian (Università Vita-Salute San Raffaele Milano), Paulo Sousa (Queen's University, Belfast), Noel Struchiner (Pontifical Catholic University of Rio de Janeiro), Vera Tripodi (University of Turin), Naoki Usui (Mie University), Alejandro Vázquez del Mercado (UNAM, Mexico), Giorgio Volpe (University of Bologna), Hrag A. Vosgerichian (American University of Beirut), Xueyi Zhang (Southeast University, P. R. China), Jing Zhu (Xiamen University).

David Rose et al., *The Ship of Theseus Puzzle* In: *Oxford Studies in Experimental Philosophy*. Edited by: Tania Lombrozo, Joshua Knobe, and Shaun Nichols, Oxford University Press (2020). © David Rose et al.
DOI: 10.1093/oso/9780198852407.003.0007

is only meant to illustrate (not to support) the proposition that the content of thoughts depends on historical facts. Another function of cases is to *provoke* the reader, that is, to elicit puzzlement in order to motivate philosophical inquiry. Metaphysical cases such as the statue of clay case are often meant to fulfill this provocative function.

To fulfill a provocative function, a thought experiment must meet the following condition (which we will call "Ambivalence"): Readers should feel inclined to assert two prima facie inconsistent propositions. This ambivalence is instrumental in leading readers to philosophize about the philosophical issue raised by this thought experiment (be it identity, persistence, constitution, etc.). Ambivalence refers to a psychological fact—that is, it is a psychological fact that readers are so inclined—and psychological methods can be used to assess whether a thought experiment successfully provokes. A thought experiment fails to fulfill its provocative function if it elicits a single, obvious answer.

If a provocative thought experiment is meant to provoke not just readers from a particular cultural background, but all or most readers, it must fulfill a second condition (which we will call "Universality"): It must elicit an ambivalent state of mind in readers of all demographic, particularly of all cultural, backgrounds.

In this chapter, we examine whether one of the most venerable thought experiments in metaphysics, the Ship of Theseus case, successfully fulfills its provocative function.[2] The Ship of Theseus case is an ancient puzzle about persistence. It emerges in partial form in the writings of the Greek biographer Plutarch (1914) and is fleshed out in its modern form by Hobbes (1839):

> For if, for example, that ship of Theseus, concerning the difference whereof made by continued reparation in taking out the old planks and putting in new, the sophisters of Athens were wont to dispute, were, after all the planks were changed, the same numerical ship it was at the beginning; and if some man had kept the old planks as they were taken out, and by putting them afterwards together in the same order,

---

[2] We will remain neutral about whether the Ship of Theseus case also has an argumentative function and about whether it successfully fulfills it.

had again made a ship of them, this, without doubt, had also been the same numerical ship with that which was at the beginning; and so there would have been two ships numerically the same, which is absurd.

(De Corpore II, p. 11)

The issue is this: On the one hand, it seems that the Ship of Theseus can survive the gradual replacement of parts and so it seems that the ship made by gradually replacing the parts (we'll call it "Replacement") is indeed the original ship. On the other hand, when all of the original parts are assembled in the same form as the original ship, it seems that the ship made from the original parts (we'll call it "Original Parts") is indeed the original ship. Both can't be the original ship. So which one is the original ship—the Ship of Theseus—Replacement or Original Parts?

Many philosophers have viewed this case as presenting a genuine puzzle arising from two opposite inclinations to judge: The "continuity of form" between the original ship and Replacement leads us to think that Replacement is the original ship, while the "continuity of matter" between the original ship and Original Parts leads us to think that Original Parts is the original ship. These two criteria for re-identifying objects pull in opposite directions (Rea, 1995, p. 532; see also, e.g., Hirsch, 1982; Hughes, 1997; Lowe, 1983; Nozick, 1981; Scaltsas, 1980; Sider, 2001; Simons, 1987; Wiggins, 1980).

Some philosophers who think the Ship of Theseus case presents a genuine puzzle about identity even doubt that the puzzle has a solution. For instance, Scaltsas (1980) claims that "the example of Theseus's ship... [is an] actual paradox .... [T]here is no sharply defined hierarchy of sufficiency conditions [for artifact identity], so that in cases of conflict we are not always in a position to determine whether the new object is identical to the initial one or not. The reason is that the cases of conflict are so rare in everyday life...Hence, our intuitions are blunt when it comes to making such decisions" (p. 152). In a similar vein, Wiggins (1980) claims that the Ship of Theseus case is "irreclaimably paradoxical" (p. 97).

By contrast, other philosophers deny that the Ship of Theseus case presents a genuine puzzle. Smart (1973), in particular, holds that thinking that the continuity of matter criterion for identity is important has led to "false beliefs—(1) that this condition [i.e., the continuity of matter criterion] applies to the Ship of Theseus case and (2) that it either outweighs or is outweighed by the continuity of form condition" and this has "been responsible for generating a puzzle where no real puzzle or need for a decision exists" (p. 27). The "obvious solution," according to Smart, is that Replacement is the original ship and the "existing rules of identity" prove to be "perfectly adequate for this unusual case" yielding "a non-arbitrary and clear-cut decision" (1972, p. 148).[3]

Our goal in this chapter is to examine whether the Ship of Theseus case is a genuine puzzle that can fulfill the provocative function. We won't address the question of how objects actually persist through part alterations. To use the terminology of Machery (2017), we are not concerned with the material problem of persistence. Nor will we examine the metaphilosophical question of whether the judgments elicited by the Ship of Theseus case can somehow be brought to bear on philosophical theorizing about identity. Instead, we examine whether Ambivalence and Universality hold for the Ship of Theseus case, i.e., whether the Ship of Theseus case elicits contradictory inclinations to judge and whether it does so across demographic groups.

1. Sailing the Ship of Theseus across the Globe

Our strategy for addressing whether the Ship of Theseus case fulfills its provocative function was to conduct a cross-cultural study. The case we used, which is modeled on the Ship of Theseus case, was adapted from Rose (2015):

John is an accomplished woodworker and sailor, whose lifelong hobby is building rowboats by hand. He built his first rowboat—which he named "Drifter"—thirty years ago. Over the years there has been wear

---

[3] It is not entirely clear how to understand Smart's claim that the Ship of Theseus puzzle has an "obvious solution." An anonymous reviewer points out that Smart's claim may not be about our *judgments* about persistence: It may not be a psychological claim. Rather, Smart may be merely saying that one of the two options is clearly the correct one. We believe that Smart's claim that there is an "obvious solution" can be understood in several ways, including in a non-psychological way. However, one way of understanding it is psychological: On this reading, Smart is saying that the case isn't puzzling, and that one of the two options strikes the reader as being correct. In any case, we take this claim as a psychological thesis worth exploring in its own right, especially since it bears on the provocative function of philosophical cases and on whether the Ship of Theseus case can fulfill this function.

and tear, and every single one of the original planks in that rowboat has been replaced.

John—never one to throw anything out—has stored all of the original planks in his shed over the years. Last month John—realizing that he had accumulated enough old planks for a whole rowboat—took out his old plans for Drifter and assembled these old planks exactly according to his old plans. John now has two rowboats of the same design: the rowboat that resulted from gradually replacing the original planks used to build a boat thirty years ago and that now has none of its original planks, and the rowboat just built one month ago with all and only the original planks that were used thirty years ago.

John has promised two of his friends—Suzy and Andy—that they can borrow Drifter for an outing. But Suzy and Andy disagree on which of the two rowboats is actually Drifter. Andy thinks that the rowboat just built a month ago is actually Drifter since it has exactly the same planks, arranged in exactly the same way as Drifter originally had. But Suzy thinks that the rowboat that resulted from gradually replacing the original planks used to build a boat thirty years ago is actually Drifter since, even though it has all new parts, this was just the result of normal maintenance.

After reading the case, participants were asked the following comprehension question:

Comprehension. According to the story, which of the following statements is correct?

(1) The boat John built one month ago is made of new planks.
(2) The boat John built one month ago is made of thirty-year-old planks.

They were then asked the key test question:

Persistence. Please indicate whether you agree with Suzy or Andy:
(1) I agree with Suzy that Drifter is the rowboat that resulted from gradually replacing the original planks used to build a boat thirty years ago and that now has none of its original planks.

(2) I agree with Andy that Drifter is the rowboat built a month ago with the planks and plans that were used thirty years ago.

Finally, participants were asked to indicate how certain they were in their response to Persistence, on a 0–100% scale, with low numbers indicating uncertainty and high numbers indicating certainty.

Data was collected from 2,722 people across twenty-five samples, spanning twenty-two locations. The case was translated from English into seventeen different languages and presented in the dominant local language for each group. 296 people answered Comprehension incorrectly. Demographics for the remaining participants are given in Table 6.1.

Analyzing responses from the remaining 2,426 participants, we found that 64% of participants thought that Replacement was the original ship and that this differed significantly from chance $\chi^2(2426)=181.911$, $p<0.001$. We also found an effect of Site on persistence intuitions, $\chi^2(24, 2426)=113.804$, $p<0.001$, Cramer's V=.217 (Figure 6.1). We then examined, within each site, whether persistence intuitions differed from what would be expected by chance (see Figure 6.1 and Tables 6.2–6.4 in the Appendix).[4]

Finally, we examined certainty ratings. We conducted a two-way ANOVA with Persistence (Replacement, Original Parts) and Site as predictors of Certainty. We found that Persistence (Replacement, M = 78.67, SD=21.73; Original Parts, M=79.02, SD=22.21) did not predict Certainty, $F(1, 2303)=1.021$, p=.312, $\eta p^2=.000$, that Site predicted Certainty, $F(23, 2303)=6.017$, p<.001, $\eta p^2=.057$, and that there was no interaction between Persistence and Site, $F(23, 2303)=1.263$, p=.180,

---

[4] We also conducted a logistic regression analysis that included site, age, gender, the Cognitive Reflection test or CRT (Frederick, 2005), our own adapted version of the Disjunctive Thinking Test (Shafir, 1994), the 18-item Need for Cognition Scale or NFC (Cacioppo, Petty, and Kao, 1984), the 12-item Personal Need for Structure Scale or NFS (Thompson, Naccarato, Parker, and Moskowitz, 2001), and the 10-item Personality Inventory or TIPI (Gosling, Rentfrow, and Swann, 2003). The full model was significant, $\chi^2(36, N=2046)=1441.715$, $p<.000$ (Nagelkerke $R^2=0.092$). However, only site (Wald $\chi^2=41.353$, df=23, p=0.011) and CRT (Wald $\chi^2=27.865$, df=3, p<0.001) significantly predicted Persistence. We should flag, though won't pursue here, that interestingly increased reflectivity makes one even more divided (CRT=0, 76% Replacement, CRT=1, 73% Replacement, CRT=2, 59% Replacement, CRT=3, 58% Replacement). Reflection may make us suspicious of our intuitions but doesn't seem to offer a clear verdict or otherwise help us resolve the issue.

Table 6.1 Demographic information about the study's participants who answered Comprehension correctly, including countries in which data were collected, nature of the sample (students vs. non-students), and mode of survey administration (paper-pencil vs. web-based, volunteers vs. in exchange for compensation, language of the survey).

Location	Students?	Method	Payment	Language	N
Europe					
Bulgaria	N	Web-based	Volunteers	Bulgarian	81
Bulgaria	Y	Web-based	Volunteers	Bulgarian	78
France	N	Web-based	Compensation & volunteers	French	192
Germany	N	Web-based	Compensation	German	99
Italy	Y	Paper-pencil	Volunteers	Italian	90
Lithuania	N	Paper-pencil	Volunteers	Lithuanian	62
Lithuania	Y	Paper-pencil	Volunteers	Lithuanian	76
Portugal	Y	Paper-pencil	Volunteers	Portuguese	87
Spain	N	Web-based	Compensation	Spanish	122
Switzerland	N	Paper-pencil & web-based	Volunteers	French	38
Switzerland	Y	Paper-pencil & web-based	Compensation & volunteers	French	17
UK	N	Web-based	Compensation	English	136
Middle East					
Iran	N	Paper-pencil	Volunteers	Persian	100
Israel	Y	Web-based	Volunteers	Hebrew	74
Israel (Bedouin)	N	Paper-pencil	Volunteers	Arabic	38
Central & North America					
Mexico	N	Paper-pencil	Volunteers	Spanish	50
USA	N	Web-based	Compensation	English	110
South America					
Brazil	Y	Paper-pencil	Volunteers	Portuguese	73
Colombia	N	Paper-pencil	Volunteers	Spanish	56
East Asia					
China	Y	Paper-pencil	Volunteers	Chinese	73
China	Y	Paper-pencil	Volunteers	Chinese, Simplified	84
China	N	Web-based	Compensation	Chinese, Simplified	95
Hong Kong	Y	Web-based	Compensation	Chinese, Traditional	86
Japan	N	Web-based	Compensation	Japanese	89
Japan	Y	Paper-pencil	Volunteers	Japanese	92
South Korea	N	Web-based	Compensation	Korean	74
Mongolia	Y	Paper-pencil	Volunteers	Mongolian	77
South & Southeast Asia					
Indonesia	Y	Paper-pencil	Compensation	Indonesian	85
India	Y	Paper-pencil	Volunteers	Bengali	92

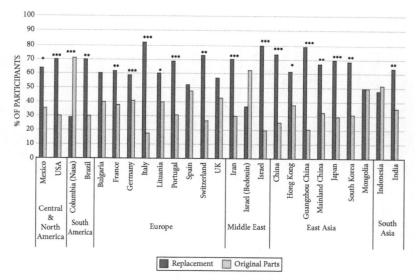

Figure 6.1 Rates of persistence intuitions with results against chance (50%) for each site.

Note: * = *p* <.05, ** = *p* <.01, *** = *p* <.001.

ηp^2=.012 (Figure 6.2).[5] Moreover, for each site, Certainty ratings were significantly different from chance regardless of whether people thought Replacement or Original Parts was the original ship (see Table 6.3 in the Appendix).

Two things bear emphasizing. First, in some sites, participants clearly judge that Replacement is the original ship (e.g., Italy, 82%), in other sites participants are divided (e.g., Mongolia, 50%), while in

---

[5] Colombia is excluded from this analysis since our collaborator who collected data from the indigenous Nasa people of Colombia indicated that participants would have difficulty representing degrees of certainty on an abstract numerical scale. For certainty, the Nasa were give a 7-point scale as follows:

   (1) Completely unsure
   (2) Unsure
   (3) Somewhat unsure
   (4) Neutral
   (5) Somewhat sure
   (6) Sure
   (7) Completely sure

There was no effect of Persistence on Certainty (Replacement, M=6.43, SD=0.813; Original Parts, M=6.12, SD=0.991), F(1, 54)=1.247, p=.269, ηp^2=0.023.

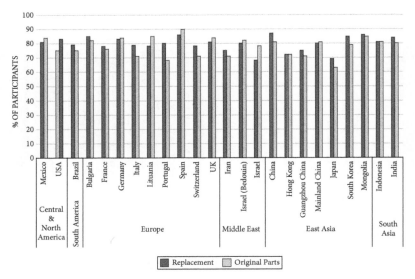

Figure 6.2 Certainty ratings for persistence intuitions for each site.

others participants clearly judge that Original Parts is the original ship (e.g., Colombia, 71%).[6] Second, regardless of whether participants judged that Replacement or Original Parts was the original ship, participants were highly certain in their judgment (Replacement, 68%–87%; Original Parts, 63%–90%).

2. The Puzzle Reassessed

To repeat a point made in the introduction, we focus exclusively on the psychological question of whether the Ship of Theseus case is a genuine puzzle—one that can support its provocative use in philosophical discussions—and not on the nature of persistence itself or the justification

---

[6] The responses of our Bedouin participants were similar to those of our participants in Colombia who were members of the indigenous Nasa tribe. 63% of the Bedouins judged that Original Parts was the original ship. This isn't different from chance (p=.10) but the power of the test is very low because of the small sample size (only 38).

for the use of thought experiments in philosophy. So, does the Ship of Theseus present a genuine puzzle about persistence due to conflicting intuitions based on two criteria for permanence, continuity of form, and continuity of matter, pulling in opposite directions (Ambivalence), and does it present a puzzle in all cultures (Universality)?

Let's begin with Ambivalence. Against the claim that the Ship of Theseus case is a genuine puzzle, it might be pointed out that the vast majority of people, across a wide range of sites and languages, clearly thought that Replacement was the original ship. So, perhaps, the Ship of Theseus case is not that puzzling after all.

However, first, we shouldn't dismiss the answers based on continuity of matter so quickly. Even though the majority of sites judged that Replacement was the original ship, 68% (13/19) of the sites that tended to judge that Replacement was the original ship gave majority ratings that fell within the 60%–70% range. That leaves quite a sizable minority—in the 30%–40% range—who thought that Original Parts was the original ship. It is doubtful that people giving these minority answers misunderstood the case or the questions, and it would be an unsupported speculation to propose that they fall victim to some kind of error that fails to reflect anything about the criteria that constitute their concept of persistence. It is also clear that they did not answer randomly since those that settled on the minority answer tended to be highly confident in their judgment.

What about Universality? The first thing to notice is that five sites (Bulgaria, Spain, the UK, Mongolia, and Indonesia) were clearly divided in the sense that the proportion of responses that Replacement is identical to the original boat did not significantly differ from chance. Among the sites that were not so divided, the consensus among two groups from traditional societies in our sample—the Nasa of Colombia and the Bedouins of Israel—was that continuity of matter was more relevant in determining which ship was the Ship of Theseus.[7] For

---

[7] An anonymous reviewer suggests that the cultural variability we find might be due to "noise." We acknowledge that this is a possibility but think it unlikely for two reasons. First, our findings cohere with those presented by Lucy (1992) who found that Yucatec-speaking Maya classify objects on the basis of material while English speakers do so on the basis of shape or form. This suggests that there is a general difference in classification styles by those in more industrialized and more traditional societies. And this coheres with our findings suggesting that those in more traditional societies such as the Nasa and the Bedouins, trace persistence on

those groups as for those where the modal answer is based on continuity of form a sizable minority gave the opposite answer, and people in the minority were confident in their answer, suggesting that in all cultures we have looked at people are ambivalent when they read the Ship of Theseus case.

Our results do indeed suggest that the Ship of Theseus case is a puzzle: People across cultures are ambivalent about what to say in response to the case. But they do not suggest it is one that feels unsolvable or that it is "irreclaimably paradoxical," placing us in a permanent state of indecision. If this were the case, then we should have found that people were divided on whether Replacement or Original Parts was the Ship of Theseus and that they were not very confident in the option they ultimately settled on. But this is not at all what we found. The majority of sites offered a clear verdict and did so quite confidently.[8]

Perhaps then, we do have two conflicting criteria, "continuity of form" and "continuity of matter" that constitute our concept of persistence and pull us in opposite directions. But people tend to settle on one answer or another and do so with confidence. The variability we find—e.g., with some sites clearly judging that Replacement is the original ship, others being divided, and others clearly judging that Original Parts is the original ship—is plausibly due to people placing different weight on which criterion to use in determining which of the two ships is the original ship. The only remaining question would be what determines

---

the basis of original material and those in more industrialized societies such as the USA and China trace persistence on the basis of form. At least some of the diversity we find is plausibly due to these more general differences in classification styles and not mere "noise." Second, if the diversity we have uncovered is attributable to mere "noise," then we should also expect this to be reflected in certainty ratings, but people were overall highly confident in their persistence judgment. So, taken together, we think it is implausible that the diversity we have uncovered is simply due to "noise."

[8] An anonymous reviewer suggests that the Ship of Theseus case might be a puzzle because of the high confidence associated with each of the contradictory answers. Our findings do indicate that people are highly confident in their judgments, but they don't suggest that people are highly confident in two conflicting judgments: that the original ship is Replacement and that the original ship is Original Parts. Instead, different people make different judgments and they are highly confident in the judgment they arrive at.

which criterion receives more weight in a given context.[9] For any proposed answer, we would flag that it needs to explain the variability we found both within and across cultures. But these are matters that fall beyond the scope of this chapter. At this point, our results suggest that there are two criteria that constitute our concept of persistence and these two criteria receive different weightings in settling matters concerning persistence. And this seems to cohere best with the psychological view that the Ship of Theseus is a genuine puzzle but one that people can solve to their satisfaction. The Ship of Theseus case does elicit puzzling judgments across a wide range of cultural groups speaking very different languages. It fulfills its provocative use.

3. Conclusion

Does the Ship of Theseus case present a genuine puzzle about persistence? That is, does it elicit puzzling judgments that support its provocative use? We set out to examine this question by conducting a cross-cultural study involving nearly 3,000 people across twenty-two locations, speaking eighteen different languages. Our results are hard to square with the proposal that there really is no puzzle at all. They also speak against the proposal that there is a genuine puzzle but one that feels unsolvable, perhaps because our intuitions are "blunt" and "irreclaimably paradoxical." Our results seem to cohere best with the view that there are two criteria—continuity of form and continuity of matter—that constitute our concept of persistence and these two criteria receive different weightings in settling matters concerning persistence.

---

[9] An anonymous reviewer points out that the context of use of the boat—Andy and Suzy wanting to take Drifter out—may be playing a role in people's judgments about persistence. The reviewer also notes that adding "both Original Parts and Replacement are the original ship" and "neither Original Parts nor Replacement is the original ship" as response options could be illuminating, especially since some philosophers have defended views in line with these options (see, e.g., Gallois, 2016; Pickup, 2016). We think these are excellent directions for future research.

4. Appendix

Table 16.2 Logistic regression results for Persistence 1.

Variable	β	SE	p	Odds ratio	Odds ratio 95% CI
Age	.00	.00	.61	1.00	[.99, 1.01]
Gender[a]	−.06	.10	.53	.94	[.77, 1.14]
Europe					
Bulgaria[b]	.13	.25	.60	1.13	[.70, 1.86]
Germany[b]	−.13	.31	.69	.88	[.48, 1.63]
Italy[b]	.39	.31	.22	1.48	[.80, 2.73]
Lithuania[b]	.12	.27	.66	1.13	[.66, 1.94]
Portugal[b]	−.30	.32	.35	.74	[.40, 1.40]
Spain[b]	.33	.28	.23	1.40	[.81, 2.40]
Switzerland[b]	−.48	.38	.21	.62	[.30, 1.30]
UK[b]	.04	.27	.88	1.04	[.62, 1.76]
North America					
Mexico[b]	−.26	.37	.49	.77	[.37, 1.60]
USA[b]	−.33	.30	.27	.72	[.40, 1.30]
South America					
Brazil[b]	−.32	.33	.33	.73	[.40, 1.40]
Columbia[b]	1.07	.39	.007	2.90	[1.35, 6.26]
Middle East					
Iran[b]	−.28	.30	.34	.75	[.42, 1.40]
Israel (Bedouins)[b]	.683	.42	.11	1.98	[.86, 4.55]
Israel [b]	−.50	.37	.18	.61	[.30, 1.25]
Asia					
China[b]	−.07	.352	.84	.93	[.47, 1.86]
Guangzhou China[b]	−.37	.35	.27	.69	[.35, 1.37]
Mainland China[b]	−.19	.33	.56	.83	[.44, 1.57]
Hong Kong[b]	.07	.34	.83	1.08	[.55, 2.01]
India[b]	−.16	.33	.62	.85	[.45, 1.62]
Japan[b]	−.89	.36	.01	.41	[.20, .83]
Mongolia[b]	.20	.37	.58	1.22	[.61, 2.50]
South Korea[b]	−.23	.25	.36	.79	[.48, 1.31]
Disjunctive thinking[c]	.06	.11	.56	1.06	[.86, 1.62]
CRT (=1)[d]	.02	.16	.93	1.02	[.74, 1.40]
CRT (=2)[d]	.57	.16	<.001	1.76	[1.29,2.41]
CRT (=3)[d]	.66	.16	<.001	1.93	[1.42, 2.62]
NFC	−.13	.10	.17	.88	[.73, 1.06]
NFS	.07	.08	.38	1.07	[.92, 1.26]
Extraversion	.04	.04	.32	1.04	[.97,1.11]
Agreeableness	.02	.05	.62	1.02	[.93, 1.12]
Conscientiousness	.03	.05	.47	1.03	[.95, .1.23]
Neuroticism	.04	.04	.27	1.04	[.97, 1.13]
Openness to experience	−.03	.05	.52	.97	[.87, 1.07]

Note: a: reference class, males; b: reference class, France; c: reference class, correct answer; d: reference class, CRT score = 0.

Table 6.3 Test of persistence judgments against chance (50%) for each site.

Sample	Persistence (χ^2) (p-value)
Central and North America	
Mexico	3.920*
USA	17.600***
South America	
Columbia	10.286***
Brazil	11.52**
Europe	
Bulgaria	6.849**
France	10.083**
Germany	15.705***
Italy	37.378***
Lithuania	5.681*
Portugal	12.517***
Spain	.295
	.587
Switzerland	11.364**
UK	2.941
	.086
Middle East	
Iran	16.000
	***
Israel (Bedouin)	2.632
	.105
Israel	26.162***
East Asia	
China	16.781***
Hong Kong	4.651*
Guangzhou China	27.429***
Mainland China	11.463**
Japan	29.442***
South Korea	10.595**
Mongolia	.013
	.909
South Asia	
Indonesia	.106
	.745
India	7.348**

Note: * = $p < .05$, ** = $p < .01$, *** = $p < .001$.

Table 6.4   Test of certainty judgments against chance for each site.

Sample	Replacement (t-value) (p-value)	Original Parts (t-value) (p-value)
Central and North America		
Mexico	8.056***	7.881***
USA	11.458***	9.395***
South America		
Columbia	11.979***	13.549***
Brazil	9.025***	6.424***
Europe		
Bulgaria	17.947***	11.067***
France	13.393***	8.639**
Germany	15.705***	10.033***
Italy	12.671***	2.885*
Lithuania	10.096***	13.618***
Portugal	10.010***	3.521**
Spain	13.844***	17.200***
Switzerland	9.229***	3.705**
UK	12.178***	11.986***
Middle East		
Iran	8.734***	4.698***
Israel (Bedouin)	6.638***	9.230***
Israel	4.109***	3.731**
East Asia		
China	17.863***	7.343***
Hong Kong	7.388***	5.862***
Guangzhou China	11.478***	5.234***
Mainland China	14.223***	9.253***
Japan	8,828***	4.115***
South Korea	15.876***	5.247***
Mongolia	15.596***	11.125***
South Asia		
Indonesia	10.979***	13.641***
India	13.459***	9.088***

Note: * = $p <.05$, ** = $p <.01$, *** = $p <.001$.

Acknowledgments

This publication was made possible through the support of a grant from the Fuller Theological Seminary/Thrive Center in concert with the John Templeton Foundation. The opinions expressed in this publication are those of the author(s) and do not necessarily reflect the views of the Fuller Thrive Center or the John

Templeton Foundation. We also thank Tatsuya Kameda (The University of Tokyo) and Kazuhisa Todayama (Nagoya University) for their help with data collection and two anonymous reviewers for comments.

References

Cacioppo, J. T., Petty, R. E., and Kao, C. F. (1984). The efficient assessment of need for cognition. *Journal of Personality Assessment*, 48, 306–7.

Frederick, S. (2005). Cognitive reflection and decision making. *The Journal of Economic Perspectives*, 19, 25–42.

Gallois, A. (2016). Identity over time. In Edward N. Zalta (ed.), *The Stanford Encyclopedia of Philosophy*. https://plato.stanford.edu/archives/win2016/entries/identity-time/.

Gosling, S. D., Rentfrow, P. J., and Swann, W. B., Jr. (2003). A very brief measure of the Big Five Personality domains. *Journal of Research in Personality*, 37, 504–28.

Hirsch, E. (1982). *The Concept of Identity*. Oxford: Oxford University Press.

Hobbes, T. (1839). *The English Works of Thomas Hobbes, Vol. 1: Concerning Body*. Ed. William Molesworth. London: John Bohn.

Hughes, C. (1997). Same-kind coincidence and the Ship of Theseus. *Mind*, 106, 53–67.

Lucy, J. A. (1992). *Grammatical Categories and Cognition: A Case Study of the Linguistic Relativity Hypothesis*. Cambridge: Cambridge University Press.

Lowe, E. J. (1983). On the identity of artifacts. *The Journal of Philosophy*, 80, 220–32.

Machery, E. (2017). *Philosophy within Its Proper Bounds*. Oxford: Oxford University Press.

Nozick, R. (1981). *Philosophical Explanations*. Cambridge, MA: Harvard University Press.

Pickup, M. (2016). A situationist solution to the Ship of Theseus puzzle. *Erkenntnis*, 81, 973–92.

Plutarch (1914). *Plutarch's Lives*. English translation by Bernadotte Perrin. Cambridge, MA: Harvard University Press; London, William Heinemann Ltd.

Rea, M. (1995). The problem of material constitution. *Philosophical Review*, 104, 525–52.

Rose, D. (2015). Persistence through function preservation. *Synthese*, 192, 97–146.

Scaltsas, T. (1980). The Ship of Theseus. *Analysis*, 40, 152–7.

Shafir, E. (1994). Uncertainty and the difficulty of thinking through disjunctions. *Cognition*, 50, 403–30.

Sider, T. (2001). *Four Dimensionalism*. Oxford: Oxford University Press.

Simons, P. (1987). *Parts: A Study in Ontology*. Oxford: Oxford University Press.

Smart, B. (1972). How to reidentify the Ship of Theseus. *Analysis*, 32, 145–8.

Smart, B. (1973). The Ship of Theseus, the Parthenon and disassembled objects. *Analysis*, 34, 24–7.

Thompson, M. M., Naccarato, M. E., Parker, K. C. H., and Moskowitz, G. (2001). The personal need for structure (PNS) and personal fear of invalidity (PFI) scales: Historical perspectives, present applications and future directions. In G. Moskowitz (ed.), *Cognitive Social Psychology: The Princeton Symposium on the Legacy and Future of Social Cognition* (pp. 19–39). Mahwah, NJ: Erlbaum.

Wiggins, D. (1980). *Sameness and Substance*. Cambridge: Cambridge University Press.

Williamson, T. (2007). Philosophical knowledge and knowledge of counterfactuals. *Grazer Philosophische Studien*, 74, 89.

7

False Memories and Quasi-Memories are Memories

Vilius Dranseika
Kaunas University of Technology

1. Introduction: The Factivity Constraint and the Strong Previous Awareness Condition

In this chapter, I present new data bearing on two constraints that are often taken to be essential features of our ordinary use of 'remembering' and 'having a memory': the factivity constraint and the strong previous awareness condition.[1] Let me introduce these two constraints in turn.

The factivity constraint. The first constraint on the ordinary use of 'remember' is the so-called factivity constraint. Werning and Cheng write: "It is [...] widely agreed that 'remember' comes with a presupposition of the factivity of the intentional object that the state referred to by 'remember' is directed to" (2017: 8). Put simply, the claim is that one can be truly said to 'remember' some event only if that person originally *experienced* or *observed* that event (e.g., Holland 1954; Malcolm 1963; Martin and Deutscher 1966; Chisholm 1989; Bernecker 2008). Any non-factive use of 'remember', then, is said to be a mistaken or figurative attribution of memory.

There are some dissenting voices, however. For example, Hazlett claims that non-factive "uses of 'knows', 'learns', 'remembers', and 'realizes' are unexceptional, and do not strike ordinary people as deviant" (2010: 501), while de Brigard argues that

---

[1] My discussion in this chapter is limited to applicability of these two constraints to ascriptions of autobiographic episodic memories.

Vilius Dranseika, *False Memories and Quasi-Memories are Memories* In: *Oxford Studies in Experimental Philosophy*. Edited by: Tania Lombrozo, Joshua Knobe, and Shaun Nichols, Oxford University Press (2020). © Vilius Dranseika. DOI: 10.1093/oso/9780198852407.003.0008

Perhaps the most obvious argument against the factivity constraint is the simple fact that competent speakers just don't abide by it when they use the word 'remembering' [...] The distinction between seeming to remember and actually remembering only makes sense from the point of view of epistemology, but this is because the philosopher has already confined her notion of remembering to veridical memories—a decision that isn't grounded in the way competent speakers use the word 'remembering'. (2017: 130–1)

The strong previous awareness condition states that remembering presupposes identity between the person who remembers an event and the person who originally experienced that event.

In the present form and under the present label, this constraint was articulated by Sydney Shoemaker in his discussion of quasi-memories, in his 1970 paper "Persons and their pasts":

Quasi-remembering, as I shall use the term, includes remembering as a special case. One way of characterizing the difference between quasi-remembering and remembering is by saying that the former is subject to a weaker previous awareness condition than the latter. Whereas someone's claim to remember a past event implies that he himself was aware of the event at the time of its occurrence [i.e. remembering is subject to the strong previous awareness condition], the claim to quasi-remember a past event implies only that someone or other was aware of it. (271)

Shoemaker's goal in introducing the notion of quasi-remembering—as well as Derek Parfit's, who later adopted this term in his book *Reasons and Persons* (1984)—was to answer one of the most influential arguments against the memory criterion of personal identity. This argument—mostly associated with Joseph Butler—claims that it is not possible to analyze personal identity in terms of autobiographical memory, for the latter presupposes the former. The notion of quasi-memory was designed to provide a criterion of personal identity that both preserves the spirit of the memory criterion and avoids the circularity charge, since quasi-memory does not presuppose that the person who quasi-remembers an event is the same person as the one who originally experienced that event.

Thus understood, remembering is a species of quasi-remembering—all memories are quasi-memories, but not all quasi-memories are memories. As described by Parfit, "ordinary memories are a sub-class of quasi-memories. They are quasi-memories of our own past experiences" (1984: 219).[2] With these definitions, according to Shoemaker, it is possible to "defend the spirit of the claim that memory is a criterion of personal identity" (1970: 281) by rewriting memory criterion as a quasi-memory criterion.

Shoemaker hints at the possibility, however, that the ordinary sense of 'remember' is not bound by the strong previous awareness condition. In discussing this possibility, he introduces two senses of 'remember'— 'remember$_s$' for a strong sense of remembering that presupposes the strong previous awareness condition and 'remember$_w$' for a weak sense of remembering, quasi-remembering being one version of weak remembering. Shoemaker then writes: "In the actual world, people remember$_s$ whatever they remember$_w$, and this makes it difficult to settle the question of whether it is the weak or the strong sense of 'remember' that is employed in ordinary discourse" (1970: 281). Shoemaker then claims that if "in its ordinary use 'remember' means 'remember$_w$'," then this would allow us to defend not only the spirit but also the letter of the claim that memory is a criterion of personal identity (1970: 281).

There is a link between the strong previous awareness condition and the factivity constraint. Violation of the strong previous awareness condition constitutes a partial violation of the factivity constraint—"veridical quasi-memory" (Shoemaker 1970: 273) or "accurate quasi-memory" (Parfit 1984: 219) preserves factivity concerning the quasi-remembered event and violates factivity concerning who was the subject of the original experience.

In the present chapter, I discuss the results of a set of four studies conducted with Lithuanian participants, which collectively suggest that indeed the ordinary use of 'remember' and 'having a memory of' is not bound by either the factivity constraint or the strong previous awareness condition. To the best of my knowledge, this is the first attempt to

---

[2] For similar purposes, Penelhum (1967) introduces a different term 'retrocognition,' where retrocognition and memory constitute disjoined classes—no memory is retrocognition and no retrocognition is memory. Otherwise retrocognition does not differ from quasi-memories.

address empirically the question whether these two constraints are features of our ordinary concept of memory.

2. Study 1: Quasi-Memories and Artificial Memories

Study 1 was designed to check whether study participants will consider cases of quasi-remembering and cases of artificial memories as cases of remembering. If they do, this would constitute a violation of the factivity constraint (in the case of artificial memory) and the strong previous awareness condition (in the case of quasi-memory).

Participants. 291 undergraduate students at a Lithuanian university (78% females, 20% males, 2% chose 'other/prefer not to answer'; mean age: 20.0; age SD = 2.85; age range 18–51) took part in this pen-and-paper study.

Materials. Three vignettes were constructed and presented in a between-subjects design: quasi-memory (referred to as Q in the vignette below), artificial memory (A), and true memory (T) as a control condition. Differences between vignettes are presented in square brackets. Original materials in Lithuanian language for all studies reported in this chapter can be obtained from the author.

Imagine that it is now the year 2086 and scientists have invented a technology that allows one [to install human memories (for Q and T)/to create artificial memories and to install such memories (for A)] into biological storage devices created for this purpose. This technology also allows one to transfer such memories into the brains of other people. A person, into whose brain such [other people's (for Q and T)/artificial (for A)] memories are transferred, cannot distinguish such transferred memories from their own memories. Also, no available technologies can distinguish such memories from others. This technology at the moment is experimental and secret, but it is already sometimes used as an educational tool, since it provides an easy way to transfer knowledge that was memorized by another person. It is also sometimes used as a means to improve psychological well-being by transferring pleasant [memories of other people (for Q and T)/ artificial memories (for A)].

Imagine that Albertas is a teenager who had a lot of [other people's (for Q and T)/artificial (for A)] memories transferred into his brain in his childhood. Albertas does not know and has no reason whatsoever to suspect that such memory transfer was performed on him. [Not all his memories, however, are transferred memories of other people. Some of his memories are from the period before memory transfer (only in T)]. One of [the transferred (for Q and A)/such original (for T)] memories is about tasting rowan-berries in childhood. When someone asks Albertas whether he has ever tasted rowan-berries, Albertas replies with confidence: "Yes, I clearly remember eating rowan-berries when I was a child."

After reading the vignette, participants were asked to answer two questions about memory and knowledge on a six-point Likert scale, anchored at 1 (Completely disagree) and 6 (Completely agree). The first question was "Do you agree that Albertas **remembers** that he has tasted rowan-berries when he was a child?" and the second one reads 'knows' instead of 'remembers.'

Results. The results of Study 1 are presented in Figure 7.1.

Remembers probes. In all three scenarios—quasi-memory, artificial memory, and true memory, one-sample t-tests indicated that participants' agreement that Albertas remembers that he has tasted rowan-berries when he was a child was above the middle-point of the scale: for quasi-memory (M = 4.87, SD = 1.72, t(96) = 7.83, p <.001, d = 0.795); for artificial memory (M = 4.70, SD = 1.87, t(95) = 6.28, p <.001, d = 0.641); and for true memory (M = 5.19, SD = 1.37, t(97) = 12.2, p <.001, d = 1.23).

For knowledge probes, quasi-memories were not considered to be the basis for knowledge. One-sample t-test indicated that participants' agreement that Albertas knows that he has tasted rowan-berries when he was a child was below the middle point of the scale in the quasi-memory scenario (M = 3.08, SD = 1.95, t(96) = 7.83, p =.037, d = 0.215). Responses were no different from the midpoint of the scale in the other two cases: for artificial memory (M = 3.27, SD = 2.10, t(95) = 1.07, p =.287,

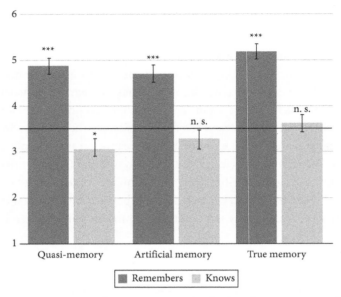

Figure 7.1 Agreement of participants with whether the agent remembers and knows that he has tasted rowan-berries when he was a child.

Note: The black horizontal line indicates the middle of the scale (3.5). Error bars represent standard errors.

d = 0.109); and for true memory (M = 3.61, SD = 1.84, t(97) = 0.605, p =.547, d = 0.061).

In all three cases, paired-sample t-tests indicated that scores on 'remembers' scale were higher than on 'knows' scale: for quasi-memory (M = 4.87, SD = 1.72 *versus* M = 3.08, SD = 1.95, t(96) = 7.83, p <.001, d = 0.579); for artificial memory (M = 4.70, SD = 1.87 *versus* M = 3.27, SD = 2.10, t(95) = 4.08, p <.001, d = 0.417); and for true memory (M = 5.19, SD = 1.37 *versus* M = 3.61, SD = 1.84, t(97) = 6.54, p <.001, d = 0.661).

Independent-sample t-tests indicated that scores on the 'remembers' scale did not differ for quasi-memories (M = 4.87, SD = 1.72) and artificial memories (M = 4.70, SD = 1.87), t(191) = 0.65, p =.516, d = 0.094. Also, an independent-sample t-test indicated that scores on the 'remembers' scale did not differ for quasi-memories and true memories (M = 5.19, SD = 1.37), t(183) = 1.47, p =.143, d = 0.211. Levene's test indicated unequal variances (F = 8.88, p =.003), so degrees of freedom were adjusted from 193 to 183. Also, an independent-sample t-test indicated that scores on the 'remembers' scale were lower for artificial memories than for true memories, t(174) = 2.10, p =.037, d = 0.303. Levene's test indicated unequal variances (F = 16.91, p <.001), so degrees of freedom were adjusted from 192 to 174.

Discussion. The main result of Study 1 is that study participants were willing to say that the agent 'remembers' both in case of artificial memory (violating the factivity constraint) and of quasi-memory (violating the strong previous awareness condition).

3. Study 2: Dream Memories

One limitation of Study 1 is that it employs unusual science fiction scenarios. In Study 2, I attempted to use a much more mundane scenario of misidentified dream resulting in a false memory. Unfortunately, it is not possible to come up with mundane scenarios to test the strong previous awareness condition, so Study 2 is limited to testing the factivity constraint.

Participants. 203 online participants took part in a study (60% females, 37% males, 3% chose 'prefer not to answer/other'; mean age: 30.4; age SD = 7.42; age range 18–60). Participants for this study (as well as for Studies 3 and 4) were recruited via advertisements on several Lithuanian popular science Facebook pages.

Materials. Three versions of a vignette were used that varied how much time has passed since the misidentified dream that resulted in a false memory. This was done in order to see whether participants will be more likely to say that the agent 'has a memory' in case of older false memories, the idea being that older false memories will be perceived as integrated into the agent's mental economy to a larger extent. The vignettes read as follows:

Six months ago [ten years ago; yesterday] Ona was attending Algis' twentieth birthday party. Thinking of that party, Ona has a vivid image in her mind of Regina inadvertently spilling red wine all over Jonas, followed by an image of Regina's horrified expression at the mishap, and of Jonas sitting on the grass by the drinks table, completely drenched.

However, no such event in fact occurred during Algis' birthday party. Instead, what happened was just that Ona, very excited about the party, on the same night had a dream of Jonas having wine spilled all over him, and she came to believe that this event occurred, not in her dream, but in reality.

When today a friend asked Ona whether she attended Algis' twentieth birthday party six months ago [ten years ago; yesterday], Ona replied: "Yes, I attended Algis' twentieth birthday party. Jonas was also there. I remember him having wine spilled all over him."[3]

After reading the vignette, participants were asked to indicate their agreement with the claim "Ona has a memory of Jonas having wine spilled all over him during a party" on a seven-point Likert scale, anchored at 1 (Completely disagree) and 7 (Completely agree).

Results. Independent-sample t-tests indicated that scores on 'has a memory of' scale did not differ between groups: yesterday (M = 4.91, SD = 2.26) versus six months (M = 5.16, SD = 2.23): t(135) =.643, p =.521, d =.110; yesterday versus ten years (M = 4.82, SD = 2.20): t(131) =.239, p =.812, d =.041; and six months versus ten years: t(134) =.892, p =.374, d =.153. Thus participants were pooled for the subsequent analysis.

One-sample t-test indicated that participants' agreement with a claim "Ona has a memory of Jonas having wine spilled all over him during a party" was above the middle point of the scale: M = 4.97, SD = 2.22, t(202) = 6.19, p <.001, d = 0.434. In fact, 7 (Completely agree) was a modal answer, covering 38% of cases.

Discussion. Study 2 looked at the factivity constraint using a more mundane scenario. Participants tended to agree that misidentified dreams were memories (in violation of the factivity constraint). However, no support was found for the claim that the older the misidentified dream, the more likely it is to be considered a case of memory.

---

[3]   This vignette is loosely based on one developed by Philipp Rau.

4. Study 3: Memories and Experiences

One potential issue with the previous studies is that participants may be answering that implanted memories in an individual are memories because her experience of remembering is tantamount to the experience of remembering in a person with no implanted memories. And if people mean the experience of remembering rather than a memory (independent of its phenomenological profile), then the view that memory is factive or assumes a previous awareness condition is not refuted.[4] Study 3 was designed to look into this possibility by giving participants a choice to indicate that what is described is not a case of having a memory of an event but a case of having an experience of a sort that would be experienced by someone who indeed has a memory of such an event.

Participants. 252 online participants took part in a study (65% females, 32% males, 3% chose 'prefer not to answer/other'; mean age: 31.2; age SD = 8.22; age range 18–56).

Materials. For Study 3, quasi-memory and artificial memory vignettes from Study 1, and the Ona's dream ('six months ago' version) vignette from Study 2 were used. After reading quasi-memory and artificial memory vignettes, participants were asked to make the following choice:

Which of the following two descriptions is more suitable to describe this situation?

1. Even though Albertas hadn't tasted rowan-berries when he was a child, he has a memory of tasting rowan-berries.
2. Albertas does not have a memory of tasting rowan-berries. He simply has an experience like the experience of someone who has such memory.

Participants who received Ona's dream vignette were separated into two groups. The two groups received the task with slightly different wording. Namely, two different synonymous Lithuanian words for 'experience' were used: 'patiria' for one group (dream memory 1; the

---

[4] I would like to thank one of the reviewers for raising this issue.

same word was used in quasi-memory and artificial memory tasks) and 'išgyvena' for another one (dream memory 2). The task read (with different Lithuanian words for 'experiencing' for different conditions):

Which of the following two descriptions is more suitable to describe this situation?

1. Ona has a memory of Jonas having wine spilled all over him during a party, even though no such event in fact happened.
2. Ona does not have a memory of Jonas having wine spilled all over him during a party. She simply has an experience like the experience of someone who has a memory of such event.

As a result, there were four conditions (quasi-memory, artificial memory, and two variations of Ona's dream), presented in between-subjects manner.

Results. A chi-square test of goodness-of-fit was performed to determine whether the two options were equally preferred. In all four conditions, significantly more participants chose 'has a memory' answer. Quasi-memories: X^2 (1, $N = 66$) = 11.9, p <.001. 71% of participants chose 'has a memory' answer. Artificial memories: X^2 (1, $N = 60$) = 19.3, p <.001. 78% of participants chose 'has a memory' answer. Dream memory 1: X^2 (1, $N = 63$) = 7.0, p =.008. 67% of participants chose 'has a memory' answer. Dream memory 2 results were exactly identical to results in Dream memory 1: X^2 (1, $N = 63$) = 7.0, p =.008. 67% of participants chose 'has a memory' answer. The results of Study 3 are presented in Figure 7.2.

Independent sample chi-square tests of association were performed to determine whether the response patterns to the four conditions differed. No differences between groups were observed, X^2 (3, $N = 252$) = 2.68, p =.443. After pooling across conditions, a chi-square test of goodness-of-fit was performed to determine whether the two options were equally preferred. Answers were not equally distributed in the population, X^2 (1, $N = 252$) = 42.9, p <.001. Across all four conditions, 71% of participants chose 'has a memory' answer.

Discussion. In all four conditions, participants were more likely to choose an option ascribing a memory of an event than an option ascribing only an experience of having a memory.

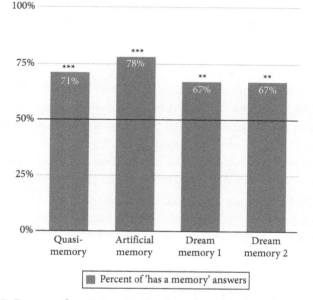

Figure 7.2 Percent of participants who chose 'has a memory' answer.

Note: The black horizontal line indicates proportion of the answers that could be expected to obtain by chance alone (50%).

5. Study 4: Memories, Money, and Guns

Study 4 was designed to look into another potential objection—namely, that non-factive memories are not memories in the same way as false money is not money or a false gun is not a gun.

To this effect, Cheng and Werning write:

In psychology, the adjective-noun combination "false memory" is often used to refer to a false mnemonic representation. The use of this phrase by psychologists is sometimes interpreted as if memory in psychology would not be regarded as factive. However, this conclusion would be justified only if "false" were an intersective adjective, for which the inference from "x is AN" to "x is N" is valid. The more plausible interpretation, we think, is that "false" in "false memory" is a privative adjective like "false" in "false money" or "fake" in "fake gun". For privative adjectives, the inference is not valid: false money is not money, a fake gun is not a gun and, likewise, false memory is not a case of memory. (2016: 1351, n.1)

I decided to run a study to look into this.

Participants. 455 online participants took part in a study (63% females, 34% males, 3% chose 'prefer not to answer/other'; mean age: 30.8; age SD = 7.88; age range 18–60). All participants who took part in either Study 2 or Study 3 (no participants overlap between Studies 2 and 3) also took part in Study 4. Study 4 was presented on a separate page and participants were not allowed to return to the previous study.

Materials. Participants were asked to indicate on the seven-point Likert scale (anchored at 1 (Completely disagree) and 7 (Completely agree)) the extent to which they agree or disagree with each of the following three claims:

A false memory is still a memory.
A fake—toy—gun is still a gun.[5]
False money is still money.

Results. One-sample t-tests were conducted for all three scenarios—memory, gun, and money. In the case of memory, the mean agreement was above the middle point of the scale: $M = 4.47$, $SD = 2.08$, $t(454) = 4.83$, $p < .001$, $d = 0.226$. In the case of gun, mean agreement did not differ from the middle point of the scale: $M = 3.96$, $SD = 2.17$, $t(454) = 0.39$, $p = .697$, $d = 0.018$. While in the case of money, mean agreement was below the middle point of the scale: $M = 2.96$, $SD = 2.07$, $t(454) = 10.71$, $p < .001$, $d = 0.502$.

Paired-samples t-tests indicated that scores for 'memory' were higher than for 'gun': $t(454) = 4.73$, $p < .001$, $d = 0.222$ and 'money': $t(454) = 14.1$, $p < .001$, $d = 0.659$.

Modal answer was 7 (Completely agree) for memories (selected by 22% of participants) and 1 (Completely disagree) for guns (20%) and money (38%).

---

[5] The word 'toy' was added to the statement about the gun because otherwise 'fake gun' in Lithuanian language would likely be interpreted as 'an exact copy of a given gun' (e.g., a counterfeit but indistinguishable from the original and fully functional copy of an old gun produced in order to sell it to a gullible gun collector).

Discussion. In Studies 1–3, I found that recalling other people's memories or artificial memories is considered to be 'remembering' or 'having a memory'. This additional brief study suggests that, contrary to what Cheng and Werning (2016) suggested, study participants were willing to agree that false memories are memories. This is in line with other studies reported in this chapter, where participants were willing to say that the agent remembers in situations where factivity constraint on memory was violated. However, one limitation of Study 4 is that—in contrast to Studies 1, 2, and 3—it was conducted on study participants who already had taken part in another study on memory.

6. General Discussion

The present set of studies suggests that the factivity constraint and the strong previous awareness condition are not essential features of our ordinary use of 'remembering' and 'having a memory of'. Concerning the factivity constraint, artificial memory and misidentified dream memory vignettes involve violations of factivity, and in all these cases study participants tended to agree that the agent 'remembers' (Study 1) or 'has a memory' (Studies 2 and 3). The fact that study participants tended to agree that the agent 'remembers' (Study 1) and 'has a memory' (Study 3; quasi-memory condition) in cases of having implanted other people's memories, suggests that the ordinary notion of memory is not bound by the strong previous awareness condition either.

These findings, of course, should be taken as only the first preliminary and very limited step in the direction of better understanding of constraints that rule our ordinary notion of remembering. Among limitations of this study, I would like to stress the very limited set of experimental vignettes used, the fact that it is unclear whether the results would generalize to other languages than Lithuanian, as well as that some of the vignettes were based on science fiction scenarios.

In summary, the data provided in this chapter provide some evidence to motivate skepticism concerning whether the factivity constraint and the strong previous awareness condition are essential features of our ordinary use of 'remember'.

There is also an intriguing possibility that the uses of 'remember' documented in this chapter reflect a relatively recent conceptual development that can perhaps be associated with exposure to such ideas in pop culture. The present methods are not suitable to address this question and one would rather need to use historical linguistic corpora to see whether they contain examples of non-factive uses of 'remembers' or 'has a memory of.'

Acknowledgments

I would like to thank Phillip Rau, Vytautas Valatka, and two anonymous reviewers for valuable suggestions and Phyllis Zych Budka for proofreading the manuscript.

References

Bernecker, S. (2008). *The Metaphysics of Memory*. Dordrecht: Springer.

Cheng, S. and Werning, M. (2016). What is episodic memory if it is a natural kind? *Synthese*, 193(5): 1345–85.

Chisholm, R. M. (1989). *Theory of Knowledge*, 3rd edition, Englewood Cliffs, NJ: Prentice-Hall.

De Brigard, F. (2017). Memory and imagination. In S. Bernecker and K. Michaelian (eds.), *The Routledge Handbook of Philosophy of Memory*. London: Routledge, pp. 127–40.

Hazlett, A. (2010). The myth of factive verbs. *Philosophy and Phenomenological Research*, 80(3): 497–522.

Holland, R. F. (1954). The empiricist theory of memory. *Mind*, 63(252): 464–86.

Malcolm, N. (1963). *Knowledge and Certainty*. Ithaca, NY: Cornell University Press.

Martin, C. B. and Deutscher, M. (1966). Remembering. *Philosophical Review*, 75(2): 161–96.

Parfit, D. (1984). *Reasons and Persons*. Oxford: Oxford University Press.

Penelhum, T. (1967). Personal identity. In P. Edwards (ed.), *The Encyclopedia of Philosophy, Volume 6*. New York: Macmillan, pp. 95–107.

Shoemaker, S. (1970). Persons and their pasts. *American Philosophical Quarterly*, 7(4): 269–85.

Werning, M. and Cheng, S. (2017). Taxonomy and unity of memory. In S. Bernecker and K. Michaelian (eds.), *The Routledge Handbook of Philosophy of Memory*. London: Routledge, pp. 7–20.

8

In Our Shoes or the Protagonist's?
Knowledge, Justification, and Projection

Chad Gonnerman
University of Southern Indiana

Lee Poag
University of Southern Indiana

Logan Redden
University of Southern Indiana

Jacob Robbins
University of Southern Indiana

Stephen Crowley
Boise State University

1. Introduction

That knowledge (K) entails justification (J) is widely accepted by philosophers. In view of the importance historically assigned to concepts in philosophy, we might ask, "Does the ordinary concept concur? Does the folk concept of knowledge treat justification as necessary for its deployment?" If it does, then, in cases where the protagonist's belief is clearly unjustified, we might expect to see a very strong *un*willingness on the part of ordinary people to attribute knowledge to the protagonist. Yet this is not what Sackris and Beebe (2014) observed. Across nine vignettes, they witnessed a sizeable tendency on the part of their participants to attribute knowledge in cases of unjustified true belief. On the basis of these results, we might conclude that the ordinary concept does

Chad Gonnerman, Lee Poag, Logan Redden, Jacob Robbins, and Stephen Crowley, *In Our Shoes or the Protagonist's? Knowledge, Justification, and Projection* In: *Oxford Studies in Experimental Philosophy.* Edited by: Tania Lombrozo, Joshua Knobe, and Shaun Nichols, Oxford University Press (2020). © Chad Gonnerman, Lee Poag, Logan Redden, Jacob Robbins, and Stephen Crowley.
DOI: 10.1093/oso/9780198852407.003.0009

not treat justification as necessary for knowledge, or, as we will often put it, that the K entails J thesis is not part of the folk concept. But there are reasons to be wary of this inference. A common assumption in the cognitive sciences, one with which we operate in this chapter, is that concepts are in-the-head structures that appear in a wide range of processes, including categorization processes (Machery, 2009; Murphy, 2004). It follows that, to be reasonably confident that the observed attribution rates show us that the folk concept of knowledge does not regard justification as necessary for its deployment, we must be reasonably sure that the attributions stem from the concept itself. Rival hypotheses must be ruled out. One of these is the possibility that the knowledge attributions observed by Sackris and Beebe stemmed largely from protagonist projection, a phenomenon in which a speaker uses words that the protagonist might use to describe her own situation and the listener interprets the speaker accordingly. Our results suggest that, however participants are engaging with Sackris and Beebe's materials, they are not interpreting the relevant knowledge claims projectively, at least not at appreciable rates. Thus, our results help to support Sackris and Beebe's conclusion to this extent: they go some way towards ruling out an alternative account of what drives the positive attributions that they witnesses. With that said, at the end of chapter, we will stress various reasons for being wary about drawing the inference that the folk concept of knowledge does not treat justification as necessary for its deployment on the basis of results like those reported by Sackris and Beebe.

2. Background

Inspired by Sartwell's (e.g., 1991, 1992) attempts at dislodging the widespread assumption among philosophers that knowledge is more than true belief, Sackris and Beebe (2014) conducted a series of studies to explore whether the folk accept the K entails J thesis. Their results suggest an outsized willingness to attribute knowledge in two types of cases where justification is missing. The first are cases involving a true belief improperly grounded in a dream or a delusion. For instance, some participants received a vignette about Jordan who comes to believe that 125 is the square root of 15,625 because that is what the demonic voices in his head told him. Sackris and Beebe report that, across five cases of this sort, over 50% of their participants attributed knowledge. The second type of case explored by Sackris and Beebe is Sartwell's "knew it all along" cases. Here, participants received vignettes in which a protagonist forms a belief that gets vindicated, though at the time of formation the preponderance of evidence had by the protagonist speaks against the belief. For instance, in one vignette, participants learn about John who mulishly believes that his daughter is innocent of a crime in the face of strong incriminating evidence, with further evidence eventually coming in that corroborates his belief. In response to these vignettes, Sackris and Beebe report means around the scale's midpoint. This is a far cry from the basement-level responses we might expect if the folk concept of knowledge treats justification as necessary for its deployment.

While suggestive of a folk rejection of the K entails J thesis, work on the "cognitive aspects of survey methodology" gives some reason for pause. This work urges us to think of survey interactions as conversations, and thus as subject to principles of the sort that govern everyday interactions (e.g., Schwarz, 1996). Accordingly, a number of experiments indicate that participants sometimes interact with survey materials in ways that align with Grice's (1975) cooperative principle. One example comes from Schwarz, Strack, and Mai (1991). They report that correlations between participant assessments of how satisfied they are with their marriage and how satisfied they are with their life are weaker when participants first receive the marriage question than when they first see the life question. This finding can be interpreted in Gricean terms. The maxim of quantity prohibits conversational contributions that are either over- or under-informative. Lies of omission would be an example of the latter. If some such maxim guides participants when taking surveys, we might expect them to reinterpret the second of two questions if they see it as asking for information that is too similar to that given in response to the first. According to Schwarz et al. (1991), this is precisely what is happening in their study. The claim is that when participants see the marriage question followed by the life question, they tend to re-interpret the latter in order to minimize repetition. In effect, the question becomes "Apart from your marriage, how satisfied are you with your life?" Other studies strike a similar theme. Yan (2005) identifies close to thirty studies of participants responding in ways that accord with Grice's maxims (see also Conrad et al., 2014). It is thus reasonable to wonder to what extent conversational principles are at play in experimental philosophy. If they are, then the results of such studies might fail to reflect the significance assigned to them by experimental philosophers. We should expect as much in particular if conversational principles drive participants to interpretations of the relevant probes that go unrecognized by the experimenters.

To illustrate how Grice's maxims might get a grip in experimental philosophy, consider a cooperative participant assigned to one of Sackris and Beebe's delusion cases. After reading a story about an agent who believes everything the voices in his head tell him, including a random mathematical truth, the participant is asked, "Does the agent know this random claim?" If she is operating with something like Grice's maxim of quantity, she might balk at answering the question as literally interpreted. She might find herself (non-consciously) thinking, "It's just so obvious that the agent doesn't know, so it'd be uninformative for me to say as much." In a similar vein, when asked, "What did you do today?" unless joking, we don't say "Woke up!" because, as Schwarz (1999) notes while appealing to the maxim of quantity, that goes without saying. Maybe, in the minds of many, that the delusional agent does not know also goes without saying. If so, then our cooperative participant might go casting about for another interpretation of the question, one whose answer is less apparent. Or, to take a different route to the same possibility, suppose that ignorance is a norm of (some forms of) asking, as many claim (e.g., Hawthorne, 2004). Then, questions with perfectly clear answers should invite nonliteral readings. Such will happen, Whitcomb (2017) claims, if you ask someone who doesn't know that you are a philosopher whether the earth is the earth. According to him, regular folk are apt to think that you are joking or asking a question that calls for a metaphorical interpretation.

Assuming for the moment that conversational principles can lead to nonliteral interpretations of questions asked in experimental philosophy, what might a nonliteral interpretation look like in a study like Sackris and Beebe's? Holton (1997) reveals a possibility. Consider "She sold him a pig in a bag. When he got home he discovered it was really a cat" (p. 627). Like the punch line in a joke that violates expectations created by the set-up, the second sentence forces a nonstandard interpretation of the first sentence. Given what the second sentence says, obviously, the swindler did not sell her buyer an actual pig. And, ultimately, we don't interpret it as if she did. Instead, on Holton's picture, what we do is we interpret the sentence as oriented to the buyer's point of view. It describes the transaction using words that he might have used to describe it at the time. A rough paraphrase of the interpretation we end up with might be "She sold him *what he thought at the time was* a pig in a bag." That this interpretation is a nonliteral interpretation of the original sentence is, we think, reasonably clear. As Jackson (2016, pp. 985–6) writes, commenting on Holton's "Everyone was given a gold ring that turned out be brass," "I don't think the semantic theory should say that 'gold' sometimes means *gold*, and sometimes means *taken by some salient person x to be gold*. Rather, the latter meaning is sometimes recovered pragmatically as a conversational implicature." Much same seems true of the literal meaning of 'pig' and the interpretation that we end up with in response to the animal-in-the-bag sentence. The phenomenon at play here is what Holton calls *protagonist projection* (for detailed discussion, see Stokke, 2013).[1] And he thinks that it can arise with uses of 'knows', as in 'She knew that he would never let her down, but, like all others, he did.' What we have here, according to Holton, is not a violation of factivity; it is a narrator putting himself in the shoes of the protagonist and reporting from her perspective.

Although embraced by many (e.g., Currie, 2010, p. 139n27; DeRose, 2009, pp. 16–17; Nagel, 2013, p. 286n11), not everyone has accepted Holton's account of non-factive uses of 'know' (e.g., Dahlman, 2017; Tsohatzidis, 1997). Still, that we sometimes adopt the perspective of others in narrative contexts has empirical support. Horton and Rapp

---

[1] To minimize confusion, there is a related phenomenon in the philosophical literature from which we must distinguish protagonist projection. It is the curse of knowledge, also called epistemic egocentrism (Nagel 2010; for empirical studies, see Alexander et al., 2014). The two are not the same. The curse of knowledge is a phenomenon that arises in mindreading. It involves projecting one's own appreciation of privileged information onto a relatively naive perspective, or, roughly speaking, mistakenly taking her to know what one knows. If Goldman (2006, pp. 165–6) is right, the curse of knowledge reflects a "quarantine violation" in the processes of constructing a model of the mental states of the mindreading target. Protagonist projection, on the other hand, is a phenomenon in language use and interpretation. In all likelihood, it stems from the pragmatics of language use and interpretation, "the study of meaning in context" (Scott-Phillips, 2015, p. xiii).

(2003) report that response times to objects that are not visible from the perspective of a central character in a story are slower than to objects visible from her perspective. It is as if participants were "seeing" the objects through the character's eyes. Moreover, Buckwalter (2014) reports some telling results with respect to uses of 'knows.' He gave participants sentences of the sort that Hazlett (2010) uses to argue against the factivity of 'knows.' An example is 'Everyone knew that stress caused ulcers, before two Australian doctors in the early 80s proved that ulcers are actually caused by bacterial infection.' Buckwalter then asked participants to indicate which description best describes what was meant by 'everyone knew': (a) everyone thought they knew vs. (b) everyone really did know. 91% opted for (a), the projective reading.

The rival hypothesis that this empirical work presents for Sackris and Beebe's work is straightforward. When asked whether a belief grounded in delusion or dream, or a belief in a loved one despite the odds, amounts to knowledge, everyday conversational principles (or perhaps other mechanisms) may encourage participants to engage in protagonist projection. Many might end up interpreting the probe—the ascription to which participants indicate their agreement or disagreement—as capturing the very words that the protagonist might use to describe her situation. If so, then agreement to a probe so interpreted is not to assent to the proposition that the protagonist *knows*. It is to assent to something like the claim that the protagonist *thinks she knows*. Thus, if the assent is concept-driven—that is, primarily the product of conceptual processing operating over concepts retrieved from long-term memory, and possibly assembled "on the fly" (Barsalou, 1987)—then the assent won't stem from the participant's concept of knowledge. It will be her concept of thinking that one knows. And so, from this participant, we won't have evidence that her concept of knowledge rejects K entails J, but that her concept of thinks that one knows rejects K entails J.

3. Experiment 1

Experiment 1 is an initial attempt to explore whether the rates of knowledge attributions observed in Sackris and Beebe's studies stemmed from protagonist projection to an appreciable degree.[2] The thought underlying this experiment is a simple one. If many participants did engage in protagonist projection in their studies, then, when given a response option that paraphrases the projective interpretation, those participants should prefer it to a simple knowledge attribution. So, after seeing vignettes of the sort used by Sackris and Beebe, we should see a decreased tendency to agree with a knowledge attribution of the form "S knows that *p*" when the other option is a projective paraphrase than when it is simply the option to disagree. Such, it seems, is the strategy for controlling for protagonist projection in experimental epistemology (e.g., Buckwalter, 2014; Machery et al., 2017; Nagel et al., 2013; Rose et al., 2019). In this experiment, we explore whether the prediction bears out.

3.1 Participants, materials, and procedure

Two hundred fifty-one participants were recruited through M-Turk. Prior to analysis, exclusion criteria were determined. Those who failed the attention check, who reported that they were not fluent in English, who did not complete the survey, or who may have taken the survey more than once as indicated by repeated IP addresses, were cut from the main analyses of the paper. This determination resulted in a sample size of $N = 186$ (Age $M = 34.39$, Female = 41.9%).

All participants saw the following vignette from Sackris and Beebe (2014):

Brian is a 10-year-old boy who has just begun to study geometry. One night he goes to sleep and dreams that the square of the hypotenuse of a right triangle is equal to the sum of the squares of its other two sides.

---

[2] It is unclear whether participants who agree with sentences of the form 'S knows that *p*' while assigning a projective interpretation to the sentences are best described as giving the experimenter a *knowledge* attribution. A more apt description might be that these participants gave something like a *thinks-one-knows* attribution. Perhaps, then, we shouldn't write about observed rates of knowledge attributions but rates of agreement to probes designed to assess whether participants think that the protagonist knows the relevant proposition. But that would be quite cumbersome. Here, we will simply stick with 'knowledge attributions,' using it to pick out indications of agreement to experimenter probes of the sort just described. As best as we can tell, nothing hinges on this stipulation.

On the basis of this dream, he comes to believe the Pythagorean Theorem. A few days later in school his teacher introduces the Pythagorean Theorem for the first time in class. Brian thinks to himself "I already knew that the square of the hypotenuse of a right angle is equal to the sum of the squares of its other two sides."

After an attention question, participants in the first condition received a *standard probe*: "Please indicate whether you agree or disagree with the following claim: 'Brian already knew that the Pythagorean Theorem is true.' (i) Agree; (ii) Disagree." Participants in the second condition received a *projective probe*: "Which do you think best describes Brian in the story? (i) Brian thought he already knew that the Pythagorean Theorem is true; (ii) Brian really did already know that the Pythagorean Theorem is true." In each condition, the probe was followed by a question asking participants to indicate how confident or unconfident they were in their response using a fully anchored six-point scale ranging from "very unconfident" to "very confident."

3.2 Results and discussion

A Pearson chi-square test revealed a statistically significant relationship between probe type and knowledge attributions: $\chi^2(1, N = 186) = 22.17$, $p < .001$, $\varphi = .35$). Participants were less likely to attribute knowledge when given the projective probe (40.4%) than when given the standard probe (74.7%) (Figure 8.1). Binomial tests indicate that the proportion of participants attributing knowledge in the projective condition was marginally lower than .50, $p = .070$ while the proportion attributing knowledge in the standard condition was higher than .50, $p < .001$.

We also used a procedure from Starmans and Friedman (2012) to generate composite scores from responses to the knowledge probes and the confidence measures. Indications of agreement to the knowledge probes were coded as +1; disagreement, as −1. These scores were then multiplied by the corresponding confidence rating. For each participant, this gave us a *composite score*, ranging from −6 to +6. An independent samples *t*-test was then performed. It revealed a difference in composite

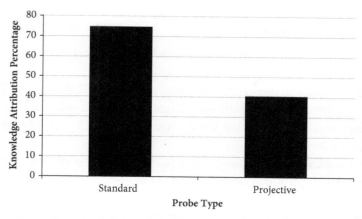

Figure 8.1 Percentage of knowledge attributions for standard probe and projective probe groups in Experiment 1.

scores across conditions (projective: $n = 99$, $M = -0.87$, $SD = 4.63$; standard: $n = 87$, $M = 2.36$, $SD = 4.07$): $t(184) = 5.06$, $p < .001$, $d = .75$. Moreover, a one sample t-test revealed that the composite score in the projection condition was marginally lower than the scale's midpoint while that in the standard condition was statistically higher than the midpoint (projective: $t(98) = 1.87$, $p = .065$; standard: $t(86) = 5.41$, $p < .001$).

This experiment revealed a decreased willingness to attribute knowledge when given a response option that paraphrases the projective interpretation. This is what we should find if many participants did engage in protagonist projection when given vignettes of the sort used by Sackris and Beebe. Thus, this experiment provides some preliminary evidence for thinking that the knowledge attributions observed by Sackris and Beebe stemmed partly from protagonist projection, though perhaps not completely, since over 40% of the participants attributed knowledge in the projective condition. It is reasonable to worry that this percentage is too high to support the projection hypothesis as articulated earlier—as the claim that the rates of attributions observed by Sackris and Beebe were *largely* driven by protagonist projection. Still, it is only one experiment. Before any firm conclusions are drawn, we should see whether similar results emerge in other cases. Experiment 2 explores this by using Sartwell's "knew it all along" cases.

4. Experiment 2

4.1 Participants, materials, and procedure

Two hundred thirty-eight participants were recruited through M-Turk as part of another experiment. Exclusion criteria were similar to Experiment 1. The resulting sample size was N = 173 (Age M = 35.78, Female = 50.9%).

Participants were randomly assigned to one of two vignettes, which were taken from Sackris and Beebe (2014):

MICKEY: The team of doctors responsible for treating Sandra's cancer told Sandra's husband, Mickey, that there was virtually no chance she should be able to beat the cancer and survive for more than a few months. In spite of what the doctors told him, Mickey was convinced that she would beat the cancer. In the end, Mickey's wife survived the cancer and remained cancer free for more than 35 years.

JOHN: John's daughter has been accused of murder. Even though she lacks a strong alibi and the police have compelling evidence against her, John feels that she must be innocent. After several very stressful weeks, the actual murderer finally comes forward and confesses.

After two attention questions, participants in the first condition received a *standard probe*. To illustrate, when it comes to *Mickey*, they were asked, "Do you agree or disagree that Mickey knew all along that his wife would survive the cancer?" Participants in the second condition received a *projective probe*. For example, "In your view, which of the following sentences better describes Mickey' situation? (i) Mickey really did know all along that his wife would survive the cancer; (ii) Mickey merely thought all along that he knew his wife would survive the cancer." These probes were then followed by a confidence measure of the sort used in Experiment 1.

4.2 Results and discussion

Table 8.1 shows the percentage of knowledge attributions in each of the four conditions. Binomial tests indicate that the proportion of

Table 8.1 Percentages of knowledge attributions.

	Standard	Projective	Row
Mickey	66.7	25.9	43.8
John	81.8	31.8	53.2
Column	73.3	28.6	

Table 8.2 Logistic regression for variables predicting knowledge attributions.

	B(S.E.)	95% C.I. for Odds Ratio		
		Lower	Odds Ratio	Upper
Probe (P)	2.27*** (0.56)	3.25	9.64	28.64
Story (S)	−0.29 (0.45)	0.31	0.75	1.81
P × S	−.52 (0.72)	0.15	0.59	2.41

Note: *** p <.001.

participants attributing knowledge in the two projective conditions was lower than .50, p <.001 while the proportion attributing knowledge in the two standard conditions was higher than .50, p <.001.

A logistic regression was performed to explore the effects of probe type, story type, and their interaction on attributions of knowledge. The model was statistically significant, $\chi^2(3) = 37.94$, p <.001. It explained 26.3% (Nagelkerke R^2) of the variance and correctly classified 72.3% of cases.

As Table 8.2 shows, only the coefficient for probe type was significant. Neither a main effect of story type (p =.521) nor an interaction of probe type and story type (p =.465) was observed on knowledge attributions.

Composite scores, calculated as before, reveal a similar pattern. We conducted a 2 × 2 ANOVA with probe type and story type as between-subject factors. The analysis revealed a main effect of probe type on composite scores, $F(1, 169) = 44.13$, p <.001, η^2 =.20. A main effect of story type was not observed, $F(1, 169) = 2.56$, p =.112, η^2 =.01, nor was an interaction between probe type and story type, $F(1, 169) = 0.13$, p =.715, η^2 <.01. In addition, one-sample t-tests indicate that, in the standard conditions, the mean is statistically above the scale's midpoint

Table 8.3 Mean composite scores and standard deviations.

	Standard	Projective	Row
Mickey	1.57 (4.45)	−2.70 (4.45)	−0.83 (4.91)
John	2.91 (3.84)	−1.86 (4.71)	0.18 (4.94)
Column	2.16 (4.22)	−2.33 (4.56)	

$(t(74) = 4.43, p < .001)$, while, in the projective conditions, the mean is statistically below the midpoint $(t(98) = 5.08, p < .001)$.

Table 8.3 summarizes the mean composite scores and standard deviations.

It appears that a decreased tendency to attribute knowledge in projective conditions extends to "knew it all along" cases. This finding provides additional evidence that many participants in Sackris and Beebe's studies engaged in protagonist projection when responding to their knowledge probes.

5. Experiment 3

While the previous two experiments generated results that were consistent with the projection hypothesis, and thus provided some evidence in favor of the hypothesis, certainly more evidence is preferable. There are other predictions worthy of exploration here. For instance, if participants are driven to projective interpretations because of Gricean mechanisms or an ignorance norm that they take to be operative in the survey context, we might expect a greater willingness to agree to the standard probe in cases of delusion when the belief is false than when it is true. After all, if the sheer obviousness of the lack of knowledge in the original cases, along with the thought that the questioner couldn't possibly be interested in something so obvious, is what drives participants to a protagonist projection, then we might expect that we will push more participants towards the projective interpretation if we make the lack of knowledge even more apparent. This should manifest itself as a *greater* inclination to agree with the standard probe when the belief is false than when it is true. Experiment 3 examines this possibility.

5.1 Participants, materials, and procedure

Ninety-one participants were recruited through Prolific. Exclusion criteria were similar to previous experiments. This resulted in a sample size of $N = 75$ (Age $M = 31.23$, Female = 56.0%).

Participants were randomly assigned to one of two vignettes, which were based on a delusion case from Sackris and Beebe (2014):

True Belief [*False Belief*]:   Ryan is a student, born and raised in Canada. He has recently become highly delusional. He claims that demons are talking to him inside his head and that they tell him all sorts of things. Ryan believes everything the demons tell him. One of the things the demons tell him is that Bill Morneau [Martin] is the Canadian Minister of Finance. Ryan has never followed Canadian politics very closely, but he comes to believe that Bill Morneau [Martin] is the Canadian Minister of Finance on this basis. It turns out, of course, that Bill Morneau really is [Martin is *not*] the current Canadian Minister of Finance.

Participants received a standard probe in both conditions: "Do you agree or disagree that Ryan knows that Bill Morneau [Martin] is the current Canadian Minister of Finance?" The probe was followed by an expanded but still fully anchored confidence measure, which now included a midpoint (1 = "very unconfident," 4 = "neither confident nor unconfident," 7 = "very confident"). Participants were then asked to respond to an attention check.

5.2 Results and discussion

A Pearson chi-square test found that participants were more likely to attribute knowledge in *True Belief* (72.2%) than in *False Belief* (20.5%): $\chi^2(1, N = 75) = 22.20$, $p < .001$, $\varphi = .52$ (Figure 8.2).

Looking at the composite scores, an independent samples *t*-test delivered a result similar to the chi-square test. They were larger in *True Belief* ($n = 36$, $M = 2.36$, $SD = 5.04$) than in *False Belief* ($n = 39$, $M = -3.67$, $SD = 4.49$): $t(73) = 5.48$, $p < .001$, $d = 1.28$.

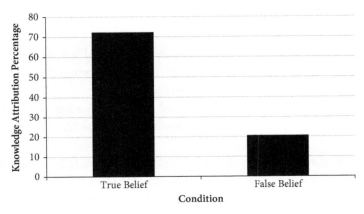

Figure 8.2 Percentage of knowledge attributions for true belief and false belief groups in Experiment 3.

These results appear to cut against the projection hypothesis, at least to the extent that it has been motivated by work on the cognitive aspects of survey methodology. If Gricean mechanisms or a norm of ignorance governing speech acts of asking drove many participants in Sackris and Beebe's studies to a projective interpretation of their knowledge probes, then, at first blush at least, it seems that we should have seen a greater tendency to attribute knowledge in *False Belief* than in *True Belief*. Again, if a literal response to the question of whether the protagonist knows in the case of an unjustified true belief is seen as setting up an answer that is seen as being too under-informative for a conversational contribution (and thus would amount to a violation of the maxim of quantity) or seen as too obvious (and thus would be a violation of a norm of ignorance on acts of asking), all the more should be true of an unjustified false belief. Yet this is not what we observed. In line with other work in experimental epistemology (e.g., Nagel et al., 2013; Turri et al., 2015), our results indicate that participants are less likely to attribute knowledge when an unjustified belief is false than when it is true.

Still, we shouldn't be hasty. Perhaps the results we observed can be explained in a manner consistent with the projection hypothesis. For instance, there may be something about the false belief case that suppresses, blocks, or bypasses the activation of Gricean machinery or an ignorance norm. At the moment, we are at a loss as to what this may be. But, given how little research has been done on the potential influences of conversational principles in experimental philosophy, our lack of ideas on this front should not carry much argumentative weight.

Another response to the results of this study is to hold on to the claim that projection is happening in Sackris and Beebe's studies but claim that the underlying mechanisms are neither Gricean maxims nor a norm of ignorance governing certain forms of asking. Something else may be the driver. Although certainly possible, it is worth noting that adopting this response in the unfolding dialectic does come at a cost. It involves abandoning many of the considerations sketched in Section 2 for taking the projection hypothesis seriously in the first place. Absent these, the possibility that Sackris and Beebe's results stem from protagonist projection begins to look less probable. True, Experiments 1 and 2 can fill some of the evidential gap opened up by this dialectical move—but only some. Here, too, rival hypotheses concerning what drives the observed effects must be ruled out. Perhaps the best dialectic move open to the person pushing the projection hypothesis is to find some nuance in the conversational principles at play in studies like Sackris and Beebe's that would predict the results just reported. We certainly welcome suggestions.

6. Experiment 4

The thought behind Experiment 4 is that if a prominent tendency to engage in protagonist projection manifested itself in Sackris and Beebe's studies, then, when given cases of the sort that they used, along with suitable controls, an interaction effect should emerge. Specifically, we should see that there is a decreased tendency to attribute knowledge to the protagonist as we move from a standard to a projective probe that is greater in the case of an *unjustified* true belief than in a case a *justified* true belief. This experiment is an attempt to see whether this prediction bears out.

6.1 Participants, materials, and procedure

We used Prolific to recruit three hundred eighty-one participants. Exclusion criteria were similar to the previous experiments. This resulted in a sample size of $N = 288$ (Age $M = 32.13$, Female = 33.7%).

Participants were randomly assigned to one of four vignettes, which we based on two delusion cases from Sackris and Beebe (2014):

Sunil Justified [*Sunil Unjustified*]: Sunil is an exchange student who has recently become very studious [delusional]. He remarks to a friend that an esteemed professor of political science is teaching his class on American politics [that a malevolent demon from the netherworld is communicating with him inside his head]. Sunil believes most everything his professor tells him during class lectures [the demon tells him throughout the day]. One of the things his professor [the demon] tells him is that Mike Pompeo is the current U.S. Secretary of State. Sunil has never followed American politics very closely, but he comes to believe that Mike Pompeo is Secretary of State on this basis. It turns out, of course, that Mike Pompeo really is the current U.S. Secretary of State.

Jordan Justified [*Jordan Unjustified*]: Jordan, a college-aged student, has recently become very studious [delusional]. He remarks to a friend that an esteemed professor of mathematics is teaching the class [that a demon is communicating with him inside his head]. Jordan believes most everything his professor tells him during class lectures [the demon tells him throughout the day]. One of the things that his professor [the demon] tells him is that 125 is the square root of 15,625, and he comes to believe that 125 is the square root of 15,625 on this basis. It turns out that 125 really is the square root of 15,625.

Besides two attention checks, participants received either a standard probe or a projective probe. To illustrate, in the Sunil cases, the standard probe read: "Do you agree or disagree that Sunil knows that Mike Pompeo is the current U.S. Secretary of State?" The projective probe went: "In your view, which of the following sentences better describes Sunil's situation? (i) Sunil really does know that Mike Pompeo is the current U.S. Secretary of State; (ii) Sunil only thinks he knows that Mike Pompeo is the current U.S. Secretary of State." The probes were then followed by a seven-point confidence measure of the sort used in Experiment 3.

Table 8.4 Logistic regression for variables predicting knowledge attributions.

	B(S.E.)	95% C.I. for Odds Ratio		
		Lower	Odds Ratio	Upper
Probe (P)	3.08*** (0.70)	5.57	21.74	84.89
Justification (J)	0.30 (0.42)	0.59	1.35	3.05
Story (S)	−0.08 (0.45)	0.38	0.93	2.24
P × J	−1.20† (0.63)	0.09	0.30	1.03
P × S	−1.47* (0.66)	0.06	0.23	0.84
S × J	0.85 (0.58)	0.75	2.35	7.38

Note: † p <.10, * p <.05, *** p <.001.

6.2 Results and discussion

A logistic regression was performed to explore the effects of probe type, story type, and justification status on participants' attributions of knowledge. The model also included terms for the three two-way interactions. The model was statistically significant, $\chi^2(6)$ = 42.77, p <.001. It explained 19.2% (Nagelkerke R^2) of the variance and correctly classified 70.1% of cases.

Table 8.4 shows that a main effect of probe type on knowledge attributions emerged, as did an interaction effect of probe type and story type. Neither a main effect of justification status (p =.477) nor of story type (p =.863) was observed. The same is true of an interaction of probe type and justification status (p =.056) and an interaction of justification status and story type (p =.144).

Composite scores were analyzed using a full-factorial $2 \times 2 \times 2$ ANOVA with probe type, justification status, and story type as between-subject subject factors. The analysis revealed a main effect of probe type on composite scores, $F(1, 280)$ = 38.98, p <.001, η^2 =.12. Neither a main effect of justification status nor a main effect of story type was observed (justification status: $F(1, 280)$ = 1.02, p =.315, η^2 <.01; story type: $F(1, 280)$ = 0.05, p =.832, η^2 <.01). An interaction effect of probe type and justification status did emerge, $F(1, 280)$ = 4.05, p =.045, η^2 =.01. The remaining interactions were non-significant (probe type × story type:

Table 8.5 Mean composite scores and standard deviations collapsed across story types.

	Standard	Projective	Row
Justified	3.58 (3.69)	−0.49 (4.85)	1.33 (4.80)
Unjustified	3.16 (3.60)	1.07 (4.65)	2.05 (4.31)
Column	3.35 (3.63)	0.34 (4.79)	

$F(1, 280) = 2.92$, $p = .088$, $\eta^2 = .01$; justification status × story type: $F(1, 280) = 1.53$, $p = .217$, $\eta^2 < .01$; probe type × justification status × story type: $F(1, 280) = 0.52$, $p = .471$, $\eta^2 < .01$).

Table 8.5 summarizes the descriptives for the four conditions that remain after collapsing across the two types of stories.

Analyses of simple effects revealed that participants were less inclined to attribute knowledge in response to the projective probe than the standard probe in the justified and unjustified cases, $F(1, 280) = 30.81$, $p < .001$, $\eta^2 = .10$ and $F(1, 280) = 10.02$, $p = .002$, $\eta^2 = .04$. In addition, these analyses did not find that, in response to the standard probe, participants were less inclined to attribute knowledge in the unjustified cases than the justified cases, $F(1, 280) = 0.46$, $p = .499$, $\eta^2 < .01$, though participants were *more* likely to agree to the projective probe in the unjustified cases compared to the justified ones, $F(1, 280) = 5.07$, $p = .025$, $\eta^2 = .02$.

At first blush, these results are encouraging for the projection hypothesis: we found an interaction effect of probe type and justification status. Closer inspection, however, reveals that the interaction effect did not go in the predicted direction (Figure 8.3). Again, if the protagonist projection hypothesis is true, then the decreased tendency to attribute knowledge to the protagonist as we move from the standard to the projective probe should be greater in the unjustified cases than in the justified cases. In our study, we saw the reverse. For example, the difference between the mean composite scores in the unjustified true belief cases was 2.09. In the justified true belief cases, it was 4.07.

7. Conclusion

Sackris and Beebe report the results of a series of studies that puts some empirical pressure on the claim that the folk concept of knowledge treats

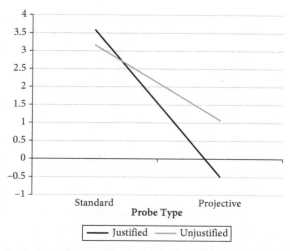

Figure 8.3 Probe type by justification status interaction on composite scores in Experiment 4.

justification as necessary for its deployment. It is reasonable, however, to wonder to what extent the knowledge attributions they observed largely stemmed from protagonist projection. On the whole, the results of this chapter suggest that the extent is not all that extensive. Although the first two experiments reported here did deliver results that are consistent with the projection hypothesis, the last two did not. In our view, those two are more probative of the hypothesis, for two reasons. First, the theoretical and empirical frameworks that motivate Experiments 3 and 4 are largely independent of each other. So, the fact that both delivered disconfirmatory results amounts to a potent consideration against the hypothesis. Second, the results of Experiments 1 and 2, while in line with the projection hypothesis, are explicable in other ways. For instance, if something like the generalized context model (GCM) or its prototype equivalent—two formal models of categorization and category learning (for GCM, see Nosofsky, 2011; for the prototype model, see Minda and Smith, 2011)—extends to the folk concept of knowledge and the associated categorization processes, then it could be that the projective probe triggers a tightening of the concept's sensitivity parameter, thereby requiring a greater degree of similarity between the concept and the target for a positive verdict to emerge (Nosofsky and Johansen, 2000). Of course, only further empirical research will tell. Whatever the most plausible alternative explanation is, the projection hypothesis doesn't look so likely in view of the constellation of considerations just adduced. And so, when it comes to Sackris and Beebe's conclusion that the folk concept of knowledge does not treat justification as necessary for its deployment, our results help to strengthen their conclusion to this extent: they go some way toward ruling out an alternative account of the knowledge attributions that they observed.

With that said, there are various reasons to be wary about drawing the inference that folk concept of knowledge does not treat justification as necessary for its deployment on the basis of results like those reported by Sackris and Beebe. Many important questions remain unanswered. Experiments 1, 2, and 4 show that, in cases like those explored by Sackris and Beebe, how one asks the question about the protagonist's possible state of knowledge influences the rates of attributions observed. This result is similar to other results reported in experimental epistemology, including in Gettier, salience, and stakes cases (Buckwalter, 2014; Machery et al., 2017; Nagel et al., 2013; Rose et al., 2019). Which of the two ways of asking is better for probing the contents of the folk concept? If protagonist projection is occurring at appreciable rates, it is the projective probes because they help to control for unwanted interpretations of the relevant knowledge claims. If the GCM story just gestured at is right, the answer may be that both question formats are perfectly fine because the probe-driven dip in knowledge attributions simply reflects different similarity gradients used in applying the one concept to the vignette. And, surely, there are other possibilities as well. Ultimately, the answer to the question of which prompt format we should prefer when probing the folk concept of knowledge using vignettes partly depends on what explains the dip in knowledge attributions observed as we move from a standard to a projective probe. At the moment, we are largely in the dark as to what this explanation may be, at least when it comes to cases of the sort explored in this chapter. But this is definitely an issue worthy of further exploration.

Moreover, before we draw any firm conclusions about the folk concept of knowledge from results like those reported here and by Sackris and Beebe, we must exert greater effort at controlling for or otherwise ruling out various forms of experimental noise. Experimentally determining whether the folk concept of knowledge treats justification as necessary for its application is in part the task of designing experiments that trigger responses that stem from categorization processes operating over this concept. If X% of our participants indicate that S knows that p in case C, we cannot simply assume that all of these indications have the appropriate etiology. To name just a few alternatives, some appreciable portion of the positive indications may reflect random or non-serious responding (Aust et al., 2013), outcome bias (Gerken, 2018), background knowledge (Machery, 2009), yea-saying (Lavrakas, 2008), or demand characteristics (Powell et al., 2014). Or, to cite one final complication, it may be that many of the attributions of knowledge observed here and by Sackris and Beebe come from participants who, to the chagrin of countless epistemologists, take the belief in question to be justified. The possibility is perhaps not as crazy as it might initially seem. After all, participants might find themselves thinking, what are the odds of, say, a delusional agent randomly picking out the one correct name from many billions of possibilities for the current U.S. Secretary of State, unless he somehow picked up the name from his environment, maybe by walking past a newsstand or something? Naturally, attributions of knowledge in the absence of justification counts as evidence against K entails J being part of the attributor's concept of knowledge only if the attributor takes the case to be devoid of justification. Such are examples of the noise that we must control for or rule out before any firm conclusions are drawn about the contents of the folk concept on the basis of results like those reported here and in Sackris and Beebe's paper. So, yes, we agree that Sackris and Beebe's results, along with ours, do make the claim that the folk concept of knowledge rejects the K entails J thesis a decent bet at the moment. We just recommend exercising some caution when determining how much to place on the bet until further work comes out on matters like those discussed in this paragraph and the previous one.

Acknowledgments

For helpful discussions, comments, and pointers, the authors thank Melissa Gonnerman, Luke Parker, and audience members of the 2018 Buffalo Experimental Philosophy Conference, especially Josh Alexander, James Beebe, Kathryn Francis, Ángel Pinillos, and David Rose. We were also greatly aided by comments from the three anonymous reviewers and the editors of this volume.

References

Alexander, J., Gonnerman, C., and Waterman, J. (2014). Salience and epistemic egocentrism: An empirical study. In J. Beebe (ed.), *Advances in Experimental Epistemology* (pp. 97–118). New York: Continuum.

Aust, F., Diedenhofen, B., Ullrich, S., and Musch, J. (2013). Seriousness checks are useful to improve data validity in online research. *Behavior Research Methods*, 45, 527–35.

Barsalou, L. (1987). The instability of graded structure in concepts. In U. Neisser (ed.), *Concepts and Conceptual Development: Ecological and Intellectual Factors in Categorization* (pp. 101–40). Cambridge: CUP.

Buckwalter, W. (2014). Factive verbs and protagonist projection. *Episteme*, 11, 391–409.

Conrad, F. G., Schober, M. F., and Schwarz, N. (2014). Pragmatic processes in survey interviewing. In T. M. Holtgraves (ed.), *The Oxford Handbook of Language and Social Psychology* (pp. 420–37). Oxford: OUP.

Currie, G. (2010). *Narratives and Narrators: A Philosophy of Stories*. Oxford: OUP.

Dahlman, R. C. (2017). The protagonist projection hypothesis: Do we need it? *International Review of Pragmatics*, 9, 134–53.

DeRose, K. (2009). *The Case for Contextualism*. Oxford: OUP.

Gerken, M. (2018). Truth-sensitivity and folk epistemology. *Philosophy and Phenomenological Research*. https://doi.org/10.1111/phpr.12515.

Goldman, A. I. (2006). *Simulating Minds: The Philosophy, Psychology, and Neuroscience of Mindreading*. Oxford: OUP.

Grice, H. P. (1975). Logic and conversation. In P. Cole and J. L. Morgan (eds.), *Syntax and Semantics: Vol. 3. Speech Acts* (pp. 41–58). New York: Academic Press.

Hawthorne, J. (2004). *Knowledge and Lotteries*. Oxford: OUP.

Hazlett, A. (2010). The myth of factive verbs. *Philosophy and Phenomenological Research*, 80, 497–522.

Holton, R. (1997). Some telling examples: A reply to Tsohatzidis. *Journal of Pragmatics*, 28, 625–8.

Horton, W. S. and Rapp, D. N. (2003). Out of sight, out of mind: Occlusion and the acceptability of information in narrative comprehension. *Psychonomic Bulletin & Review*, 10, 104–9.

Jackson, A. (2016). From relative truth to Finean non-factualism. *Synthese*, 193, 971–89.

Lavrakas, P. J. (2008). Acquiescence response bias. In P. J. Lavrakas (ed.), *Encyclopedia of Survey Research Methods* (pp. 3–4). Thousand Oaks, CA: SAGE.

Machery, E. (2009). *Doing without Concepts*. Oxford: OUP.

Machery, E., Stich, S., Rose, D., Chatterjee, A., Karasawa, K., Struchiner, N., et al. (2017). Gettier across cultures. *Noûs*, 51, 645–64.

Minda, J. P. and Smith, J. D. (2011). Prototype models of categorization: Basic formulation, predictions, and limitations. In E. M. Pothos and A. J. Willis (eds.), *Formal Approaches in Categorization* (pp. 65–87). Cambridge: CUP.

Murphy, G. L. (2004). *The Big Book of Concepts*. Cambridge, MA: MIT Press.

Nagel, J. (2010). Knowledge ascriptions and the psychological consequences of thinking about error. *Philosophical Quarterly*, 60, 286–306.

Nagel, J. (2013). Knowledge as a mental state. In T. S. Gendler and J. Hawthorne (eds.), *Oxford Studies in Epistemology, Vol. 4* (pp. 273–308). Oxford: OUP.

Nagel, J., San Juan, V., and Mar, R. A. (2013). Lay denial of knowledge for justified true beliefs. *Cognition*, 129, 652–61.

Nosofsky, R. M. (2011). The generalized context model: An exemplar model of categorization. In E. M. Pothos and A. J. Willis (eds.), *Formal Approaches in Categorization* (pp. 18–39). Cambridge: CUP.

Nosofsky, R. M. and Johansen, M. K. (2000). Exemplar-based accounts of "multiple system" phenomena in perceptual categorization. *Psychonomic Bulletin & Review*, 7, 375–402.

Powell, D., Horne, Z., and Pinillos, N. Á. (2014). Semantic integration as a method for investigating concepts. In J. R. Beebe (ed.), *Advances in Experimental Epistemology* (pp. 119–44). New York: Bloomsbury.

Rose, D., Machery, E., Stich, S., Alai, M., Angelucci, A., Berniūnas, R., et al. (2019). Nothing at stake in knowledge. *Noûs*, 53, 224–47.

Sackris, D. and Beebe, J. R. (2014). Is justification necessary for knowledge? In J. R. Beebe (ed.), *Advances in Experimental Epistemology* (pp. 175–92). New York: Bloomsbury.

Sartwell, C. (1991). Knowledge is merely true belief. *American Philosophical Quarterly*, 28, 157–65.

Sartwell, C. (1992). Why knowledge is merely true belief. *Journal of Philosophy*, 89, 167–80.

Schwarz, N. (1996). *Cognition and Communication: Judgmental Biases, Research Methods, and the Logic Conversation*. Hillsdale, NJ: Erlbaum.

Schwarz, N. (1999). Self-reports: How questions shape the answers. *American Psychologist*, 54, 93–105.

Schwarz, N., Strack, F., and Mai, H.-P. (1991). Assimilation and contrast effects in part-whole question sequences: A conversational logic analysis. *Public Opinion Quarterly*, 55, 3–23.

Scott-Phillips, T. (2015). *Speaking Our Minds: Why Human Communication is Different, and How Language Evolved to Make It Special*. London: Palgrave Macmillan.

Starmans, C. and Friedman, O. (2012). The conception of knowledge. *Cognition*, 124, 272–83.

Stokke, A. (2013). Protagonist projection. *Mind & Language*, 28, 204–32.

Turri, J., Buckwalter, W., and Blouw, P. (2015). Knowledge and luck. *Psychonomic Bulletin and Review*, 22, 378–90.

Tsohatzidis, S. L. (1997). More telling examples: A response to Holton. *Journal of Pragmatics*, 28, 629–36.

Whitcomb, D. (2017). One kind of asking. *The Philosophical Quarterly*, 67, 148–68.

Yan, T. (2005). Gricean effects in self-administered surveys (unpublished doctoral dissertation). University of Maryland, College Park, MD.

9

I Owe You an Explanation

Children's Beliefs about When People Are Obligated to Explain their Actions

Shaylene Nancekivell
University of North Carolina at Greensboro

Ori Friedman
University of Waterloo

You do not normally have to explain your actions to others. For instance, when grocery shopping, you are not obligated to tell other shoppers why you are using a cart instead of a basket, or why you chose one brand of cereal over another. However, you might owe other shoppers an explanation if you intentionally block their path with your cart. Understanding when explanations are owed is important for our daily social interactions. For instance, if you neglected to explain why you blocked your fellow shoppers, you might be perceived as inconsiderate and rude. Conversely, if you needlessly explained your purchases to the other shoppers, you might be viewed as odd.

People's judgments about when explanations are owed are informative about the social norms involved in communication. Recent work in experimental philosophy has focused on norms that govern the content of communicative utterances. For example, much work shows that people feel that assertions should express knowledge, and these norms likely exist to prevent people from misleading or misinforming others (e.g., Turri, 2015, 2016, 2017). In contrast to these norms, obligations to explain actions are discourse obligations (Traum and Allen, 1994). Discourse obligations determine *when* certain things should be said.

Shaylene Nancekivell and Ori Friedman, *I Owe You an Explanation: Children's Beliefs about When People Are Obligated to Explain their Actions* In: *Oxford Studies in Experimental Philosophy*. Edited by: Tania Lombrozo, Joshua Knobe, and Shaun Nichols, Oxford University Press (2020). © Shaylene Nancekivell and Ori Friedman.
DOI: 10.1093/oso/9780198852407.003.0010

They include apologies and responses to questions, and may often function to ensure that people avoid conflicts, and maintain relationships. In this chapter, we examine whether people feel individuals are obligated to explain actions that directly interfere with others' goals. People feel they are autonomous and have self-determination rights that entitle them to pursue their goals without being subject to interference. For example, adults and children feel people are entitled to make self-relevant decisions, even when their decisions are opposed by authority figures (e.g., Helwig, 1997; Killen and Smetana, 1999; Lagattuta et al., 2010; Nucci, 1981; Nucci and Weber, 1995; Ruck et al., 1998). Actions that directly interfere with others' goals encroach on their autonomy, and may warrant explanation.[1] This proposal is inspired by the philosopher Stanley Benn's (1975) claim that people are obligated to explain their actions when they interfere with others' freedom to act (see also Benn and Weinstein, 1971).

The proposal that explanations may sometimes be owed to others is broadly consistent with research showing that adults mostly provide explanations spontaneously, without being prompted or asked to do so (Malle, 1999, 2004; Wong and Weiner, 1981). Our proposal that explanations are sometimes motivated by obligations extends this idea by specifying one factor that may lead people to generate explanations without being prompted.

To examine our proposal, we tested whether young children judge that agents have to explain their actions when they directly interfere with others' goals. We anticipated that young children might succeed in recognizing that people owe explanations in such situations because from infancy they find goals very salient, and recognize when goals are interfered with (Hamlin, 2013; Kuhlmeier, 2013; Woodward, 2009). Investigating this in young children is also promising as it can increase knowledge of children's awareness of how explanations enter into their social interactions.

Much recent research on children's explanations has examined how generating explanations benefits children's causal reasoning (Legare and Lombrozo, 2014; Rittle-Johnson et al., 2008; Walker et al., 2014; for a

---

[1] This proposal does not imply that directly interfering with others' goals is the *only* action that creates such obligations. For example, people could also be obligated to explain their actions when they break existing agreements, commitments, or promises (see Gräfenhain et al., 2009 for related work).

review see Legare, 2014). For example, explaining how a toy works helps 3-year-olds remember new causal information about how it works (Legare and Lombrozo, 2014). Related research has examined children's ability to evaluate the quality of causal explanations. These studies show that preschoolers prefer explanations which are simple and highly probable (Bonawitz and Lombrozo, 2012) and place little trust in explanations that are circular and contain no causal information (Baum et al., 2008; Mercier et al., 2014; see also Corriveau and Kurkul, 2014). Moreover, children intelligently evaluate reasons (Castelain et al., 2016; Koenig, 2012). For example, they prefer reasons provided by powerful people, and do not like reasons based on guesses (Castelain et al., 2016; Koenig, 2012). Together, these studies are informative about the relation between explanations and children's causal reasoning, and how children evaluate speakers' testimony. However, they say less about their expectations for the ways in which explanations *should* enter social interactions. For instance, such studies are informative about children's evaluative abilities, but are fairly uninformative about their beliefs about *when* and *why* people should explain their actions to others.

Only a few studies have examined children's use of explanations in these kinds of social interactions. These studies have predominantly used naturalistic observation methods to examine when toddlers and preschoolers provide explanations and justifications (e.g., Dunn and Munn, 1987; Goetz, 2010; Orsolini, 1993; Veneziano and Sinclair, 1995; for exceptions see Köymen et al., 2014; Köymen et al., 2016). They mainly conclude that young children provide explanations when they are in disputes with others (e.g., arguing over whose turn it is to play a game; Dunn and Munn, 1987; Goetz, 2010; Orsolini, 1993), or when making joint-decisions (e.g., deciding where to place a toy; Köymen et al., 2014; Köymen et al., 2016). However, these studies do not reveal whether children recognize that people (including themselves) are sometimes *obligated* to explain their behavior.

1.   Present Studies

We report three experiments. In all experiments, children saw brief vignettes and then judged whether a character in each vignette had to explain their actions. We chose this approach, rather than examining when children explain their actions, as it could be difficult to induce children to interfere with others' goals. We also favored an approach in which children evaluated third parties, as children's decisions to generate explanations could depend on many factors besides their notions of when explanations are owed.

Our experiments include children in two age groups, 3–4 and 5–6 years. We chose these ages ranges because children's social cognition undergoes much development between ages 3 and 6. On the one hand, we anticipated that young children might succeed in recognizing that people owe explanations in such situations because children are skilled at *evaluating* reasons (Koenig, 2012), and goal interference is very salient to young children (Hamlin, 2013; Kuhlmeier, 2013; Woodward, 2009). At the same time, this understanding might show delayed development as younger children sometimes fail to apply their understanding of "theory of mind" (which includes reasoning about goals) when making other kinds of judgments (e.g., Bradmetz and Schneider, 1999; Pesowski et al., 2016; Richert and Lillard, 2002). For example, young preschoolers often neglect to apply their understanding of intent when judging whether actions are wrong or should be punished (e.g., Cushman et al., 2013; Zelazo et al., 1996).

2. Experiment 1

2.1 Methods

Participants. We tested 88 children: 44 3–4-year-olds (M = 4;2, range = 3;1–4;10, 20 girls) and 44 5–6-year-olds (M = 5;11, range = 5;0–6;11, 23 girls). Two additional children were tested, but excluded for not answering the test question. In all experiments, children were individually tested at preschools, daycares, and schools.

Materials and Procedure. Children were told a story narrated by the experimenter, accompanied by pictures shown on a laptop computer; stories were also conveyed in this way in the subsequent experiments. Children were randomly assigned to hear one of two versions of the story, which varied in whether an agent's action did or did not interfere with another character's goal (see Figure 9.1 for sample slides and scripts from all experiments). In the "interference" version, a boy wanted to sit in the larger of two chairs, but a girl took this chair so that she could reach a box of toys on a high shelf. In the "non-interference" version, the boy wanted to sit in the smaller chair, and the girl again took the larger chair to reach the box. After hearing the story, children were asked a yes/no test question about whether the girl was obligated to explain her

EXPERIMENT 1

Look here are two chairs. And up here is a box of toys. Look here is a boy. The boy wants to sit on the **[blue/green]** chair. Which chair does the boy want to sit on? So he goes to sit down. Just before he sits down a girl comes. The girl wants the box of toys but she can't reach. So she goes and gets the blue chair to stand on. *Why did she get the chair? Does the girl have to tell the boy that?*

EXPERIMENT 2

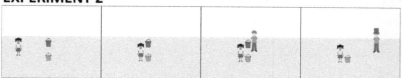

Here are two buckets. And look here is a girl. The girl wants to play with the **[purple/orange]** bucket. Which bucket does the girl want to play with? So she goes to play with it. Just before she does, a boy comes. The boy takes the purple bucket and puts it on his head. He puts the purple bucket on his head because he wanted to pretend he is a robot. Why did he do that? **[*Does the boy have to tell the girl that? / Does the girl want to know that?*]**

EXPERIMENT 3

Look, here are some kids and they are in a library. And Look, this boy is going to read the blue book. He is going to read it. This boy is going to read the orange book. He is going to read it. Let's see what happens. This girl takes the orange book from the boy. She takes it because it's her favorite story. Does the girl have to tell *this* boy she took it because it's her favourite story?

Figure 9.1   Sample stimuli and story scripts for all three experiments.

Table 9.1 Proportion of comprehension questions passed in Experiments 1 and 2.

	Condition	3–4-year-olds	5–6-year-olds
Experiment 1	Interference	0.98	1.00
	Non-interference	0.93	1.00
Experiment 2	Interference, owes question	0.92	
	Interference, desires question	0.79	
	Non-interference, owes question	0.88	
	Non-interference, desires question	0.86	

actions to the boy.[2] The story also included two comprehension questions. If children did not answer these questions, or answered them incorrectly, then all relevant information was repeated, and the questions were asked again. If children did not answer the comprehension questions correctly after three tries, the experimenter continued testing (see Table 9.1 for rates of success). The comprehension questions allowed us to highlight important information in our stories. Some of these questions were more linguistically demanding (i.e., why questions) than our test questions (i.e., yes/no questions), so we analyzed children's responses regardless of whether they passed the comprehension questions. The same comprehension questions and prompting procedure were used in Experiment 2.

2.2   Results and discussion

We examined whether children were more likely to say the agent owed an explanation when she interfered with the other character's goal compared with when she did not.[3] A generalized linear model for binary

---

[2] In this experiment, and those subsequent, children occasionally said "I don't know" or remained silent when asked the test question. Children who responded "I don't know" (4 of 200 children across all experiments) were prompted with "What do you think?"; if they said "I don't know" again, or remained silent, their answer of "I don't know" was kept. Children who were silent (5 of the 200 children across all experiments) for the initial test question were prompted three times, first with "What do you think?," second with "Just guess," and third with a repetition of the test question.

[3] Data from all experiments are available at https://osf.io/hr683/?view_only=195733ff14754 b18964dd187ea8644fe.

logistic data with the between-subject factors *story-version* (interference, non-interference) and *age* (3–4-year-olds, 5–6-year-olds) revealed a main effect of story-version, Wald $X^2(1)$ = 14.15, p <.001, with children more likely to say the agent was obligated to explain her action when she interfered with the other character's goal (82% of responses) compared with when she did not interfere (41% of responses). There was a marginally significant effect of age, Wald $X^2(1)$ = 3.01, p =.083, and the interaction between condition and age was not significant, p =.599.

These findings suggest that young children consider whether an agent interferes with others' goals when deciding whether the agent has to explain their actions. To ensure these findings are robust, in the next experiment, we sought to replicate our findings using different storylines in which the reasons for interfering with another's goal were less transparent. The next experiment also addressed a potential concern with our findings: Instead of considering whether the agent owed an explanation, children might have asked themselves whether the other character *desired* an explanation. We felt this is a plausible concern because for young children, desires are salient motivators of behavior (Bartsch and Wellman, 1989). To address this concern, the next experiment compares judgments of whether the agent owed an explanation to judgments of whether the other character wanted an explanation of the agent's action. Because there were no significant effects of age in Experiment 1, Experiment 2 only included children in our younger age range (i.e., 3–4-year-olds).

3.   Experiment 2

3.1   Methods

Participants. We tested 72 3–4-year-olds (M = 4;1, range = 3;2–4;11, 35 girls).

Materials and Procedure. Children were randomly assigned to one of four conditions in a 2 × 2 between-subjects design manipulating *story-type* (interference, non-interference) and *question-type* (explanation-owed, explanation-desired). In each condition, children heard two stories where an agent either did or did not interfere with another character's goal. In the first story, a boy wanted to sit in a certain chair, and a girl either took this chair (interference) or another chair that was beside it (non-interference); in contrast with Experiment 1, these chairs were the same size, making the agent's motivation less transparent. In the second story, a girl wanted to play with a certain bucket, and a boy either took this bucket (interference) or another bucket that was beside it (non-interference). Immediately after each story, children were asked a test question which either concerned whether the second agent was obligated to explain their actions (explanation-owed) or whether the other character wanted to know why the agent acted as they did (explanation-desired).

3.2   Results and discussion

We anticipated that children would be more likely to say the agent owed an explanation when they interfered with the other character's goal. However, children might not show a similar effect of interference when judging whether the other character desired an explanation. The agent's motivation was not transparent in both versions of the story, so it is possible that children expected the other character to want to know the reasons for the agent's actions regardless of whether the agent interfered.

To examine these possibilities, we entered children's "yes" responses into a generalized estimating equations (GEE) model (binary logistic) with the predictors *story-type* (interference, non-interference) and *question-type* (explanation-owed, explanation-wanted). There were no main effects, both ps =.678, but there was a significant interaction between story-type and question-type, Wald $X^2(1) = 8.28$, p =.004. To follow-up on this interaction, we ran pairwise comparisons to examine whether children's responses varied by story-type when they answered each question. Children were more likely to agree the agent had to explain her actions when she interfered with a goal (72% of responses) than when she did not (36% of responses), p =.014. Crucially, a similar effect did not arise when children were asked whether the other character wanted an explanation. Instead, there was a marginally significant effect in the opposite direction, p =.055.

These findings suggest that young children consider whether an agent interferes with others' goals when deciding whether the agent has to explain their actions. The results also show that children differentiate between situations where explanations are owed and where they might be desirable (i.e., where someone might be curious to know what is going on).

However, the findings so far do not examine whether children understand the *specificity* of the agent's obligation to explain their action. Children might feel that an agent who interferes with goals must explain their actions, but without knowing who it is owed to. For example, children could feel the explanation is owed anyone who witnessed the agent's actions. Hence, in our final experiment, we examined whether young children recognize that the agent specifically owes an explanation to the person whose goal was interfered with, and not to others.

In this final experiment, we returned to testing young and older groups of children (i.e., as 3–4-year-olds and 5–6-year-olds). Unlike Experiment 2, which used a similar design to Experiment 1, this experiment used a new test question, and employed a different within-subjects design.

4. Experiment 3

4.1 Methods

Participants. We tested 40 children: 20 3–4-year-olds (M = 4;0, range = 3;2–4;9, 13 girls) and 20 5–6-year-olds (M = 5;9, range = 5;0–6;11, 9 girls).

Materials and Procedure. In a within-subjects design, children were told two stories in which an agent interfered with the goals of a second character, but without interfering with the goals of a third character. In the first story, two boys were going to read books in a library, and a girl took the book one of the boys wanted. In the second story, two girls were going to play with puzzles, and a boy took the puzzle one of the girls was going to play with. After each story, children were asked whether the agent owed an explanation to the "victim," and whether the agent owed an explanation to the "observer." We counterbalanced the order of these questions across the two stories and across participants.

We did not include a comprehension question in this experiment as we did not want to highlight one object and character more than the other. For example, asking children to point to which book the girl wants would have led them to point to the book right beside the target boy.

4.2   Results and discussion

In this experiment, children could indicate that an explanation was owed to the victim, to the observer, to both of these characters, or to neither. To examine whether children understand that explanations are specifically owed to the person whose goal is disrupted, we entered children's responses into a GEE model (binary logistic) with the within-subjects factor *addressee* (victim, observer) and the between-subjects factor age (3–4-year-olds, 5–6-year-olds). There was a main effect of addressee, *Wald* $X^2(1)$ = 28.60, p <.001, in which children were more likely to say that an explanation was owed to the victim (84% of responses) than to the observer (34% of responses). There was a marginally significant effect of age, *Wald* $X^2(1)$ = 2.79, p =.095, and the interaction between addressee and age was not significant, *Wald* $X^2(1)$ = 1.18, p =.278. These results suggest young children have some understanding of the specificity of obligations to explain actions that interfere with others.

5.   General Discussion

Philosophical and adult psychological work suggests that the ability to recognize when explanations are owed is important for evaluating the fairness of actions, maintaining relationships, and preventing conflict (e.g., Bobocel and Zdaniuk, 2005; Malle, 2004; Turri, 2015, 2016, 2017). Our findings reveal that by 3 years of age, children recognize when explanations are owed to others. They appreciate that people are obligated to explain their actions when they interfere with others' goals (Experiments 1 and 2), and that these explanations are owed to the person whose goal was frustrated, but not to observers (Experiment 3).

Our findings support the proposal, inspired by Stanley Benn (1975), that actions that directly interfere with others' goals and encroach on their autonomy, warrant explanation. They also build on prior work investigating people's awareness of norms that govern the content of communicative utterances (e.g., Turri, 2015, 2016, 2017) by demonstrating that in early childhood, people are already aware of a discourse obligation (Traum and Allen, 1994) governing *when* explanations are required.

5.1   Developmental relevance

Our findings have implications for understanding children's development. First, our finding that children recognize one situation in which explanations are owed, suggests that they may recognize other situations like this. For example, children might judge that people owe explanations if they break social commitments, such as not keeping a promise. Similarly, children might judge that people owe explanations when they violate conversational maxims, as when they lie and disregard the Gricean maxim of quality (see Grice, 1975). Children as young as 3 years old recognize when these kinds of violations occur, so they may have the prerequisite knowledge to judge that explanations are owed (see Gräfenhain et al., 2009 for work on social commitments, and Eskritt, Whalen, and Lee, 2008 for work on Gricean violations). If children also recognize that explanations are owed in these cases, it would suggest a broader theory according to which people owe explanations whenever they violate social obligations. On this view, interfering with others' goals and freedoms is just one such violation.

Second, our findings hint at an intriguing progression in children's understanding of how explanations enter into social interactions. As adults, we are aware of many reasons for explaining our actions to others. Besides generating explanations because they are owed, we may also explain our actions for self-interested reasons such as to avoid blame, maintain our reputations, and manage how others view us (Malle, 2004; Malle et al., 2000; see also Malle and Knobe, 1997 for related work on intentions). For example, if you are late for a meeting, but make no attempt to explain why, others could conclude that you are unreliable or that you are indifferent to their convenience and welfare. However, they might be less likely to conclude this if you explain that you were late because of factors outside your control.

However, recent work suggests that young preschoolers are unlikely to understand these other motivations for explaining actions. For example, children do not appear to understand the reputational consequences of actions until they are 6, or possibly 5 years old (for an excellent review see Silver and Shaw, 2018). As such, our findings suggest that children's understanding of when people are *obligated* to explain their actions likely emerges *before* their awareness of *self-interested* reasons that might prompt explanation. This suggestion is counter to traditional accounts of development which posit the reverse developmental trajectory. Most notably, Kohlberg (1973) proposed a pattern of development where young children understand moral considerations such as *obligations* to others, *after self-beneficial motives* for actions (e.g., avoiding punishment). It must be noted, though, that our findings only hint at this developmental progression, and further work is needed to carefully explore it.

5.2   Potential concerns

One potential concern with our study is that children may not have really felt that the agents in our vignettes were *obligated* to explain their actions. For instance, children could have interpreted our test questions as instead asking whether the agent should have to explain their actions, or whether the agent was expected to explain their actions. Similarly, children's judgments could reflect the belief that it would be socially beneficial for the agent to explain their actions—this might appease the victim, and serve to excuse the interfering actions. Although our findings cannot conclusively rule out these alternatives, the differences between these related possibilities are not great. These interpretations of the question are all normative and all rely on normative reasoning about explanation.

Another potential concern is that children might have been reasoning about ownership and not goals during our task. Prior work shows that young children recognize that ownership governs the acceptability of actions, and that owners have a right to decide how their property is used (Neary, Friedman, and Burnstein, 2009; Nancekivell and Friedman,

2014, 2017; Schmidt et al., 2013). In our experiments, children could have felt that explanations were owed to the victims because their ownership rights were violated (i.e., not because of interference with their goals). However, we believe this is unlikely. In Experiments 1 and 2, this ownership-violation account requires children to think that the victim owned the object they intended to use, but not the other object. However, previous work suggests that children do not infer ownership from an agent's intention to use an object (e.g., Neary et al., 2009 Experiment 2; see also Shaw et al., 2012). Children do sometimes infer ownership from physical proximity and contact (e.g., Blake et al., 2012; Friedman and Neary, 2008); however, the victim was equally close to both of the objects. If children inferred ownership in this way, they should judge the agent would explain themselves regardless of which object they took. We did not find this. Also, in Experiment 3 the characters were in a library, so it is unlikely that children thought that any of the characters owned the books. Notably, *even if* children did infer ownership, our finding would still be broadly consistent with Stanley Benn's account, as rights to one's property could be construed as an extension of our freedom to act autonomously (for a philosophical discussion, see Humphrey, 1992).

A final and related concern is that children's responses were based on expectations that agents are more likely to owe explanations to someone they are already interacting with, than to someone they have not yet interacted with. This is a plausible concern in Experiment 3 because the agent moved closer to the victim than to the other person who was present. However, Experiments 1 and 2 used between-subjects designs in which children saw the exact same slides regardless of whether the agent interfered with a goal or did not. Hence, it is implausible that children construed an interaction in one condition, but not the other. Moreover, the scripts did not describe any verbal or physical interaction between the agent and the victim. Finally, in Experiment 2, this alternative account struggles to explain why children's judgments about whether an explanation was desired did not significantly differ across condition.

5.3 Open questions

We expected that people would adhere to a goal-based principle in judging when explanations are owed. However, as discussed above, Benn

(1975) suggests that people need to explain their actions when they interfere with others' *freedom*. A strict interpretation of this account means that people owe explanations when they interfere with others' ability to make choices, even when they do not specifically interfere with others' goals. This account is also plausible given that children can reason about free choice and recognize factors that constrain it (e.g., Chernyak et al., 2019; Kushnir et al., 2015). Although the present findings are equally explained by both accounts, the current experiments only directly test the narrower goal-based account.

Another question raised by our findings is whether obligations to explain actions are related to obligations to apologize. At first, it might seem that explanations and apologies are required in the same situations. For example, the agent in our vignettes probably owed apologies alongside owing explanations. However, we suspect people are often obligated to explain their actions, even when they do not owe an apology. For example, when a parent grabs their child's hand to prevent the child from touching a hot stove, they might not owe the child an apology. But the parent may need to explain why they interfered with the child's goal. Similar intuitions might also arise when paternalistic actions benefit adults. Although we have not yet tested this prediction, it at least raises the possibility that obligations to explain and apologize depend on different communicative norms.

We close by considering a further question on the nature of owed explanations. Our investigation focused on *when* people are obligated to explain their actions. As such, we did not address factors that affect the quality of these explanations, or factors that make these explanations satisfying. From childhood, people evaluate the quality of explanations (e.g., Baum et al., 2008; Bonawitz, and Lombrozo, 2012). For example, they prefer simple explanations containing a single cause over more complex explanations, and likewise dislike circular explanations which reiterate the question being asked (Baum et al., 2008; Bonawitz and Lombrozo, 2012). However, additional considerations might influence how people evaluate explanations that are produced under obligation. One possibility is that the "mode" of explanation may be particularly important. For instance, explanations referring to mental states are especially informative about people's motivations for actions (Malle et al., 2000), while explanations referring to skills and facilitating circumstances are more informative about how people came to complete their actions (Malle et al., 2000). When we are obligated to explain our actions to others, we may be expected to inform others of our motivations, and therefore refer to our mental states. For example, after blocking a fellow grocery store shopper with your cart, others might judge your explanation as more satisfying if you mention your mental states (e.g., I didn't mean to block you; I didn't know you were there) than if you refer to external circumstances enabling your actions (e.g., the wheels on my cart are jammed; my hair fell in front of eyes).

6. Conclusion

In sum, our findings are informative about people's recognition that others are sometimes obligated to explain their actions to others. The findings show that young children aged 3–6 are aware of one type of discourse obligation (i.e., one kind of situation where people are obligated or required to say something; Traum and Allen, 1994). The present research also highlights that early in development people are aware of certain ways that explanations enter into social interactions, and that this recognition is crucial for their social functioning.

References

Bartsch, K. and Wellman, H. (1989). Young children's attribution of action to beliefs and desires. *Child Development, 60,* 946–64.

Baum, L. A., Danovitch, J. H., and Keil, F. C. (2008). Children's sensitivity to circular explanations. *Journal of Experimental Child Psychology, 100,* 146–55.

Benn, S. I. (1975). Freedom, autonomy and the concept of a person. *Proceedings of the Aristotelian Society, 110,* 109–30.

Benn, S. I. and Weinstein, W. L. (1971). Being free to act, and being a free man. *Mind, 80,* 194–211.

Blake, P. R., Ganea, P. A., and Harris, P. L. (2012). Possession is not always the law: With age, preschoolers increasingly use verbal information to identify who owns what. *Journal of Experimental Child Psychology, 113,* 259–72.

Bobocel, D. R. and Zdaniuk, A. (2005). How can explanations be used to foster organizational justice. *Handbook of Organizational Justice*, *1*, 469–98.

Bonawitz, E. B. and Lombrozo, T. (2012). Occam's rattle: Children's use of simplicity and probability to constrain inference. *Developmental Psychology*, *48*, 1156–64.

Bradmetz, J. and Schneider, R. (1999). Is Little Red Riding Hood afraid of her grandmother? Cognitive vs. emotional response to a false belief. *British Journal of Developmental Psychology*, *17*, 501–14.

Castelain, T., Bernard, S., der Henst, V., and Mercier, H. (2016). The influence of power and reason on young Maya children's endorsement of testimony. *Developmental Science*, *19*, 957–66.

Chernyak, N., Kang, C., and Kusnir, T. (2019). The cultural roots of free will beliefs: How Singaporean and U.S. children judge and explain possibilities for action in interpersonal contexts. *Developmental Psychology*, *55*, 866–76.

Corriveau, K. H. and Kurkul, K. E. (2014). "Why does rain fall?": Children prefer to learn from an informant who uses noncircular explanations. *Child Development*, *85*, 1827–35.

Cushman, F., Sheketoff, R., Wharton, S., and Carey, S. (2013). The development of intent-based moral judgment. *Cognition*, *127*, 6–21.

Dunn, J. and Munn, P. (1987). Development of justification in disputes with mother and sibling. *Developmental Psychology*, *23*, 791–8.

Eskritt, M., Whalen, J., and Lee, K. (2008). Preschoolers can recognize violations of the Gricean maxims. *British Journal of Developmental Psychology*, *26*, 435–43.

Friedman, O. and Neary, K. R. (2008). Determining who owns what: Do children infer ownership from first possession? *Cognition*, *107*, 829–49.

Goetz, P. J. (2010). The development of verbal justifications in the conversations of preschool children and adults. *First Language*, *30*, 403–20.

Gräfenhain, M., Behne, T., Carpenter, M., and Tomasello, M. (2009). Young children's understanding of joint commitments. *Developmental Psychology*, *45*, 1430–43.

Grice, H. P. (1975). Logic and conversation. In P. Cole and J. L. Morgan (eds.), *Syntax and Semantics Vol. 3: Speech Acts* (pp. 41–58). New York: Academic Press.

Hamlin, J. K. (2013). Moral judgment and action in preverbal infants and toddlers: Evidence for an innate moral core. *Current Directions in Psychological Science*, *22*, 186–93.

Helwig, C. C. (1997). The role of agent and social context in judgments of freedom of speech and religion. *Child Development*, 68, 484–95.

Humphrey, N. (1992). *A History of the Mind: Evolution and the Birth of Consciousness*. New York: Simon & Schuster.

Killen, M. and Smetana, J. G. (1999). Social interactions in preschool classrooms and the development of young children's conceptions of the personal. *Child Development*, 70, 486–501.

Koenig, M. A. (2012). Beyond semantic accuracy: Preschoolers evaluate a speaker's reasons. *Child Development*, 83, 1051–63.

Kohlberg, L. (1973). Continuities in childhood and adult moral development revisited. In Paul B. Baltes and K. Warner Schaie (eds.), *Life-Span Developmental Psychology* (pp. 180–207). New York: Academic Press.

Köymen, B., Mammen, M., and Tomasello, M. (2016). Preschoolers use common ground in their justificatory reasoning with peers. *Developmental Psychology*, 52, 423–9.

Köymen, B., Rosenbaum, L., and Tomasello, M. (2014). Reasoning during joint decision-making by preschool peers. *Cognitive Development*, 32, 74–85.

Kuhlmeier, V. A. (2013). The social perception of helping and hindering. In M. D. Rutherford and V. A. Kuhlmeier (eds.), *Social Perception: Detection and Interpretation of Animacy, Agency, and Intention* (pp. 283–303). Cambridge, MA: MIT Press, 283–303.

Kushnir, T., Gopnik, A., Chernyak, N., Seiver, E., and Wellman, H. M. (2015). Developing intuitions about free will between ages four and six. *Cognition*, 138, 79–101.

Lagattuta, K. H., Nucci, L., and Bosacki, S. L. (2010). Bridging theory of mind and the personal domain: Children's reasoning about resistance to parental control. *Child Development*, 81, 616–35.

Legare, C. H. (2014). The contributions of explanation and exploration to children's scientific reasoning. *Child Development Perspectives*, 8, 101–6.

Legare, C. H. and Lombrozo, T. (2014). Selective effects of explanation on learning during early childhood. *Journal of Experimental Child Psychology*, 126, 198–212.

Malle, B. F. (1999). How people explain behavior: A new theoretical framework. *Personality and Social Psychology Review*, 3, 23–48.

Malle, B. F. (2004). *How the Mind Explains Behavior: Folk Explanations, Meaning, and Social Interaction*. Cambridge, MA: MIT Press.

Malle, B. F. and Knobe, J. (1997). Which behaviors do people explain? A basic actor-observer asymmetry. *Journal of Personality and Social Psychology*, 72, 288–304.

Malle, B. F., Knobe, J., O'Laughlin, M., Pearce, G. E., and Nelson, S. E. (2000). Conceptual structure and social functions of behavior explanations: Beyond person–situation attributions. *Journal of Personality and Social Psychology*, 79, 309–26.

Mercier, H., Bernard, S., and Clément, F. (2014). Early sensitivity to arguments: How preschoolers weight circular arguments. *Journal of Experimental Child Psychology*, 125, 102–9.

Nancekivell, S. E. and Friedman, O. (2014). Mine, yours, no one's: Children's understanding of how ownership affects object use. *Developmental Psychology*, 50, 1845–53.

Nancekivell, S. E. and Friedman, O. (2017). "Because it's hers": When preschoolers use ownership in their explanations. *Cognitive Science*, 41, 827–43.

Neary, K. R., Friedman, O., and Burnstein, C. L. (2009). Preschoolers infer ownership from "control of permission." *Developmental Psychology*, 45, 873–976.

Nucci, L. (1981). Conceptions of personal issues: A domain distinct from moral or societal concepts. *Child Development*, 52, 114–21.

Nucci, L. and Weber, E. K. (1995). Social interactions in the home and the development of young children's conceptions of the personal. *Child Development*, 66, 1438–52.

Orsolini, M. (1993). "Dwarfs do not shoot": An analysis of children's justifications. *Cognition and Instruction*, 11, 281–97.

Pesowski, M. L., Denison, S., and Friedman, O. (2016). Young children infer preferences from a single action, but not if it is constrained. *Cognition*, 155, 168–75.

Richert, R. A. and Lillard, A. S. (2002). Children's understanding of the knowledge prerequisites of drawing and pretending. *Developmental Psychology*, 38, 1004–15.

Rittle-Johnson, B., Saylor, M., and Swygert, K. E. (2008). Learning from explaining: Does it matter if mom is listening? *Journal of Experimental Child Psychology*, 100, 215–24.

Ruck, M. D., Abramovitch, R., and Keating, D. P. (1998). Children's and adolescents' understanding of rights: Balancing nurturance and self-determination. *Child Development*, 69, 404–17.

Schmidt, M. F., Rakoczy, H., and Tomasello, M. (2013). Young children understand and defend the entitlements of others. *Journal of Experimental Child Psychology*, *116*, 930–44.

Shaw, A., Li, V., and Olson, K. R. (2012). Children apply principles of physical ownership to ideas. *Cognitive Science*, *36*, 1383–403.

Silver, I. M. and Shaw, A. (2018). Pint-sized public relations: The development of reputation management. *Trends in Cognitive Sciences*, *22*, 277–9.

Traum, D. R. and Allen, J. F. (1994). Discourse obligations in dialogue processing. In J. Pustejovsky (ed.), *Proceedings of the 32nd Annual Meeting on Association for Computational Linguistics* (pp. 1–8). Stroudsburg, PA: Association for Computational Linguistics. doi: 10.3115/981732.981733.

Turri, J. (2015). Knowledge and the norm of assertion: A simple test. *Synthese*, *192*, 385–92.

Turri, J. (2016). *Knowledge and the Norm of Assertion: An Essay in Philosophical Science*. Cambridge: Open Book Publishers.

Turri, J. (2017). Experimental work on the norms of assertion. *Philosophy Compass*, *12*, e12425.

Vaish, A., Carpenter, M., and Tomasello, M. (2011). Young children's responses to guilt displays. *Developmental Psychology*, *47*, 1248–62.

Veneziano, E. and Sinclair, H. (1995). Functional changes in early child language: The appearance of references to the past and of explanations. *Journal of Child Language*, *22*, 557–81.

Walker, C. M., Lombrozo, T., Legare, C. H., and Gopnik, A. (2014). Explaining prompts children to privilege inductively rich properties. *Cognition*, *133*, 343–57.

Wong, P. T. and Weiner, B. (1981). When people ask "why" questions, and the heuristics of attributional search. *Journal of Personality and Social Psychology*, *40*, 650–63.

Woodward, A. L. (2009). Infants' grasp others' intentions. *Current Directions in Psychological Science*, *18*, 53–7.

Zelazo, P. D., Helwig, C. C., and Lau, A. (1996). Intention, act, and outcome in behavioral prediction and moral judgment. *Child Development*, *67*, 2478–92.

10

The Relevance of Alternate Possibilities for Moral Responsibility for Actions and Omissions

Pascale Willemsen
University of Zurich[1]

1. The Principle of Alternate Possibilities and the Action/Omission Asymmetry

Can an agent be morally responsible for an outcome she could not have avoided? The *Principle of Alternate Possibilities* (PAP) states that for an agent to be morally responsible, the agent must have been able to do other than performing the action she actually performed. Thus, if we figured out that an agent's action and its consequences were fully necessitated so that the agent could not have done otherwise, then the agent is blameless for whatever consequences she caused by acting. This principle enjoys some great prima facie plausibility. We typically do not blame others for performing an action if we find out that she acted under severe duress or coercion, suffers from paralysing anxiety, obsessive-compulsive disorder, or was physically unable to act in any other way.

However, due to the work of Frankfurt (1969) and many others who followed (e.g., Blumenfeld, 1971; Dennett, 1984; Fischer and Ravizza, 1991, 2000; Zimmerman, 1988), PAP is the subject of an intense debate. Imagine that an evil neurosurgeon implanted a microchip into Agent's

[1] The majority of this work was completed while Pascale Willemsen was a visiting fellow at University College London and employed at Ruhr-University Bochum.

Pascale Willemsen, *The Relevance of Alternate Possibilities for Moral Responsibility for Actions and Omissions* In: *Oxford Studies in Experimental Philosophy*. Edited by: Tania Lombrozo, Joshua Knobe, and Shaun Nichols, Oxford University Press (2020). © Pascale Willemsen.
DOI: 10.1093/oso/9780198852407.003.0011

brain with the help of which he is able to perfectly predict Agent's decisions and to manipulate these decisions and the subsequent actions. Agent is about to shoot Victim, and the neurosurgeon wants Victim's death. In the unlikely event that Agent decides against shooting Victim, the neurosurgeon will intervene and make Agent shoot Victim anyway. As a consequence, Agent will shoot and kill Victim no matter what. Agent cannot *not* shoot Victim. As a matter of fact, though, Agent never wavers in his decision and shoots Victim without the neurosurgeon's intervention. Call this case *Shooting*. In such a case, so many have argued, Agent is morally responsible for Victim's death, even though Agent could not have *not* shot Victim (Blumenfeld, 1971; Dennett, 1984; Fischer and Ravizza, 1991, 2000; Zimmerman, 1988). Thus, PAP cannot be true, as alternative possibilities are not *necessary* for moral responsibility.

While many philosophers are convinced that so-called Frankfurt-style cases like Shooting are counterexamples to PAP, it is much less questioned when it comes to omissions. Suppose Victim is drowning, and Agent is the only person around. Agent decides not to jump into the water to help Victim, and Victim dies. However, unbeknownst to Agent, the water is infested with sharks. Had Agent tried to save Victim, the sharks would have attacked and prevented Agent from saving Victim. Again, there is no way that Agent could have saved Victim. Call cases like these *Sharks*. Is Agent morally responsible for Victim's death? Some authors have denied this (e.g., Clarke, 1994; McIntyre, 1994). In order to be morally responsible for the consequences of an omission, so it is argued, the agent needs to be able to perform a relevant action that would have prevented the outcome. Thus, PAP seems to be true in cases of omissions.

Based on contrasting cases like Shooting and Sharks, it has been concluded that there is a moral asymmetry between actions and omissions with respect to the role of alternative possibilities (Clarke, 1994; McIntyre, 1994). For instance, Sartorio (2005, p. 461) describes it as follows: "whereas an agent can be responsible for an *action* even if he couldn't have done otherwise, an agent cannot be responsible for an *omission* if he couldn't have done otherwise" (emphases in original). Call claims like these the *Action/Omission Asymmetry Thesis* (AOAT).

2. Structure and Aim of the Chapter

In this chapter, I empirically investigate whether non-philosophers' moral evaluations provide evidence in support of a moral asymmetry between actions and omissions with respect to alternative possibilities. The experimental-philosophical debate has demonstrated a significant interest in the relevance of alternative possibilities for the attribution of moral responsibility. Researchers have provided evidence that agents are often held responsible in the absence of alternative possibilities (Bear and Knobe, 2016; Buckwalter and Turri, 2015; Feltz and Cova, 2014; Henne et al., 2016; Miller and Feltz, 2011; Nahmias et al., 2005, 2006; Nichols, 2004; Sarkissian et al., 2010; Turri, 2017).[2] However, in doing so, researchers have had a strong focus on actions, thereby neglecting omissions.[3] As a consequence, while it is often argued that alternative possibilities are not a necessary precondition for moral responsibility for actions, we lack evidence about this relationship for omissions. The aim of this chapter is to fill this lacuna and empirically investigate what non-philosophers think about the relevance of alternative possibilities for omissions.

To set the stage for the subsequent experiments, I will first outline the relevant arguments against AOAT (Sections 3 and 4). From these arguments, I will infer empirically testable predictions about which factors determine moral responsibility in the absence of alternative possibilities. I present four pre-registered experiments to test these predictions. In Experiment 1, I test whether the absence of alternative possibilities affects non-philosophers' moral judgments about an agent's action and the consequences resulting from it. In Experiment 2, I test the same experimental manipulation for omissions. In both Experiment 1 and 2, I strongly rely on the cases discussed in the philosophical literature. Since philosophers have put so much argumentative weight on these cases, we should test exactly those cases to see how philosophical

---

[2] Note that these papers start off from various research questions. While some researchers are interested in the connection between free will and alternative possibilities, others are interested in the so-called ought-implies-can principle. What unites these studies is that they all collect data on whether participants blame the agent despite the lack of alternative possibilities.

[3] One notable exception is Miller and Feltz (2011). In two experiments, they investigate the relevance of alternative possibilities for actions and omissions, using Frankfurt-style cases.

thought experiments play out when asking for the folk's opinion. In Section 7, I discuss the methodological and philosophical shortcomings of those cases, and, consequently, my own experiments. I argue that the philosophical debate has not provided us with cases that allow for methodologically sound experiments. For this reason, the experiments will necessarily be limited with respect to the conclusions we can draw from them. In Experiment 3, I attempt to create a novel design that fixes those problems, and I will test this design using two types of scales.

3. Objections against the Action/Omission Asymmetry

Several arguments have been presented against AOAT. Before engaging with them more closely, we need to disentangle the meaning of PAP and specify how it applies to AOAT.

PAP has played a crucial role in the free will and moral responsibility debate. Following Frankfurt (1969), it is often formulated like this:

(PAP):   An agent is morally responsible for what she has done only if she could have done otherwise.

But what does it mean to be responsible for something one has done, and what is required for it to be the case that she could have done otherwise (see Miller and Feltz, 2011 for a similar discussion)? According to one understanding of PAP, free will and moral responsibility require that an agent's action must result from her own choice among a variety of options. Consequently, an agent acted freely and is morally responsible if there were alternative courses of actions the agent could have chosen instead. Note that this understanding focuses on the agent's *action* and, in particular, the *situational circumstances when initiating the action*. Call this the *Principle of Alternative Actions* understanding of PAP. In the philosophical tradition, many arguments for incompatibilist positions concerning free will have relied on the assumption that the Principle of Alternative Actions is true and, thus, if determinism is true, free will is conceptually impossible (Ginet, 1982; Keil, 2007; van Inwagen, 1975; Wegner, 2003). As free will is typically considered a necessary precondition for moral responsibility, the lack of alternative possibilities implies the lack of moral responsibility (McKenna and Coates, 2016; O'Connor, 2016).

Second, a different understanding of PAP does not focus on the circumstances under which the action was initiated, but it takes the action to be defined by its *consequences* (for such an understanding of PAP, see, among others: van Inwagen, 1983, 1999; Sartorio, 2005). An agent is morally responsible for *killing* a man, if the consequence of her action is the death of a person, and if this death could have been prevented. If the victim would have died no matter what, the agent is not morally responsible. Call this the *Principle of Alternative Outcomes* or, as Miller and Feltz (2011) call it, the *Principle of Possible Prevention*. In Shooting, Agent could not have prevented Victim's death, because of the evil neuroscientist. As a consequence, Agent could not have done otherwise in the sense that he could have avoided killing the Victim. Victim's death was without alternatives. In Sharks, Agent could not have prevented Victim's death because the sharks would have attacked him. As a consequence, Agent could not have done otherwise in the sense that he could not have saved the child. Again, Victim's death was without alternatives.

It is this latter understanding of PAP that builds the starting point for the philosophical debate about AOAT. The asymmetry consists in the claim that while in both cases the outcome could not have been prevented, Agent is morally responsible and blameworthy when the death was brought about by an action (Shooting), and he is not morally responsible and blameworthy when it was brought about by an omission (Sharks).

When reading Sharks, did you have the intuition that Agent *is* morally responsible? If you did, you might think that there is no asymmetry after all, as alternative possibilities are irrelevant in both Sharks and Shooting. Defenders of AOAT agree with you that Agent is morally responsible and that he deserves blame for something. For instance, it is not denied that he is morally responsible and blameworthy for his *decision* not to save the child, for *not even trying*, for his *malicious thoughts* about the child, etc. However, the crucial point is that he is neither responsible nor blameworthy for the child's *death*. Why not? Because the death is something that he could not have prevented, and when it comes to omissions, alternative possibilities concerning the outcome are necessary for moral responsibility and blameworthiness. Thus, for the discussion at hand, it is important to keep these different moral judgments separate and to focus on our intuitions about the agent's moral responsibility and blameworthiness *for the outcome of their actions and omissions alone.*[4]

So how convincing is AOAT? Against AOAT, Fischer and Ravizza (1991, 2000) and Fischer (1997) have objected that Shooting and Sharks are not relevantly similar. The two stories do not only differ in the type of behavior (action vs. omission), but also in the point in the causal history of Victim's death at which the relevant intervention would have occurred. In Shooting, the evil neuroscientists would have intervened on Agent's decision-making process. Had he shown the slightest tendency toward making a decision not to shoot Victim, the neuroscientists would have made sure that Agent decided to shoot Victim. In contrast, in Sharks, there would have been no intervention on the decision-making process. Agent would have decided to try to save the child and would have already initiated the relevant action when the intervention occurs. The sharks would have simply prevented Agent from succeeding in his attempt to save Victim.[5]

To ensure the relevant similarity, Fischer and Ravizza (1991) suggest a different case that better matches the structure of Shooting, namely the Frankfurt-Style Omission Case (FSOC):

Frankfurt Style Omission Case.   I see the child drowning, I think I can save him by jumping into the water, but I freely decide not to jump in. This time there are no sharks in the water, but the evil neuroscientist is

---

[4] This thought becomes relevant when designing the experiments. As an experimental researcher, you want to make sure that participants are aware that the agent could be blamed for different things and to keep them distinct when making their moral judgments. See Section 5.2 for an elaboration of how I tried to help participants keep these importantly different moral judgments apart.

[5] It might be argued that what Fischer and Ravizza are concerned with is that the two cases violate the two understandings of PAP in different ways. In Sharks, the agent could not have done otherwise as defined by the outcome (understood in line with PAP); he could have brought about the outcome in a different way (understood in line with PAP in the Garden of Forking Paths sense). He might have failed in his attempt to save the child, but the child would have died in a different way, namely in a scenario in which someone died trying to save her. In Shooting, Agent could not have altered the way he acted. Because of the neuroscientists, Agent would have performed the same bodily movement in both cases. Unfortunately, Fischer and Ravizza do not make this claim explicit.

monitoring my brain. Had I wavered in my decision, he would have made me decide not to jump in.[6]

In this case, so Fischer and Ravizza argue, Agent is morally responsible for Victim's death—even though there was no way he could have prevented the death. As a consequence, if we do contrast relevantly similar cases,[7] the asymmetry between actions and omissions with respect to the relevance of alternate possibilities disappears. If the point of intervention is chosen to be the decision-making process,[8] alternate possibilities are not necessary, neither for actions nor omissions. Thus, we can reject PAP altogether and with it AOAT.

Jeremy Byrd agrees with Fischer and Ravizza that Sharks is not an adequate contrast for Shooting. However, he disagrees on why this is. According to Byrd (2007), the point of intervention is actually irrelevant for moral responsibility judgments about these cases. However, Shooting and Sharks differ in a crucial respect, namely the kind of intervener in play. In Shooting, the intervener is an intentional human agent, whereas in Sharks, the intervener is a non-agent—it is the natural, non-agentive world not playing along. Against Fischer and Ravizza's original position, Byrd claims that only intentional human agents can play the role of a Frankfurt-style intervener. As a consequence, if the sharks were replaced by another human agent, intuitions in both the action and the omission case should be identical: First, Agent is to blame for the child's death when a human agent intervenes on either my decision-making or my behavior, diminishing my possibilities to prevent the outcome. Second, as a consequence, PAP is false as Agent is morally responsible in the absence of alternative possibilities. Third, since PAP is proven false for omissions, AOAT is false and actions and omissions are symmetric with respect to the relevance of alternative possibilities.

---

[6] Taken from Sartorio (2005).

[7] Please note that there are good reasons to doubt that Shooting and FSOC are relevantly similar. I will discuss some of those reasons in Section 6. For now, I simply reconstruct the philosophical debate.

[8] This is, of course, not trivial and an argument could be made that the right point of intervention is, in fact, the action itself, not the decision-making process. Philosophers in the moral luck debate might make such an argument.

4. Toward an Experiment

From the existing work, we can extract three different suggestions of what factors are relevant for determining the role that alternate possibilities play for moral responsibility for the consequences of actions and omissions:

1. the point of intervention (decision-making process vs. behavior),
2. the intervener (agent vs. nature), and
3. the type of behavior (action vs. omission).

Ideally, the resulting experiment would consist of eight between-subject conditions that differ with respect to the first three factors: Type of Behavior (Action vs. Omission), Intervener (Agent vs. Nature), and Point of Intervention (Behavior vs. Decision-Making). As a within-subject factor, one might want to manipulate whether the outcome could have been prevented or not, to be able to detect how much people's responses differ between those two conditions. As dependent measures, participants would be asked to express their moral evaluation of the story.

Unfortunately, things are not that simple. To avoid potential confounding variables, all eight between-subject conditions should be tested using the same cover story. Yet, the two stories that have been used in the debate so far, namely Shooting and Sharks, do not allow for adaptations to omission and action cases, respectively. What is an omission comparable to the shooting of a person? A not-stopping of a shooting? What action is comparable to not helping a drowning person? Pushing someone into deep water?[9] None of the stories used in the literature so far can easily be adapted, such that they apply equally to actions and omissions without introducing potentially relevant asymmetries. We would need to come up with an entirely new cover story that might deviate quite strongly from those stories that have mainly influenced the philosophical debate.

---

[9] For a discussion of why such contrasts are problematic, see Willemsen and Reuter (2016). In short, our legal system and our everyday practice treat cases of killing and not helping very differently in terms of their moral evaluation. This is partly explained by the fact that the rules that are violated when we kill or not help are considered differently important. Willemsen and Reuter, therefore, argue that we should only compare actions and omissions for cases in which we have less socially and culturally grounded preconceptions.

As a consequence, the results would only speak indirectly to the predictions that philosophers have made about Shooting and Sharks. For this reason, Experiment 1 and 2 will use a more direct, yet methodologically sub-optimal design and test the philosophical thought experiments used in the debate. In Experiment 3, I will then correct those flaws and use a new, methodologically sound cover story.

When we think of testing philosophical theories, one major challenge is often to translate philosophical language into empirically testable queries. For instance, in the literature, philosophers have often discussed the relevance of alternative possibilities for the abstract concept of "moral responsibility." And sometimes in these discussions, "being morally responsible for X" seems to be treated as synonymous to "being blameworthy/praiseworthy for X" (for a similar discussion, see Miller and Feltz, 2011 and Turri, 2017).[10] However, in the experimental literature on moral cognition, we often find that moral responsibility judgments might differ strongly from judgments about blameworthiness (Turri, 2017). There is no obvious reason to pay attention to one moral judgment rather than the other when testing philosophical theories. For this reason, the following experiments will ask participants to evaluate an agent's moral responsibility *and* blameworthiness. I will discuss how the results of the experiments speak to or against PAP and AOAT, and also whether it makes a difference if we consider PAP and AOAT to be about moral responsibility or blameworthiness.

5. Experiment 1: Actions

In Experiment 1, I test whether alternative possibilities are relevant factors in deciding if an agent is morally responsible and blameworthy for the consequences of his or her actions. This experiment, as well as all following experiments, were pre-registered with the Open Science Framework (https://osf.io/6bfna/). Table 10.1 summarizes the main

---

[10] Malle et al., 2014 have argued that 'responsibility' should not be used by researchers in empirical studies, as it is "hopelessly equivocal" and "collapses distinct phenomena under a single label."

Table 10.1 Experiment 1. Philosophical claims and predictions

Claim	Prediction	Held by
Alternative possibilities are not necessary for the attribution of moral responsibility (same claim for blame).	Moral responsibility ratings will be above the midpoint of the scale (4) when the agent cannot do otherwise (same predictions for blame).	AOAT, Fischer, Fischer and Ravizza, Byrd.

claims of defenders of AOAT, Fischer, Fischer and Ravizza, and Byrd, and the empirically testable predictions.[11]

5.1 Sample size rationale and participants

The tests required to evaluate the philosophical hypotheses were t-test against the midpoint of the scale. A power analysis revealed that 72 participants for each of the four between-subject conditions were needed to detect a small to medium effect ($d = 0.35$) with 90% power (one-tailed). Thus, the results are reported for the first 72 participants in each condition who completed the survey in no less than 90 seconds and passed the manipulation check (question named "Unavoidable").[12] Participants were recruited on Amazon's Mechanical Turk and received monetary compensation ($0.40). 52.8% of participants were male, 47.2% female, the mean age was 38 years ($SD = 13$). All but five participants indicated English as their native language, and all participants were located in the United States while taking the survey.

5.2 Methods

A 2 (Intervener: Agent vs. Nature) × 2 (Point of Intervention: Decision Making vs. Behavior) × 2 (Alternative Possibilities: Yes vs. No) mixed

---

[11] None of the authors makes any of these predictions explicitly. They are rather the predictions that I infer from the philosophical claims they do make. The same holds for Experiments 2 and 3 as well.

[12] 472 participants were tested, 348 of which passed the manipulation check. Only the first 288 of those participants to finish the survey were included in the analysis. Thus, 124 participants were excluded for failing the manipulation check, and 60 because of the sample size rationale.

Table 10.2 Vignettes used in Experiment 1.

	Person	Nature
Introduction	Bob[/Joe/Rob/Jack] is pointing a gun at Bill whom he detests and wants dead. Bob deliberately decides to pull the trigger, he pulls the trigger, and Bill dies.	
Decision-Making	Unbeknownst to Bob, an evil neurosurgeon has implanted a microchip into Bob's brain and is secretly monitoring his brain. Had Bob wavered in his decision to shoot Bill, the neurosurgeon would have sent a signal to Bob's brain that would have ensured that he decided to shoot Bill anyway. As a consequence, Bill would have died no matter what.	Unbeknownst to Joe, he recently got exposed to a chemical substance that affects Joe's behavior. Had Joe wavered in his decision to shoot Bill, the drug would have ensured that he decided to shoot Bill anyway. As a consequence, Bill would have died no matter what.
Behavior	Unbeknownst to Rob, an evil busybody is observing the situation and already in position to roll a large rock off a cliff onto Bill. Had Rob not shot, the evil busybody would have rolled the large rock onto Bill which would have killed him instead. As a consequence, Bill would have died no matter what.	Unbeknownst to Jack, Bill is standing right below a rock that is about to fall off a cliff. Had Jack not shot, the falling rock would have killed Bill instead. As a consequence, Bill would have died no matter what.

design was applied, with Intervener and Point of Intervention as between-participants factors and Alternative Possibilities as a within-subject factor.

First, all participants read the introduction (Table 10.2) describing an agent who shoots a victim, Bill, leading to Bill's death. After reading the introduction, participants were asked five questions[13] and provided their answers on a scale from "1" meaning "not at all" to "7" meaning "fully":

[13] Since Moral Responsibility uses the formulation most in line with the philosophical debate, this question is always presented first, on a separate page. After answering Moral Responsibility and proceeding to the following page, participants could not go back to alter their judgment. The subsequent four questions were presented in fixed order on the same page to increase awareness of the difference between, for instance, being blameworthy for one's decision vs. being responsible for the death.

Unavoidable: Please indicate if you rather agree or disagree with the following statement: "In this scenario, Bill's death was unavoidable."

Moral Responsibility: How much do you agree with the following statement? "Bob [/Joe/Rob/Jack] is morally responsible for Bill's death."

Blame (Not Trying):   How blameworthy is Bob [/Joe/Rob/Jack] for not trying to spare Bill's life?

Blame (Decision):   How blameworthy is Bob [/Joe/Rob/Jack] for his decision to shoot Bill?

Blame (Outcome):   How blameworthy is Bob [/Joe/Rob/Jack] for Bill's death?

After providing their answers, participants were randomly assigned to one of the four between-subject conditions (Table 10.2). Participants were told that this was only part of the story and asked to now read the rest of it. Participants then answered all five questions again, as well as an additional question about whether and to what extent the additional information affected their thoughts about the agent.

To speak to the question of whether the absence of alternative possibilities diminishes moral responsibility and blame, it is crucial that all participants believed Bill's death to be unavoidable in the No Alternative Possibilities Condition. For this reason, I used people's responses to the Unavoidable question as a manipulation check and a selection criterion. Only those participants who agreed that in the No Alternative Possibilities condition Bill's death was unavoidable, were accepted for analysis.

The questions Blame(Not Trying), Blame(Decision) and Blame-(Outcome) were presented on the same page. It might be argued that there are several things for which participants are inclined to blame the agent, namely for not even trying to spare Bill's life, for the decision to shoot him, and also for Bill's death (see Section 3). For the purpose of this study, it is crucial to keep these three different targets of blame separate, and more specifically to ensure that people's blame judgment for the outcome is only an evaluation concerning the *outcome*. Thus, while the question of interest is Blame(Outcome), the two additional blame questions are asked to trigger reflective thinking. But since they do not matter for the research question at hand, results are only reported for Moral Responsibility and Blame(Outcome).

5.3   Results

Figure 10.1, Figure 10.2, and Table 10.3 summarize the results of the descriptive analysis. Table 10.3 further presents the t-tests against the midpoint of the scale. The results confirm the philosophical predictions in two ways. First, in the Alternative Possibilities Yes condition (that is, the first set of ratings before alternative possibilities were restricted), both moral responsibility and blame ratings are above the midpoint of the scale and almost reach ceiling. Thus, participants clearly hold the agent responsible and consider him blameworthy for the outcome of his action. In addition, in all four Alternative Possibilities No conditions (that is, the second set of ratings, after alternative possibilities were restricted in some way), moral responsibility and blame ratings are significantly above the neutral midpoint of 4. Those results speak against PAP and in support of its critics, as alternative possibilities are not necessary for moral responsibility for actions.

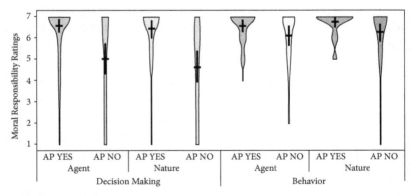

Figure 10.1 Experiment 1. Mean ratings for moral responsibility, as a function of Point of Intervention, and Intervener and Alternative Possibilities, with '1' meaning 'not at all' and '7' meaning 'fully'.

Note: Horizontal black lines represent means, vertical black lines represent 95% CI. The width of the shapes around the mean is proportional to the number of participants choosing each answer option.

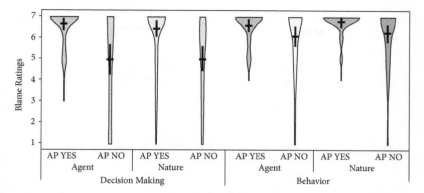

Figure 10.2 Experiment 1. Mean ratings for blame, as a function of Point of Intervention, and Intervener and Alternative Possibilities, with '1' meaning 'not at all' and '7' meaning 'fully'.

Note: Horizontal black lines represent means, vertical black lines represent 95% CI. The width of the shapes around the mean is proportional to the number of participants choosing each answer option.

To test for effects beyond philosophers' predictions, mixed-measure ANOVAs were conducted for the dependent variables moral responsibility and blame (outcome), with the within-subject condition Alternative Possibilities.

For the dependent variable moral responsibility, I found significant main effects of Point of Intervention, $F(1, 284) = 37.68$, $p < .001$, $\eta^2 = 0.117$, and of Alternative Possibilities, $F(1, 284) = 89.77$, $p < 0.001$, $\eta^2 = 0.240$. Moral responsibility ratings were higher when the Point of Intervention was the behavior, compared to when it was the agent's decision-making process. Further, moral ratings were also higher in the Alternative Possibilities Yes condition, compared to when alternative possibilities were ruled out. There was a significant two-way interaction between Point of Intervention and Alternative Possibilities, $F(1, 284) = 29.56$, $p < 0.001$, $\eta^2 = 0.094$, such that in Decision-Making moral responsibility was reduced significantly more compared to Behavior. No other main effect or interaction was significant.

Similar results were obtained for the dependent variable blame.[14] There were significant main effects of Point of Intervention, $F(1, 284) = 27.70$,

---

[14] To test whether moral responsibility and blame ratings differed significantly from each other in the Alternative Possibilities No conditions, a mixed-measure ANOVA was conducted. There was no main effect of Question, $F(1, 284) = 0.514$, $p = 0.474$. This test was not pre-registered.

Table 10.3 Experiment 1. Descriptive statistics and t-test against midpoint of the scale '4'.

		Means	SD	t	df	p (one-tailed)	d
Alternative Possibilities Yes	Moral Resp	6.59	0.898	48.929	287	<0.001	2.884
	Blame	6.61	0.904	49.028	287	<0.001	2.887
Alternative Possibilities No	Decision/Agent Moral Resp	5.07	2.26	4.015	71	<0.001	0.473
	Blame	4.93	2.352	3.358	71	<0.001	0.395
	Decision/Nature Moral Resp	4.64	2.058	2.635	71	<0.001	0.311
	Blame	5.01	2.024	4.25	71	<0.001	0.499
	Behavior/Agent Moral Resp	6.14	1.225	14.811	71	<0.001	1.747
	Blame	6.11	1.43	12.53	71	<0.001	1.476
	Behavior/Agent Moral Resp	6.28	1.292	14.964	71	<0.001	1.765
	Blame	6.24	1.284	14.782	71	<0.001	1.745

$p < 0.001$, $\eta^2 = 0.073$, and of Alternative Possibilities, $F(1, 284) = 85.94$, $p < .001$, $\eta^2 = 0.2329$. The two-way interaction between Point of Intervention and Intervener was also statistically significant, $F(1, 284) = 22.50$, $p < 0.001$, $\eta^2 = 0.073$. No other significant main effect or interaction was found.

5.4 Discussion

Experiment 1 demonstrated that alternative possibilities are not a necessary precondition for the attribution of moral responsibility in cases of actions. Experiment 1 thus provides additional evidence that the folk reject PAP as a general principle for both moral responsibility and blame. However, while alternative possibilities were not considered necessary for the attribution of moral responsibility and blame, they still have a strong effect on people's moral judgments. When participants learn that the outcome was unavoidable, their moral responsibility and blame judgments dropped notably.

6. Experiment 2: Omissions

Experiment 2 now tests whether learning that an agent could not have prevented an outcome had he intervened has an impact on the agent's moral responsibility for that outcome. Table 10.4 summarizes the hypotheses that will be tested in Experiment 2.

6.1 Sample size rationale and participants

As in Experiment 1, a power analysis revealed that 72 participants for each of the four between-subject conditions were needed to detect a small to medium effect (d = 0.35) with 90% power (one-tailed). Thus, the results are reported for the 72 participants in each condition who completed the survey in no less than 90 seconds and passed the

Table 10.4 Experiment 2. Philosophical claims and predictions.

Claim	Prediction	Held by
Alternative possibilities **are not necessary** for the attribution of moral responsibility (same claims for blame)		
if the Point of Intervention is the agent's decision-making	Moral responsibility ratings will be above 4 in all the Decision-Making/ Alternative Possibilities No conditions	Fischer & Ravizza
	(same predictions for blame)	Byrd
if the Intervener is a human agent	Moral responsibility ratings will be above 4 in all the Agent/Alternative Possibilities No conditions	
	(same predictions for blame)	
Alternative possibilities **are** necessary for the attribution of moral responsibility (same claims for blame)	Moral responsibility ratings will be below 4 in all the Decision-Making/ Alternative Possibilities No conditions (same predictions for blame)	AOAT

manipulation check (question named "Unavoidable").[15] Participants were recruited on Amazon's Mechanical Turk and received monetary compensation ($0.40). 52.4% of participants were male, 47.6% female, the mean age was 35 years ($SD = 11$). All but eight participants indicated English as their first language, and all participants were located in the United States while taking the survey.

6.2 Methods

The experimental design was completely identical to the one used in Experiment 1 with only minor modifications to the questions to match the vignettes (Table 10.5):[16]

---

[15] 417 participants were tested, 318 of whom passed the manipulation check. Only the first 288 of those participants to finish the survey were included in the analysis. Thus, 99 participants were excluded for failing the manipulation check, and 30 because of the sample size rationale.

[16] Highlights are just for illustration purposes and were not used in the actual study.

Table 10.5 Vignettes used in Experiment 2.

Introduction	While walking by the beach, Tom [/Sean/Dan/John] sees a child drowning. The beach is completely empty and there is nobody else around who could save the child. Tom believes that he could jump into the water and save the child with minimal effort and inconvenience. Tom notices that the child is the neighbor's kid who he detests and wants dead. He deliberately decides not to attempt to save the child. He decides not to jump into the water and continues his walk. The child drowns.	
	Person	**Nature**
Decision-Making	Unbeknownst to Tom, an evil neurosurgeon has implanted a microchip into Tom's brain and is secretly monitoring his brain. Had Tom wavered in his decision not to jump into the water, the neurosurgeon would have sent a signal to Tom's brain that would have ensured that Tom decided not to jump in anyway. As a consequence, the child would have died no matter what.	Unbeknownst to Sean, he recently got exposed to a chemical substance that affects Sean's behavior. Had Sean wavered in his decision not to jump into the water, the drug would have ensured that he decided not to jump in anyway. As a consequence, the child would have died no matter what.
Behavior	Unbeknownst to Dan, an evil busybody is observing the situation and controlling the gate of a cage filled with sharks. Had Dan jumped into the water, the evil busybody would have released the sharks and they would have attacked Dan and prevented him from saving the child. As a consequence, the child would have died no matter what.	Unbeknownst to John, the water is infested by sharks. Had John jumped into the water, the sharks would have attacked him and prevented him from saving the child. As a consequence, the child would have died no matter what.

Unavoidable: Please indicate if you rather agree or disagree with the following statement: "In this scenario, Bill's death was unavoidable."

Moral Responsibility: How much do you agree with the following statement? "Tom [/Sean/Dan/John] is morally responsible for the *child's* death."

Blame (Not Trying):   How blameworthy is Tom [/Sean/Dan/John] for not trying to *save the child*?

Blame (Decision):   How blameworthy is Tom [/Sean/Dan/John] for his decision *not to jump into the water to save the child?*

Blame (Outcome):   How blameworthy is Tom [/Sean/Dan/John] for the *child's* death?

6.3 Results

The results of the descriptive statistics are depicted in Figure 10.3, Figure 10.4, and Table 10.6. Table 10.6 further presents the t-tests against the midpoint of the scale. In the Alternative Possibilities Yes condition, moral responsibility and blame ratings are above the neutral midpoint, speaking in favor of the claim that agents are morally responsible and blameworthy for the outcome of their omissions if there is no lack of alternative possibilities.

In the Alternative Possibilities No condition, moral responsibility ratings do not differ significantly from the midpoint of the scale. How should we interpret cases in which ratings are not significantly different from the midpoint? First and most straightforwardly, the results could be interpreted as speaking against the AOAT, as blame and moral

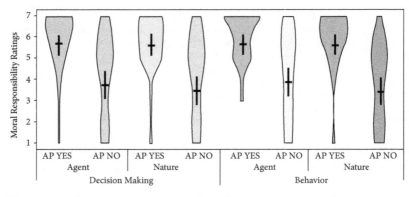

Figure 10.3 Experiment 2. Mean ratings for moral responsibility, as a function of Point of Intervention, and Intervener and Alternative Possibilities, with '1' meaning 'not at all' and '7' meaning 'fully'.

Note: Horizontal black lines represent means, vertical black lines represent 95% CI. The width of the shapes around the mean is proportional to the number of participants choosing each answer option.

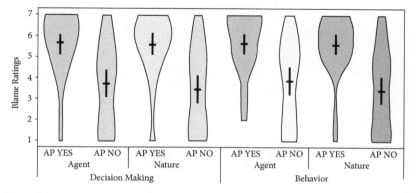

Figure 10.4 Experiment 2. Mean ratings for blame, as a function of Point of Intervention, and Intervener and Alternative Possibilities, with '1' meaning 'not at all' and '7' meaning 'fully'.

Note: Horizontal black lines represent means, vertical black lines represent 95% CI. The width of the shapes around the mean is proportional to the number of participants choosing each answer option.

responsibility ratings are not significantly below the midpoint. Further, they could be interpreted as also contradicting all those positions that argued against AOAT, as ratings are not significantly *above* the midpoint. However, failures to find a departure from the midpoint are hard to interpret. First, it is not clear that participants understand the midpoint as accurately between the extremes of the scale. Participants might alternatively use the midpoint to indicate that the agent is responsible for some aspects of his behavior, yet not for others. Second, it is not even clear that participants use the midpoint to indicate any responsibility judgment on the spectrum. Participants might have used it to indicate uncertainty, no opinion on the issue, etc. For these reasons, strong conclusions based on a failure of the means to differ from the midpoint need to be avoided.

To be able to detect effects beyond the philosophical predictions, mixed-measure ANOVAs were conducted. For the dependent variable moral responsibility, I found a significant main effect of Alternative Possibilities, $F(1, 284) = 211.05, p < 0.001, \eta^2 = 0.426$. Once participants were provided with information about the lack of alternative possibilities, moral responsibility ratings went down. No other main effect or interaction was significant.

Table 10.6 Experiment 2. Descriptive statistics and t-test against midpoint of the scale '4'.

		Means	SD	t	df	p (one-tailed)	d
Alternative Possibilities Yes							
	Moral Resp	5.94	1.288	25.577	287	**<0.001**	1.506
	Blame	5.63	1.469	18.858	287	**<0.001**	1.11
Alternative Possibilities No							
Decision/Agent	Moral Resp	4.33	1.972	1.435	71	0.078	0.167
	Blame	3.69	1.99	-1.303	71	0.099	-0.156
Decision/Nature	Moral Resp	4.13	1.942	0.546	71	0.294	0.067
	Blame	3.5	2.021	-2.099	71	**0.020**	-0.247
Behavior/Agent	Moral Resp	4.32	2.082	1.302	71	0.099	0.154
	Blame	3.92	2.047	-0.345	71	0.366	-0.039
Behavior/Agent	Moral Resp	3.83	1.875	-0.754	71	0.227	-0.091
	Blame	3.43	1.999	-2.417	71	**0.009**	-0.285

For the dependent variable blame (outcome), there was a significant main effect of Alternative Possibilities, $F(1, 284) = 229.55$, $p < 0.001$, $\eta^2 = 0.447$. No other significant main effect or interaction was found.

Going beyond the pre-registration, I further analyzed whether blame and moral responsibility judgments significantly differed from one another in the Alternative Possibilities No condition using a mixed-measure ANOVA with Question tested within-subjects. There was a statistically significant main effect of Question, $F(1, 284) = 34.20$, $p < 0.001$, $\eta^2 = 0.107$. No interaction was significant.

6.4 Discussion

Experiment 2 tested the core claim of AOAT, namely that alternative possibilities are necessary for omissions. Defenders of AOAT would predict that participants should withhold moral responsibility and blame attribution when the outcome was unavoidable. This led to the empirical predictions that moral responsibility and blame ratings should be significantly below the midpoint of the scale. Against AOAT, the results show that participants' moral responsibility ratings were not significantly below the neutral midpoint of the scale when the outcome was unavoidable. This was the case across conditions. However, ratings were also not significantly above the midpoint and therefore challenge critics of AOAT as well.

For blame, the results are significantly lower than moral responsibility judgments, and in some conditions, agreement ratings were even significantly below the midpoint of the scale. Interestingly, none of the factors that philosophers have considered relevant for the attribution of moral responsibility, namely the point of intervention and the intervener, played a role. Experiment 2, therefore, provides very mixed evidence but provides initial reason to reject AOAT.

7. Is there an Action/Omissions Asymmetry?

Experiments 1 and 2 demonstrate that for actions, alternative possibilities are not a necessary precondition for the attribution of moral responsibility and blame. Even when participants learned that an agent, whose behavior led to a bad outcome, could not have prevented the outcome, they still judged him morally responsible and blameworthy for the outcome of his actions. These results are not surprising, both in light of the theoretical arguments that have been put forward and in light of previous empirical findings.

Interestingly, the results look different for omissions. Both moral responsibility and blame ratings are not statistically different from the midpoint. These findings contradict both PAP and AOAT. In no condition did agreement ratings drop below the neutral midpoint. So is this evidence in favor of critics of AOAT? Not at all. First, in no condition were mean ratings above the neutral midpoint. Second, none of the factors that were considered relevant in the literature actually mattered. According to Fischer and Ravizza, the point of intervention was supposed to matter. When the point of intervention is the agent's decision-making, the agent should be held responsible and should be blamed for both actions and omissions. Alternative possibilities should not be necessary for these judgments. This effect did not emerge. Byrd's suggestion that the type of intervener would determine whether alternative possibilities were necessary in the omission case also failed to find support.

While these results might cause some frustration, there are at least two reasons to be optimistic. First, across conditions, the lack of alternative possibilities made people reduce their initial moral evaluation of the agent. Thus, while alternative possibilities are not necessary, they are still an important moderator for the attribution of moral responsibility and blame: whether they are present of absent changed people's moral intuitions. This effect was found for both actions and omission.

Second, the experimental design used here is, as mentioned earlier, limited. On the one hand, while it seems that AOAT should be rejected given the empirical evidence, we still do not know whether alternative possibilities are *equally* irrelevant for actions and omissions. One might believe that alternative possibilities are not necessary in cases of actions or omissions, but that the strength of their effect on moral responsibility attributions is different for actions and omissions. The experimental design does not allow for the relevant tests. On the other hand, since the cover stories are different for actions and omissions, we cannot make any claims as to whether there is a general tendency to condemn actions more strongly than omissions, nor whether actions are generally considered more causally relevant. Some philosophers have argued that an omission leading to a bad outcome is not as bad as an action leading to the same outcome (Foot, 1967), and a related empirical effect has been found (Baron and Ritov, 2004; Spranca et al., 1991; Willemsen and Reuter, 2016). For those two reasons, it is advisable to test the relevance of alternative possibilities for actions and omissions in one single experiment.

There is another reason to suspect that the cases used in Experiments 1 and 2 are ill-suited to test the hypotheses at hand, and this reason is of a methodological nature. Compare, for both actions and omissions individually, how Victim would have died, had there been an intervention. In the Action/Decision-Making condition, had the evil neurosurgeon or the drug intervened, she/it would have sent a signal to Agent's brain, so that, eventually, Agent would have killed Victim anyway. In the Action/Behavior condition, however, the counterfactual causal chain does not include Agent at all. Victim would have died, but as a result of being hit by a rock. There are other versions in the literature in which an evil bystander is already in position to shoot Victim, in case Agent decides not to. No matter how the counterfactual intervention on the agent's behavior is spelled out, the resulting causal chain does not include Agent.

There are two reasons why this difference in the causal chain might contaminate intuitions. First, we know that the underlying causal structure is an important moderator for the attribution of moral responsibility (Darley and Shultz, 1990; Malle et al., 2014; Murray and Lombrozo, 2017). The extent to which an agent is considered causally responsible affects the agent's moral responsibility for that outcome. We further know that adding causal factors to the story reduces the causal relevance of an agent to the outcome (Alicke, 1992). Against this worry, it might be objected that the causal structures are identical in terms of what *actually* happened; they only differ in the *counterfactual* scenario. The difference between action and omission conditions should, thus, be irrelevant for people's moral judgments about what actually happened. This objection, however, does not succeed. Empirical evidence suggests that people rely heavily on counterfactual thinking when evaluating a situation, both morally and causally (Gerstenberg et al., 2015; Kominsky et al., 2015; Lagnado and Gerstenberg, 2017; Lagnado et al., 2013).

In fact, people's causal judgments are largely influenced by considerations about what would have happened, had the agent acted differently. Moreover, the whole discussion about the relevance of alternative possibilities deals with the question of whether alternative, that is *counterfactual*, possibilities influence moral judgments about what actually happened. We can and, given the whole starting point of the debate, philosophers *should* expect that the counterfactual causal structure has a significant impact on participants' causal and moral evaluation. For this reason, we need to ensure that those causal structures are identical in all conditions that we want to compare directly.

When it comes to omissions, things are equally worrisome. Compare again the Decision-Making to the Behavior condition. In Decision-Making, had Agent wavered in his decision not to help the child, his decision not to help would have been caused by the neurosurgeon or the drug. As a result, the child would have died, while Agent would have been safe and sound. In Behavior, however, the counterfactual outcome differs in important respects. Had the agent tried to intervene, he would have been attacked by sharks. While the story does not explicitly state it, it is very likely that this attack would lead to Agent's death or at least severe injuries and, thus, to *two* victims instead of one. Consequently, Decision-Making and Behavior differ in the outcome of the counterfactual scenario. In addition, the fact that he would have died or been injured as well provides an objective reason for Agent not to jump into the water which might post-hoc rationalize the agent's behavior and reduce blame. Had he known about the sharks, he would have had a good, justified reason not to jump in. Such an objective reason that would have made the agent's decision understandable does not exist in Decision-Making.

Trying to transform the philosophical thought experiments that have guided the debate about the relevance of alternative possibilities into real, methodologically sound experiments reveals a devastating fact. Philosophers have built their arguments about the relevance of alternative possibilities on cases which are dramatically different in terms of their underlying causal structure, the severity of the outcomes, as well as the possibility to rationalize and excuse the agent's decision post-hoc. None of these differences is trivial or can be expected not to matter. I do not dare to decide which cases are philosophically the most interesting or relevant ones. However, philosophers who would like to stick to the traditional cases will have to make such decisions or make suggestions of how those cases can be fixed and made more parallel. Until then, philosophers and empirical researchers interested in the relevance of alternative possibilities need to be aware that intuitions often require a more complex explanation than what is currently provided. If we are further interested in extending those cases to real-world experiments, the cases available so far might not even qualify in the first place and we need novel scenarios to test our philosophical intuitions.

8. Experiment 3: Actions and Omissions

Due to the significant shortcomings of Experiments 1 and 2, it is advisable to test AOAT by using one cover story for both actions and omissions. For the reasons discussed in Sections 3 and 6, I will not try to adapt Shooting or Sharks, but use an entirely new cover story.

Willemsen and Reuter (2016) argued that many studies on the moral significance of actions and omissions suffer from a severe methodological flaw, namely that agents break different moral norms that are considered differently important. Malle et al. (2014, p. 168) have recently pointed out that "social perceivers may distinguish omissions and commissions by the norms these two actions violate." The thought experiments used in the literature typically describe cases of harming vs. not helping, or killing vs. letting die, which people do believe to differ in importance (Willemsen and Reuter, 2016). In addition, extreme and emotionally affective outcomes, such as death, severe injury, or harm to children, tend to trigger extreme moral condemnation. Such ceiling effects might conceal effects one would find if participants were not tempted to ascribe as much moral responsibility as possible. For this reason, the vignette I use is inspired by Willemsen and Reuter (2016) and describes a moderate, less emotionally affective outcome.

This experiment has two parts. Experiment 3a copies the experimental design from Experiments 1 and 2 and uses a 7-point Likert scale for moral responsibility and blame evaluations. Experiment 3b uses a

Table 10.7 Experiment 3. Philosophical claims, empirical predictions, and tests of those predictions.

Claim	Empirically Testable Prediction	Test
Agents are morally responsible for the outcomes of their actions (same claim for blame)	Moral responsibility ratings will be above 4 in the No Information condition (same prediction for blame)	t-test against 4 for DV moral responsibility
Agents are morally responsible for the outcomes of their omissions (same claim for blame)	Blame ratings will be above 4 in the No Information condition (same prediction for blame)	t-test against 4 for DV blame (outcome)
Alternative possibilities are not necessary for the attribution of moral responsibility for actions (same claim for blame)	Moral responsibility ratings will be above 4 in the Information condition (same prediction for blame)	t-tests against 4 for DV moral responsibility for the Information condition
Alternative possibilities are not necessary for the attribution of moral responsibility for omissions (same claim for blame)	Moral responsibility ratings will be above 4 in the Information condition (same prediction for blame)	t-tests against 4 for DV moral responsibility for the Information condition
Agents will be considered less morally responsible for omissions, compared to actions (same claim for blame)	There will be a main effect of Behavior for DV moral responsibility, such that means are higher for actions than for omissions (same prediction for blame)	ANOVA
Agents will be considered less causally relevant for omissions, compared to actions (same claim for blame)	There will be a main effect of Behavior for DV causation, such that means are higher for actions than for omissions (same prediction for blame)	ANOVA

binary scale to see whether small tendencies become more extreme when only two answer options are available.

8.1 Experiment 3a

Based on the results from Experiments 1 and 2, as well as the work by Willemsen and Reuter (2016), I make the empirically testable predictions shown in Table 10.7.

8.1.1 Sample size rationale and participants

As in Experiments 1 and 2, a power analysis revealed that for the most demanding statistical test (the t-test against the midpoint of the scale), 72 participants for each of the four between-subject conditions were needed to detect a small to medium effect ($d = 0.35$) with 90% power (one-tailed). Thus, the results are reported for the 72 participants in each condition who completed the survey in no less than 90 seconds and passed the manipulation check (question named "Unavoidable").[17] Participants were recruited on Amazon's Mechanical Turk and received monetary compensation ($0.40). 45.1% of participants were female, the mean age was 33 years ($SD = 11$). All but one participant indicated English as their first language, and all participants were located in the United States while taking the survey.

8.1.2 Methods

A 2 (Type of Behavior: Action vs. Omissions) × 2 (Alternative Possibilities: Yes vs. No) mixed design was applied, with Alternative Possibilities as a within-subject factor. Participants were randomly assigned to one of the two between-subject conditions (Table 10.8) and answered adapted versions of the questions used in Experiments 1 and 2 in the same order. The vignettes are based on Willemsen and Reuter (2016) and are presented in Table 10.8.

8.1.3 Results

The results of Experiment 3 are summarized in Figure 10.5, Figure 10.6, and Table 10.9. For both actions and omissions, participants' moral responsibility and blame ratings are above the midpoint of the scale, in the Alternative Possibilities Yes condition. In Alternative Possibilities No, both moral responsibility and blame ratings remain significantly above the neutral midpoint for actions. For omissions, only moral responsibility ratings are significantly above 4. For blame, however, they are not. For blame, mean ratings are only descriptively above the neutral midpoint and therefore hard to interpret. A look at the overall distribution of

---

[17] 179 participants were tested, 161 of which passed the manipulation check. Only the first 144 of those participants to finish the survey were included in the analysis. Thus, 18 participants were excluded for failing the manipulation check, and 15 because of the sample size rationale.

Table 10.8 Vignettes used in Experiment 3.

	Action	Omission
First part of the story	Peter works for a sales company. He is responsible for several tasks, like answering incoming phone calls and updating customer information on the central computer. For quite some time now, Peter is very unhappy with this job. He feels like his commitment is not appreciated and it is always others who get a promotion or salary increase. For some time now, Peter has been thinking about a way to harm the company.	
	One morning, Peter goes through his normal routine and updates customer information on the central computer, when suddenly a window pops up.	
	Peter reads the text, which states, "All customer information will be deleted. If you'd like to continue, click on 'delete.'"	Peter reads the text, which states, "In 10 seconds, all customer information will be deleted. If you'd like to abort, click on 'cancel.'"
	Peter clicks on delete immediately, as he knows that losing customer information will be a big problem for the company. Immediately,	Peter does not click on cancel, as he knows that losing customer information will be a big problem for the company. After 10 seconds,
	all customer information is deleted from the central computer. The company loses important customer information.	
Lack of Alternative Possibilities	Unbeknownst to Peter, an evil neurosurgeon has implanted a microchip into Peter's brain and is secretly monitoring his brain. Had Peter wavered in his decision to click on 'delete,' the neurosurgeon would have sent a signal to Peter's brain that would have ensured that Peter decided to click on 'delete' anyway. As a consequence, the data would have been deleted no matter what.	Unbeknownst to Peter, an evil neurosurgeon has implanted a microchip into Peter's brain and is secretly monitoring his brain. Had Peter wavered in his decision not to click on 'cancel' the data, the neurosurgeon would have sent a signal to Peter's brain that would have ensured that Peter decided not to click on 'cancel' anyway. As a consequence, the data would have been deleted no matter what.

participants' blame responses might provide some helpful insights. 56.95% of participants chose an answer option of 5, 6, or 7, indicating that they consider the agent blameworthy (only 5.56% chose the neutral midpoint).

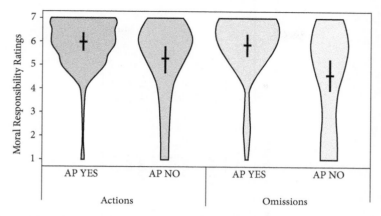

Figure 10.5 Experiment 3a. Mean ratings for moral responsibility, as a function of Type of Behavior and Alternative Possibilities, with '1' meaning 'not at all' and '7' meaning 'fully'.

Note: Horizontal black lines represent means, vertical black lines represent 95% CI. The width of the shapes around the mean is proportional to the number of participants choosing each answer option.

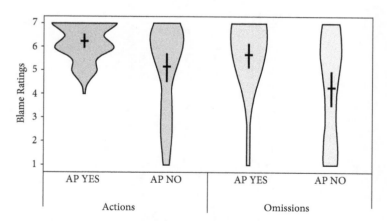

Figure 10.6 Experiment 3a. Mean ratings for blame, as a function of Type of Behavior and Alternative Possibilities, with '1' meaning 'not at all' and '7' meaning 'fully'.

Note: Horizontal black lines represent means, vertical black lines represent 95% CI. The width of the shapes around the mean is proportional to the number of participants choosing each answer option.

Table 10.9 Experiment 3. Descriptive statistics and t-tests against the midpoint of the scale.

			Means	SD	t	df	p (one-tailed)	d
Alternative Possibilities No	Action	Moral Resp	6.00	1.075	15.791	71	**<0.001**	1.86
		Blame	6.24	0.788	24.385	71	**<0.001**	2.843
	Omission	Moral Resp	5.88	1.352	11.763	71	**<0.001**	1.391
		Blame	5.68	1.412	10.069		**<0.001**	1.19
Alternative Possibilities Yes	Action	Moral Resp	5.25	1.701	6.234	71	**<0.001**	0.735
		Blame	5.15	1.881	5.199	71	**<0.001**	0.611
	Omission	Moral Resp	4.57	1.925	2.321	71	**0.006**	0.296
		Blame	4.28	2.114	1.046	71	0.073	0.132

A 2 × 2 mixed-measure ANOVA for the dependent variable moral responsibility, revealed significant main effects of Alternative Possibilities, $F(1, 142) = 36.07$, $p < 0.001$, $\eta^2 = 0.203$. The main effect of Type of Behavior is at best suggestive as it merely reaches the .05 significance level and its effect size is small, $F(1, 142) = 3.879$, $p = 0.05$, $\eta^2 = 0.0027$. The two-way interaction was not statistically significant, $F(1, 142) = 2.64$, $p = 0.107$, $\eta^2 = 0.018$.

Mirroring the results for moral responsibility, for the dependent variable blame outcome, I found a significant main effect of Alternative Possibilities, $F(1, 142) = 42.88$, $p < 0.001$, $\eta^2 = 0.232$. This time, also the main effect of Type of Behavior was significant, $F(1, 142) = 12.22$, $p = 0.001$, $\eta^2 = 0.079$. The two-way interaction was not statistically significant, $F(1, 142) = 0.708$, $p = 0.402$, $\eta^2 = 0.005$.

A mixed-measure ANOVA with the within-subject factor Question further revealed that Moral Responsibility and Blame did not differ significantly, $F(1, 142) = 3.01$, $p = 0.085$. This test was not pre-registered.

8.1.4 Interim discussion

Experiment 3a confirms the results from Experiment 1 and demonstrates that alternative possibilities are not necessary for moral responsibility and blame for actions. In addition, the results provide additional evidence that alternative possibilities are also not required for moral responsibility for omissions, as moral responsibility ratings are significantly above the midpoint. People clearly ascribe moral responsibility even if the outcome could not have been avoided. For people's blame judgments, the results are less straightforward and neither significantly above nor below the midpoint. They speak against AOAT but we are not justified in concluding that people blame an agent in the absence of alternative possibilities. For now, the empirical evidence speaks clearly against AOAT.

Using one cover story, we are now also able to detect other important differences between actions and omissions. For both actions and omissions, moral responsibility ratings drop significantly when participants learn that the outcome was unavoidable, and they do so equally strongly for actions and omissions. This suggests that alternative possibilities have the same moral responsibility-reducing effect for both types of behavior.

8.2 Experiment 3b

Experiment 3a provided initial evidence that there is no Action/ Omission Asymmetry when we consider people's moral responsibility judgment. For blame, we still lack telling evidence. It might be argued that being morally responsible or blameworthy is primarily a yes-or-no issue. Thus, to really investigate whether alternative possibilities are a necessary requirement, a binary answer format might be more adequate and informative. In addition, binary answer formats further circumvent the difficulties of interpreting ratings close to the midpoint. In Experiment 3b, I now use such a binary answer format.

8.2.1 Sample size rationale and participants

A power analysis revealed that for the most demanding statistical test (the binominal test against chance), 93 participants for each of the two between-subject conditions were needed to detect a small to medium effect (d = 0.15) with 90% power (one-tailed). Thus, the results are reported for the first 93 participants in each condition who completed the survey in no less than 90 seconds and passed the manipulation check (question named "Unavoidable").[18] Participants were recruited on Amazon's Mechanical Turk and received monetary compensation ($0.40). 53.8% of participants were male, 46.3% female, the mean age was 35 years (SD = 11). All but three participants indicated English as their first language, and all participants were located in the United States while taking the survey.

8.2.2 Methods

The vignettes are identical to the ones used in Experiment 3a and again a mixed-design was used. Participants answered all five questions that were already used in Experiments 1 to 3a, this time using a binary scale. Since Alternative Possibilities were manipulated within-subjects, all participants answered all five questions twice. The exact formulation of the questions is as follows:

---

[18] 281 participants were tested, 226 of which passed the manipulation check. Only the first 186 of those participants to finish the survey were included in the analysis. Thus, 55 participants were excluded for failing the manipulation check, and 40 because of the sample size rationale.

Please indicate if you rather agree or disagree with the following statements:

Unavoidable: In the scenario, the loss of the data was unavoidable.

Moral Responsibility: Peter is morally responsible for the data being deleted.

Blame (Not Trying):   Peter is blameworthy for not trying to save the data.

Blame (Decision):   Peter is blameworthy for his decision to click on 'delete'/not to click on 'cancel.'

Blame (Outcome):   Peter is blameworthy for the data being deleted.

8.2.3 Results

The mean ratings are shown in Figure 10.7 and Figure 10.8. In the Alternative Possibilities No condition, agreement with the moral responsibility and the blame statement are surprisingly close to chance for both Actions and Omissions. Going beyond the pre-registered tests, I compared whether agreement was significantly different for actions and for omissions. This was not the case (Moral Responsibility: χ^2 (1, $N = 186$) = 0.544, $p = 0.555$; Blame: χ^2 (1, $N = 186$) = 3.634, $p = 0.078$).

In the Action, Alternative Possibilities No condition, 58% of participants agreed that the agent is morally responsible for the data being deleted. A binominal test against chance revealed that this majority is

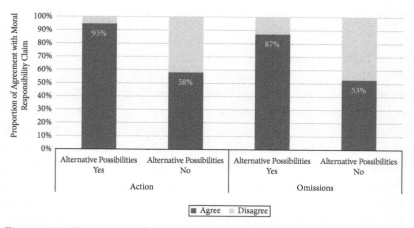

Figure 10.7 Experiment 3b. Proportion of moral responsibility judgments as a function of Type of Behavior and Alternative Possibilities.

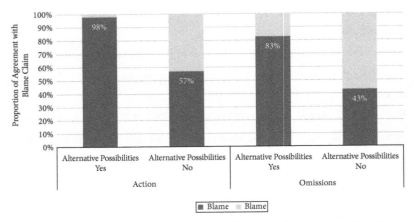

Figure 10.8 Experiment 3b. Proportion of blame judgments as a function of Type of Behavior and Alternative Possibilities.

not significant, test value = 0.5, p = 0.073, one-tailed. For the blame statement, 56.99% indicated agreement. Also this percentage is not significantly different from 50%, test value = 0.5, p = 0.107, one-tailed.

For omissions, 52.7% indicated agreement with the statement that the agent is morally responsible in the Alternative Possibilities No condition. A binominal test demonstrated that this is not significantly different from 50%, test value = 0.5, p = 0.3409. When asked about the agent's blameworthiness, 43% chose the agreement option, a proportion that is, again, not significantly different from 50%, test value = 0.5, p = 107.

8.2.4 Interim discussion

The results of Experiment 3b are surprising in three ways. First, in Experiments 1 and 3a, mean moral responsibility and blame ratings about actions were clearly above the midpoint of the scale in the No Alternative Possibilities condition. This indicates that people hold agents responsible for the consequences of their actions, even in the absence of alternative possibilities. From this, I inferred that alternative possibilities are not a necessary precondition for actions. However, the results in this experiment are much less straightforward. Only 58% of participants said that the agent was morally responsible, a proportion not significantly different from chance. In Experiment 3a, on the other hand, 76.39% chose an answer option above 4, indicating some degree of agreement. For blame, 57% said that he was blameworthy for the consequences of his action in Experiment 3b. In Experiment 3a, using a 7-point rating scale, 69.44% chose an answer option of 5, 6, or 7, indicating agreement.

Second, for omissions, switching from a rating scale to a binary scale did not provide more conclusive evidence for or against AOAT. Neither moral responsibility nor blame ratings are significantly different from 50%, making it hard to draw any reliable conclusions. At best we can say that participants are split into two groups: those who consider alternative possibilities to be necessary, and those who do not.

The third surprising finding is that the difference between actions and omissions disappeared and is now merely descriptive.

8.3 Discussion

In Experiment 3, two different types of scales were used to test whether alternative possibilities are necessary for moral responsibility and blame for the consequences of actions and omissions. Experiment 3a provided evidence that PAP is false for both types of moral judgments and for both actions and omissions. The results of Experiment 3a therefore challenge AOAT.

While Experiment 3b was conducted to provide even stronger evidence, the evidence is instead less conclusive. When the outcome was unavoidable, roughly half of participants agreed and half of them disagreed that the agent is morally responsible and to blame for the outcome. Interestingly, this effect was obtained for both actions and omissions.

It is hard to find an explanation of these differences without being merely speculative. The different scales might trigger different background assumptions or different interpretations of the test query. For instance, participants might be okay with ascribing some blame to an agent who could not have avoided the outcome, and to choose a 5 on a 7-point scale. However, participants might interpret a binary answer format as asking whether the agent is *fully* blameworthy. Here, participants who believe that the agent deserves a minimal amount of blame might choose the disagree option because they disagree that the agent is fully blameworthy. While this might be one (of many) plausible explanations, more research will be required.

9. General Discussion

Ever since the work of Harry Frankfurt, the Principle of Alternative Possibilities (PAP) has been subject to an intense philosophical debate. While many philosophers are convinced that an agent can only be morally responsible for an outcome that he could have avoided, others have rejected this idea and argued that moral responsibility is not dependent on alternative possibilities. In this chapter, I engaged with a more nuanced position, according to which alternative possibilities are not required for moral responsibility for actions, but they are required for moral responsibility for omissions. This position was dubbed the Action/Omission Asymmetry Thesis (AOAT). The aim of this chapter was to empirically test whether philosophers' intuitions about concrete thought experiments are shared by the folk, and to what extent the folk's intuitions support philosophical theory. Therefore, the main question this chapter aimed to answer is: Is there an Action/Omission Asymmetry?

Experiment 1 lent support to the position that an agent can be morally responsible for the consequences of his actions, even if those consequences could not have been avoided. Experiment 2 showed that for omissions, people's intuitions speak against AOAT and lend initial support for the position that alternative possibilities are not a necessary precondition for omissions either. For both actions and omissions, the lack of alternative possibilities had a significant effect on people's moral evaluations. Once participants learned that the outcome could not have been avoided, they held the agent much less responsible and blamed him less for the outcome. To detect whether this effect was equally or differently strong for actions and omissions, a vignette needed to be designed that works for both actions and omissions. Experiment 3 demonstrated that the effect of alternative possibilities on people's moral responsibility judgments is equally strong. When learning that the outcome could not have been avoided, people's moral responsibility judgments go down equally strongly for actions and omissions. For blame judgments, the effect of alternative possibilities was slightly stronger for omissions, compared to actions.

So is there an Action/Omission Asymmetry? The empirical study of the folk's intuitions presented in this chapter suggests that AOAT is false, but it cannot provide a definite answer and more research will be required. Here is, what I believe, we can say for sure.

First, it seems that whether we can be confident in rejecting AOAT strongly depends on which moral judgment we consider relevant for the asymmetry in the first place. If we believe that the relevant moral judgment is a judgment about moral responsibility, then we can be confident that there is no Action/Omission Asymmetry. Neither for actions nor for omissions were alternative possibilities found to be a necessary precondition for moral responsibility; people still held the agent responsible when the outcome was unavoidable. As a consequence, PAP is wrong for both actions and omissions. In contrast, if we believe that the relevant moral judgment is a judgment about blameworthiness, then the results provide a weaker basis to reject AOAT. In Experiment 2, moral responsibility and blame ratings were significantly different from one another and blame ratings tended to be below the neutral midpoint. Had only blame been tested, one might have taken this as initial evidence in support of AOAT. However, this difference disappeared in Experiment 3.

Second, no matter which moral judgment we consider, the lack of alternative possibilities always led to more moderate moral evaluations. Across conditions, a lack of alternative possibilities made the agent less morally responsible and less blameworthy. This means that while PAP fails as an analysis of conceptual necessity, it succeeds as a principle of moral psychology. Alternative possibilities do matter for moral responsibility and blame, and their absence strongly decreases both types of moral judgments. It should be noted that the within-subject design used in the experiments might partly explain the reduction of moral responsibility and blame. For instance, in the action condition, participants first read a story about an agent who shoots another person, and they are then asked to morally evaluate the agent. Afterwards, they learn that the agent could not have done otherwise. People might have understood this obvious difference as an invitation to change their previous answer. Increasing it seems implausible and was for many participants not even possible, as they already gave very extreme ratings. Thus, the only way in which changes are possible is to reduce the initial rating. It is therefore advisable to re-run the experiments with a fully between-subject design.

Finally, it seems that philosophers strongly rely on thought experiments and believe them to make for good and reliable intuition pumps. However, as this chapter has demonstrated, these thought experiments do surprisingly poorly. First and foremost, they provide inadequate experimental vignettes. The cases that have dominated the debate about moral responsibility and free will cannot be adapted in a way such that we can test actions and omissions with one and the same cover story. Once we have dealt with the problem of finding suitable vignettes, philosophical theories are sometimes hard to translate into experimental test queries. At least the authors discussed in this paper do not make a clear distinction between moral responsibility and blame. As other empirical studies as well as Experiment 2 demonstrated, the folk do. Experimental studies should do justice to such differences. Philosophers, on the other hand, should also take notice of such differences and adapt their philosophical claims in a more precise way. And finally, philosophers' intuitions about thought experiments on alternative possibilities are not shared by the folk. Neither the point of intervention nor the intervener, both factors that have been said to matter, played a role for the folk's moral intuitions.

Going beyond the philosophical theories that were tested in this chapter, the results might inspire some more general thoughts on the relevance of alternative possibilities and their relation to moral responsibility. When philosophers think about the question of whether an agent is morally responsible or blameworthy for the consequences of her behavior, they typically think about the answer as a Yes/No matter—you either are morally responsible or you are not; you are blameworthy or you are not. This way to think about it might be mistaken though. As the results of this study suggest, the folk concepts of moral responsibility and blameworthiness come in degrees. An agent is not fully morally responsible or not at all, but she might be morally responsible and blameworthy to various degrees depending, among other things, on whether the outcome could have been avoided.

If we stick to a concept of moral responsibility that operates in a dichotomous way, the question of whether there is an Action/Omission Asymmetry is hard to answer. At best we can conclude that the folk are split into two groups. For one group of participants, alternative possibilities are not a precondition, neither for actions nor for omissions, so AOAT is false. For others, alternative possibilities are only a precondition for omissions, yet not for actions; so for this group, AOAT is true. If we believe that this is the right way to think about moral responsibility, then future research will need to address the question of what it is that distinguishes these two groups. It should, however, be noted that applying a binary scale instead of a more nuanced rating scale provides its own challenges to AOAT. Asking participants to indicate agreement or disagreement with a moral responsibility claim resulted in a proportion of agreement ratings that was indistinguishable from chance—for both actions and omissions. This suggests that, when thinking of moral responsibility as a binary concept, actions and omissions do not seem to be asymmetrical at all.

In contrast, if you believe that the folk's graded concept of moral responsibility provides an important indicator as to how we should think about moral responsibility, then it seems that we should reformulate the AOAT. Instead of asking whether alternative possibilities are necessary for actions, yet not for omissions, we should ask whether moral intuitions about actions and omissions equally strongly depend on alternative possibilities. The evidence presented suggests that they are. People's moral intuitions for actions and omissions are equally strongly dependent on alternative possibilities. Why is it that for omissions, we find moral ratings that are so close to the midpoint of the scale when the outcome could not have been avoided? The reason seems to be that people tend to hold agents less morally responsible for omissions than for actions in general. This effect is called the *Omission Effect* (Cushman et al., 2012; Willemsen and Reuter, 2016) or *Omission Bias* (Baron and Ritov, 2004; Spranca et al., 1991), and has been repeatedly reported in the empirical literature. It thus comes as no surprise that the same decline in moral responsibility will bring omissions closer to the neutral midpoint compared to actions. As a consequence, ratings close to the neutral midpoint of a rating scale should not be over-valued when determining the Action/Omission Asymmetry question. The more important and illuminating question seems to be to what extent alternative possibilities affect moral intuitions about actions and omissions, and whether actions and omissions differ in this respect.

If this interpretation of the results is convincing, then the evidence in this chapter uniformly suggests that AOAT needs to be rejected. But be it convincing or not, more empirical research is required that addresses the question of whether we should think about moral responsibility and blame in a binary or graded way. Such research will be essential for all empirical research making use of these terms, and it might make an essential contribution to the philosophical debate as well.

References

Alicke, M. (1992). Culpable causation. *Journal of Personality and Social Psychology*, 63(3), 368–78.

Baron, J. and Ritov, I. (2004). Omission bias, individual differences, and normality. *Organizational Behavior and Human Decision Processes*, 94(2), 74–85. https://doi.org/10.1016/j.obhdp.2004.03.003.

Bear, A. and Knobe, J. (2016). What do people find incompatible with causal determinism? *Cognitive Science*, 40(8), 2025–49. https://doi.org/10.1111/cogs.12314.

Blumenfeld, D. (1971). The principle of alternate possibilities. *The Journal of Philosophy*, 68(11), 339–45.

Buckwalter, W. and Turri, J. (2015). Inability and obligation in moral judgment. *PLoS ONE*. Retrieved from: http://journals.plos.org/plosone/article?id=10.1371/journal.pone.0136589.

Byrd, J. (2007). Moral responsibility and omissions. *The Philosophical Quarterly*, 57(226), 56–67.

Clarke, R. (1994). Ability and responsibility for omissions. *Philosophical Studies*, 73, 195–208.

Cushman, F., Murray, D., Gordon-McKeon, S., Wharton, S., and Greene, J. (2012). Judgment before principle: Engagement of the frontoparietal control network in condemning harms of omission. *Social Cognitive and Affective Neuroscience*, 7, 888–95.

Darley, J. M. and Shultz, T. R. (1990). Moral rules: Their content and acquisition. *Annual Review of Psychology*, 41(1), 525–56.

Dennett, D. C. (1984). *Elbow Room: The Varieties of Free Will Worth Wanting*. Oxford; New York: Clarendon Press; Oxford University Press.

Feltz, A. and Cova, F. (2014). Moral responsibility and free will: A meta-analysis. *Consciousness and Cognition*, 30, 234–46. https://doi.org/10.1016/j.concog.2014.08.012.

Fischer, John M. (1997). Responsibility, control, and omissions. *The Journal of Ethics*, 1(1): 45–64.

Fischer, J. M. and Ravizza, M. (1991). Responsibility and inevitability. *Ethics*, 101(2), 258–78. https://doi.org/10.1086/293288.

Fischer, J. M. and Ravizza, M. (2000). *Responsibility and Control: A Theory of Moral Responsibility*. Cambridge: Cambridge University Press.

Foot, P. (1967). The problem of abortion and the doctrine of the double effect. In R. F. Chadwick, D. Schroeder, and P. Foot (eds.), *Applied Ethics: Critical Concepts in Philosophy* (187–98). New York: Routledge.

Frankfurt, H. G. (1969). Alternate possibilities and moral responsibility. *The Journal of Philosophy*, 66(23), 829. https://doi.org/10.2307/2023833.

Gerstenberg, T., Goodman, N. D., Lagnado, D. A., and Tenenbaum, J. B. (2015). How, whether, why: Causal judgments as counterfactual contrasts. In D. C. Noelle et al. (eds.), *Proceedings of the 37th Annual Conference of the Cognitive Science Society* (782–7). Austin, TX: Cognitive Science Society.

Ginet, C. (1982). A defence of incompatibilism. *Philosophical Studies*, 44(3), 391–400.

Henne, P., Chituc, V., De Brigard, F., and Sinnott-Armstrong, W. (2016). An empirical refutation of 'Ought' Implies 'Can'. *Analysis*, 76(3), 283–90. https://doi.org/10.1093/analys/anw041.

Keil, G. (2007). *Willensfreiheit*. Berlin: de Gruyter.

Kominsky, J. F., Phillips, J., Gerstenberg, T., Lagnado, D., and Knobe, J. (2015). Causal superseding. *Cognition*, 137, 196–209. https://doi.org/10.1016/j.cognition.2015.01.013.

Lagnado, D. A. and Gerstenberg, T. (2017). Causation in legal and moral reasoning. In Michael R. Waldmann (ed.), *Oxford Handbook of Causal Reasoning* (565–602). Oxford: Oxford University Press.

Lagnado, D. A., Gerstenberg, T., and Zultan, R. (2013). Causal responsibility and counterfactuals. *Cognitive Science*, 37(6), 1036–73. https://doi.org/10.1111/cogs.12054.

McIntyre, Alison (1994). Guilty bystanders? On the legitimacy of duty to rescue statutes. *Philosophy and Public Affairs* 23(2), 157–91. https://doi.org/10.1111/j.1088-4963.1994.tb00009.x.

McKenna, M. and Coates, D. J. (2016). Compatibilism. In E. N. Zalta (ed.), *Stanford Encyclopedia of Philosophy*. Retrieved from: https://plato.stanford.edu/archives/win2016/entries/compatibilism/.

Malle, B. F., Guglielmo, S., and Monroe, A. E. (2014). A theory of blame. *Psychological Inquiry*, 25(2), 147–86. https://doi.org/10.1080/1047840X.2014.877340.

Miller, J. S. and Feltz, A. (2011). Frankfurt and the folk: An experimental investigation of Frankfurt-style cases. *Consciousness and Cognition* 20(2), 401–14. https://doi.org/10.1016/j.concog.2010.10.015.

Murray, D. and Lombrozo, T. (2017). Effects of manipulation on attributions of causation, free will, and moral responsibility. *Cognitive Science* 41(2), 447–81.

Nahmias, E., Morris, S., Nadelhoffer, T., and Turner, J. (2005). Surveying freedom: Folk intuitions about free will and moral responsibility. *Philosophical Psychology*, 18(5), 561–84. https://doi.org/10.1080/09515080500264180.

Nahmias, E., Morris, S., Nadelhoffer, T., and Turner, J. (2006). Is incompatibilism intuitive? *Philosophy and Phenomenological Research*, 73(1), 28–53.

Nichols, S. (2004). The folk psychology of free will: Fits and starts. *Mind & Language*, 19(5), 473–502.

O'Connor, T. (2016). Free will. In E. N. Zalta (ed.), *Stanford Encyclopedia of Philosophy*. Retrieved from: https://plato.stanford.edu/archives/sum2016/entries/freewill/.

Sarkissian, H., Chatterjee, A., De Brigard, F., Knobe, J., Nichols, S., and Sirker, S. (2010). Is belief in free will a cultural universal? *Mind & Language*, 25(3), 346–58.

Sartorio, C. (2005). A new asymmetry between actions and omissions. *Noûs*, 39(3), 460–82.

Spranca, M., Minsk, E., and Baron, J. (1991). Omission and commission in judgment and choice. *Journal of Experimental Social Psychology*, 27, 75–105.

Turri, J. (2017). Compatibilism can be natural. *Consciousness and Cognition*, 51, 68–81. https://doi.org/10.1016/j.concog.2017.01.018.

van Inwagen, P. (1975). The incompatibility of free will and determinism. *Philosophical Studies*, 27(3), 185–99.

van Inwagen, P. (1983). *An Essay on Free Will*. Oxford: Clarendon Press.

van Inwagen, P. (1999). Moral responsibility, determinism, and the ability to do otherwise. *The Journal of Ethics*, 3, 341–50.

Wegner, D. (2003). *The Illusion of Conscious Will*. Cambridge, MA: MIT Press.

Willemsen, P. and Reuter, K. (2016). Is there really an omission effect? *Philosophical Psychology*, 29(8), 1142–59. https://doi.org/10.1080/09515089.2016.1225194.

Zimmerman, M. J. (1988). *An Essay on Moral Responsibility*. Totowa, NJ: Rowman & Littlefield.

11

Intuitive Expertise and
Irrelevant Options

Alex Wiegmann
University of Göttingen and Ruhr-University Bochum[1]

Joachim Horvath
Ruhr-University Bochum

Karina Meyer
University of Göttingen

1. Introduction

Thought experiments play an important role in moral philosophy. Their main methodological purposes are to develop and evaluate moral theories. With regard to the developing aspect, moral dilemmas are used to trigger moral intuitions, and these intuitions can guide the moral philosopher toward a normative moral theory.[2] As an example, consider the methodology of a leading moral philosopher, Frances Kamm (2007, p. 5):

Consider as many case-based judgments of yours as prove necessary. Do not ignore some case-based judgments, assuming they are errors,

---

[1] "Alex Wiegmann and Joachim Horvath contributed equally to this paper and should be regarded as joint first authors." Please also note that this change has ramifications for the editors' introduction, where our chapter should then be referred to as "Alex Wiegmann and colleagues", and, of course, for the table of contents as well.

[2] In this chapter, we intend to use the term 'intuition' in a largely theory-neutral way. For example, we intend to stay neutral on whether intuitions in this sense are just ordinary judgments (see, e.g., Machery, 2017) or a distinctive kind of mental states (see, e.g., Bengson, 2015; Chudnoff, 2013). Keeping the label 'intuition' still seems helpful, because much of the relevant philosophical and metaphilosophical discussion is cast in this way.

Alex Wiegmann, Joachim Horvath, and Karina Meyer, *Intuitive Expertise and Irrelevant Options* In: *Oxford Studies in Experimental Philosophy*. Edited by: Tania Lombrozo, Joshua Knobe, and Shaun Nichols, Oxford University Press (2020).
DOI: 10.1093/oso/9780198852407.003.0012

just because they conflict with simple or intuitively plausible principles that account for some subset of your case-based judgments. Work on the assumption that a different principle can account for all of the judgments. Be prepared to be surprised at what this principle is. Remember that this principle can be simple, even though it is discovered by considering many complex cases. (If the principle is complex, this would not undermine the claim that people have intuitive judgments in accord with it, since people need not be conscious of the principle to have case-based intuitive judgments.)

In a related way, thought experiments can be used to evaluate normative moral theories. If, for example, a normative moral theory is applied to concrete cases and tells us that the right action—according to the theory—stands in sharp contrast to our moral intuitions, this fact would strongly count against the theory. This kind of criticism constitutes one of the strongest arguments against consequentialist, especially utilitarian, moral theories (cf. Hooker, 2000).

Consequentialism tells us, roughly, that the morally right act is the one that has the best consequences—impartially considered. Although this principle may sound plausible in the abstract, it can sometimes prescribe actions that most lay people and moral philosophers consider morally wrong. One of the most popular thought experiments in this vein is a moral dilemma called *push dilemma*, or *footbridge dilemma* (cf. Thomson, 1985). In this kind of scenario, an out-of-control trolley is about to run over and thereby kill five people. The only possibility to save the five people consists in pushing a heavy stranger from a bridge onto the tracks, so that the heavy stranger, who will die in the collision, stops the trolley. However, most lay people (cf. Waldmann et al., 2012) and philosophers (cf. Schwitzgebel and Cushman, 2012, 2015) consider this action as morally wrong—although it brings about the best consequences. Since this thought experiment is considered as a strong counterexample to consequentialist moral theories, it does not come as a surprise that supporters of consequentialism tried to debunk the widely shared intuition that pushing the heavy man would be morally wrong. For example, Unger (1992, 1996) claims that intuitions about the push dilemma are not robust and can be changed by adding more options. To support this claim, he introduces the following case, labeled *The Heavy Skater*:

By sheer accident, an empty trolley, nobody aboard, is starting to roll down a certain track. Now, if you *do nothing about* the situation, your *first* option, then, in a couple of minutes, it will run over and kill six innocents who, through no fault of their own, are trapped down the line (just beyond an "elbow" in the track). [...] Regarding their plight, you have *one other* option: Further up the track, near where the trolley's starting to move, there's a path crossing the main track and, on it, there's a very heavy man on roller skates. If you turn a remote control dial, you'll start up the skates, you'll send him in front of the trolley, and he'll be a trolley-stopper. But, the man will be crushed to death by the trolley he then stops.   (Unger, 1996, p. 91)

Unger believes that most people consider redirecting the heavy skater as morally wrong. However, he also thinks that this intuition would change if more options were added to the scenario, as in the following case, which we will label *Four Options* (Unger, 1996, p. 90; see Figure 11.1):

By sheer accident, an empty trolley, nobody aboard, is starting to roll down a certain track. Now, if you *do nothing about* the situation, your *first* option, then, in a couple of minutes, it will run over and kill six innocents who, through no fault of their own, are trapped down the line. [...] Regarding their plight, you have *three other* options: On your *second option*, if you push a remote control button, you'll change the position of a switch-track, switch A, and, before it gets to the six, the trolley will go onto another line, on the left-hand side of switch A's fork. On that line, three other innocents are trapped and, if you change switch A, the trolley will roll over them. [...] On your *third option*, you'll flip a remote control toggle and change the position of another switch, switch B. Then, a very light trolley that's rolling along another track, the Feed Track, will shift onto B's lower fork. As two pretty heavy people are trapped in this light trolley, after going down this lower fork the vehicle won't only collide with the onrushing empty trolley, but, owing to the combined weight of its unwilling passengers, the collision will derail the first trolley and both trolleys will go into an uninhabited area. Still, the two trapped passengers will die in the collision. On the other hand, if you don't change switch B, the lightweight trolley will go along B's upper fork and, then, it will bypass the empty trolley, and its

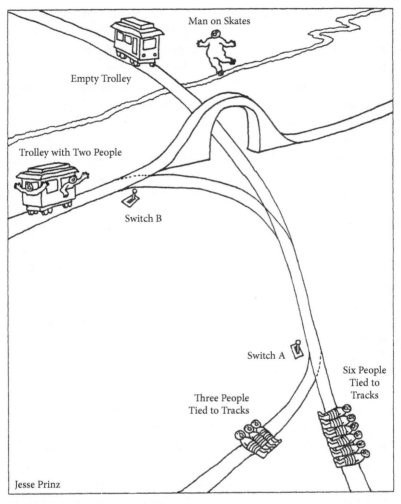

Figure 11.1 "Diagram for the Switches and the Skates" (original illustration of the several-option case).

Source: Reprinted by permission of Oxford University Press, USA from *Living High and Letting Die: Our Illusion of Innocence* (p. 89), by Peter Unger, 1996, New York: Oxford University Press.

two passengers won't die soon. [...] Finally, you have a *fourth option*: Further up the track, near where the trolley's starting to move, there's a path crossing the main track and, on it, there's a very heavy man on roller skates. If you turn a remote control dial, you'll start up the skates, you'll send him in front of the trolley, and he'll be a trolley-stopper. But, the man will be crushed to death by the trolley he then stops.

In this several-option case, Unger claims most people would consider redirecting the heavy skater as the morally right thing to do.

Wiegmann and Meyer (2015) tested Unger's idea with a push dilemma (labeled *Two Options*) and a several-option scenario (labeled *Six Options*) that also included the option to push a heavy stranger from a bridge (see Figure 11.2).[3] These two scenarios were presented following each other in randomized order. The two main findings were: First, when one considers only the scenarios that were presented first, participants were more likely to choose the push option in Six Options than in Two Options. Second, participants' responses to the first scenario influenced their responses to the second scenario insofar as they tended to choose the same option for both scenarios. For example, when participants received Two Options after Six Options, they were more likely to choose the push option in both scenarios than when Two Options was presented first.

Since adding intermediate options to the push dilemma arguably should not increase participants' moral preferences for pushing the heavy man from the bridge, the addition of intermediate options works as a morally irrelevant factor here (see, e.g., Huber et al., 1982, for only one of several non-moral settings in which adding an option increases

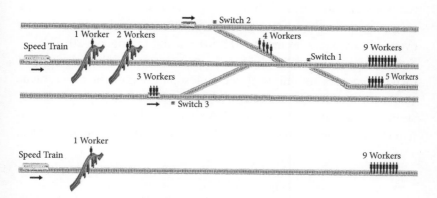

Figure 11.2 Illustration of the six-option case (on top) and the two-option case (below).
Source: Wiegmann and Meyer, 2015 (copyright by Alex Wiegmann and Karina Meyer).

---

[3] For another study testing Unger's claim, see Weijers (2015) and Weijers et al. (ms).

the choices for an option that has been available before; more on this in Section 4). Hence, the paradigm of two-option versus several-option cases provides a framework for testing whether the moral intuitions of lay people and experts are influenced by morally irrelevant factors. An Unger-style several-option scenario is also a less familiar version of the standard *trolley cases*, since it has triggered comparatively little discussion so far.[4] This may help to forestall worries about testing expert ethicists with all-too-familiar cases, which may not fully engage their intuitive expertise (cf. Horvath and Wiegmann, 2016; Rini, 2015).

2. Intuitive Expertise and the Expertise Defense

Since intuitive expertise is a well-researched psychological phenomenon in its own right (see, e.g., Kahneman and Klein, 2009), doing experiments on Unger's several-option case with experts in moral philosophy would require no special motivation or justification. But as it happens, the issue of intuitive expertise also turns out to be vitally important for recent debates in philosophical methodology. These debates were mainly triggered by the new movement of *experimental philosophy*, which started its life in the early 2000s with an empirical investigation of intuitions about philosophical thought experiments, in particular by using survey-based methods from psychology and the social sciences (for an overview, see, e.g., Alexander, 2012; Sytsma and Livengood, 2016).[5]

A number of critical findings from experimental philosophy suggest that lay people's intuitions about philosophical thought experiments vary with factors that are seemingly irrelevant to their proper evaluation, such as cultural background (Machery et al., 2004), affective content (Nichols and Knobe, 2007), order of presentation (Liao et al., 2012;

---

[4] Further evidence for this claim might be that Unger's original presentation of several-option cases in "Causing and Preventing Serious Harm" (1992) has only ten citations on Google Scholar, and Kamm's critical discussion "Grouping and the Imposition of Loss" (1998) has only two citations (as of September 6, 2018). It should be noted that the relevant material by Unger and Kamm was later included in monographs (Kamm, 2007; Unger, 1996) that have far higher citation rates. However, the issue of several-option cases does not seem to be among the more influential themes from these two books.

[5] However, experimental philosophy has broadened its scope considerably since its beginnings (see, e.g., Machery and O'Neill, 2014; Sytsma and Livengood, 2016).

Swain et al., 2008), or heritable personality traits (Feltz and Cokely, 2009). On the basis of these and related findings, experimental philosophers of a "restrictionist" stripe have challenged the epistemic trustworthiness of intuitions about philosophical thought experiment cases (see, e.g., Alexander et al., 2009; Alexander and Weinberg, 2007; Feltz and Cokely, 2012; Machery, 2017). If successful, this challenge might have far-reaching consequences for a number of key philosophical debates, for example, about knowledge or free will, since it is not clear how these debates should proceed without appeals to intuitions about thought experiments.[6]

It is no wonder, then, that other philosophers have forcefully responded to the experimental restrictionist challenge in various ways (see, e.g., Horvath, 2010; Kauppinen, 2007; Ludwig, 2007; Nagel, 2012; Sosa, 2007, 2009). An especially interesting and much-discussed response is the so-called *expertise defense* (for recent surveys, see Horvath and Wiegmann, 2016; Nado, 2014). The basic idea is that professional philosophers are experts concerning the intuitive evaluation of thought experiment cases. Based on this idea, problematic results about lay people's intuitions are regarded as irrelevant to philosophical practice, because professional philosophers are expected to be largely resistant to the influence of irrelevant factors on their thought experiment intuitions (see, e.g., Devitt, 2011; Hales, 2006; Horvath, 2010; Ludwig, 2007; Williamson, 2011).

There are different ways of motivating the expertise defense, and thus different ways of providing prima facie support for the crucial claim that the intuitions of professional philosophers are resistant to the influence of irrelevant factors because of their intuitive expertise in evaluating thought experiment cases.

One way is by appealing to an analogy between professional philosophers and the professional practitioners of other disciplines, such as lawyers, mathematicians, or physicists (cf. Hales, 2006; Ludwig, 2007; Sorensen, 2014; Williamson, 2005, 2007, 2011). Since the latter are rightly regarded as experts in their field, philosophers should be regarded as experts in their own field as well, which typically includes the intuitive evaluation of thought experiment cases in their area of expertise.

---

[6] For skepticism about the methodological centrality of intuitions about thought experiments in philosophy, see Cappelen (2012) and Deutsch (2015); see Nado (2016) for a recent reply.

Another way is to appeal to a general presumption of expertise for professional practitioners of any respectable intellectual discipline, including philosophy (cf. Horvath, 2010; Williamson, 2011). Although this general presumption is defeasible, even by empirical evidence, it would still suffice to shift the burden of proof to the critics of philosophers' intuitive expertise.

A third way of supporting the expertise defense appeals to specific cognitive skills of professional philosophers that might explain why their intuitions are less susceptible to the influence of irrelevant factors than those of lay people. For example, it seems plausible that professional philosophers are more sensitive to various conceptual distinctions that are crucial for the evaluation of thought experiment cases in their area of expertise (cf. Hofmann, 2010; Horvath, 2010; Ludwig, 2007; Williamson, 2007).

None of these ways of supporting the expertise defense is uncontroversial, and each faces problems and challenges of its own (for discussion, see Hitchcock, 2012; Horvath, 2010; Nado, 2015; Rini, 2014; Weinberg et al., 2010). However, one point deserves special attention: What an argument in support of the expertise defense needs to show is not just that philosophers are experts in one sense or other—which they surely are—but rather that they have the quite specific intuitive expertise for evaluating philosophical thought experiments, an expertise of a kind that would make their intuitions largely resistant to the influence of irrelevant factors (Weinberg et al., 2010).

There are direct and indirect strategies for assessing this key claim about philosophers' intuitive expertise (Schulz et al., 2011). Indirect strategies, such as the one by Weinberg et al. (2010), rely on general findings about genuine expertise in other fields or disciplines (see, e.g., Ericsson et al., 2006). On that basis, they suggest various ampliative inferences from general findings about expertise to the alleged intuitive expertise of professional philosophers. A problem with indirect strategies of this kind is that paradigm cases of intuitive expertise in psychology, such as fire ground commanders (Klein et al., 1986), or nurses in neonatal intensive care units (Crandall and Getchell-Reiter, 1993), are strikingly disanalogous to thought-experimenting philosophers (cf. Horvath and Wiegmann, 2016). So, at the present stage of the debate, direct strategies for assessing the expertise defense seem more promising, that is, strategies that rely on experimental studies with professional philosophers.

In light of the experimental restrictionist challenge, the most straightforward direct strategy would be to test whether the intuitions of professional philosophers are equally susceptible to the influence of irrelevant factors as those of lay people (for somewhat different approaches, see, e.g., Beebe and Monaghan, 2018; Carter et al., 2015; Carter et al., ms; Horvath and Wiegmann, 2016; Machery, 2012; Sytsma and Machery, 2010). So far, there are only a few studies of this kind (Hitchcock and Knobe, 2009; Schulz et al., 2011; Schwitzgebel and Cushman, 2012, 2015; Tobia, Buckwalter, and Stich, 2013; Tobia, Chapman, and Stich, 2013), and we will briefly summarize their main results in the following.

To begin with, the study by Hitchcock and Knobe (2009) investigates intuitive judgments about actual causation, that is, judgments of the form "Peter caused the window to break." With respect to judgments of this kind, Hitchcock and Knobe found that "events that involve norm violations are especially likely to be selected as causes" (2009, p. 605), even by the 327 professional philosophers who took part in their study. Since facts about causation are often regarded as paradigms of objective facts—or at least as facts that are independent of normative considerations—this result might indicate that expert intuitions about actual causation vary with the irrelevant factor of normative valence (however, the discussion by Hitchcock and Knobe suggests that this interpretation would be controversial).

The study by Schulz et al. (2011) indicates that the personality trait *extraversion*—more precisely, the facet *warmth* of this personality trait—predicts compatibilist intuitions about free will even in people who are familiar with the philosophical debate about free will. However, their "Free Will Skill Test" mainly tracks rather superficial or merely historical knowledge about the philosophical debate, such as whether "Arthur Schopenhauer said that there is definitely free will" (2011, p. 1730). At best, the Free Will Skill Test thus helps to exclude participants who have little or no familiarity with the philosophical debate about free will. It is doubtful whether the study really investigates what seems most relevant for the expertise defense, namely, the intuitive expertise of professional philosophers who specialize on free will.

Schwitzgebel and Cushman (2012) present evidence that order effects about ethical cases are about as large in professional philosophers and expert ethicists as in lay people (inter alia, they studied trolley cases that are similar to those we used in our own experiment—see Section 3). In addition, they found that professional philosophers—even those who specialize in ethics—were more likely than lay people to endorse general moral principles that are in line with their order-sensitive judgments about particular cases. Schwitzgebel and Cushman suggest that this finding might be explained by philosophers' stronger tendency for post hoc rationalization.

In a follow-up study, Schwitzgebel and Cushman (2015) replicated their earlier finding that the intuitive case judgments of expert ethicists are no less sensitive to order effects than those of lay people. Their follow-up study also addresses a number of worries about their earlier study, for example, that the antecedent familiarity of expert ethicists with trolley cases or the lack of reflection in standard experimental settings might have a significant effect on their results. However, Schwitzgebel and Cushman found that neither a forced delay in combination with the appeal to reflect on the scenario, nor antecedent familiarity with the relevant philosophical issues, nor self-reported stability of relevant views, and not even self-reported expertise on the specific issues in question, had any tendency to reduce order effects in expert ethicists.

Tobia, Buckwalter, and Stich (2013) found that professional philosophers respond differently to various ethical cases depending on whether the scenario is described in a first-person or third-person way—an instance of the so-called *actor–observer bias*. For example, they investigated a standard trolley case where one option is to do nothing—and five people will be killed—and the other option is to direct the trolley to another track—and only one person will be killed. Professional philosophers' agreement that redirecting the trolley is permissible was much higher in the first-person condition (89%) than in the third-person condition (64%). Strikingly, this was almost the exact reversal of the ratings of lay people, who exhibited a higher rate of agreement in the third-person condition (90%) than in the first-person condition (65%).

The study by Tobia, Chapman, and Stich (2013) confirms the susceptibility of professional philosophers' moral intuitions to actor–observer bias, although with a set of different, "purity-related" scenarios. In addition to that, they also found that even the ratings of professional philosophers were significantly influenced by the smell of Lysol, which is strongly associated with cleanliness. The direction of the effect was once again somewhat different in professional philosophers than in lay people.

To conclude, the summarized studies do not lend much support to the expertise defense, and all of them raise at least a modicum of doubt about the intuitive expertise of professional philosophers. This may look like a devastating result for the expertise defense. However, so far only a handful of studies bear directly on the question whether professional philosophers' intuitions are more resistant to the influence of irrelevant factors than those of lay people. Therefore, more work is needed before we can draw any robust conclusions about the precise contours and limitations of philosophers' intuitive expertise (see also Buckwalter, 2016; De Cruz, 2015; Horvath and Wiegmann, 2016; Nado, 2015).

Our present study provides some of this additional work, and it does not turn out to be good news for the expertise defense. Basically, our study confirms the growing experimental consensus that the moral intuitions of philosophical experts are no less susceptible to order effects than those of lay people. Moreover, we have identified a new irrelevant factor that influences the intuitions of expert ethicists to a comparable or even greater degree than those of lay people: the availability of irrelevant additional options.

3. Experiment

The data is available online at https://osf.io/8ycfh/.

3.1 Participants

Overall, the data of 279 participants were included in our main analysis. The mean age was 34 years, 62% identified as male, 34% as female, and the remaining participants as *other* or *prefer not to say*. In this sample, 134 participants were identified as expert participants (mean age was 36 years; 68% identified as male, 25% as female, and 7% as *other* or *prefer not to say*) and 145 as lay participants (mean age 31 years; 57% male, 43% female).

Our expert participants were recruited via a call for participation that included a link which directed the participants to the online experiment. The call was distributed on an electronic mailing list for philosophers (PHILOS-L), on the Experimental Philosophy Blog (http://philosophycommons.typepad.com/xphi/), and on PEA Soup (http://peasoup.us), a blog that specializes in ethics. In order to be included as expert participants, participants had to indicate, first, that they have a PhD (64%) or MA (36%) in philosophy and, second, that moral philosophy or ethics is one of their areas of specialization (62%) or competence (38%). Furthermore, we excluded the data of participants who did not complete the survey, completed it in less than 90 seconds, or failed to answer an easy transitivity question correctly. Out of initially 278 participants, 134 met these criteria, which were not mentioned in the call for participation or during the survey.

Lay participants were recruited via a database located in the UK (Prolific Academics; cf. Palan and Schitter, 2018). Each participant received a compensation of £0.50. To ensure that lay participants differ strongly from expert participants in their level of philosophical expertise, we only included the data of participants who indicated that they had no prior experience with philosophy, or only some experience in school but not in university, and who had not participated in a trolley-style experiment before. Moreover, we excluded the data of participants who did not complete the survey, completed it in less than 90 seconds, or failed to answer an easy transitivity question correctly. Out of initially 485 participants, 145 met these criteria, which were not mentioned in the call for participation or during the survey.[7]

3.2 Design and procedure

The experiment was conducted on the Internet. Upon clicking on a link that participants received via email or in a blog post (experts), or on the Prolific Academics page (lay people), they were redirected to a website with the experiment. Participants were first presented with general

---

[7] The vast majority of excluded lay participants were excluded because they indicated that they had participated in a trolley-style experiment before.

instructions. These instructions familiarized them with the question mode, asked them to read the subsequent case descriptions carefully, and appealed to them to take the task seriously. After that, participants were randomly assigned to one of two conditions. In one condition, they saw Two Options first and then Six Options, and in the other condition, they saw Six Options first and then Two Options. Here is the exact wording of Two Options:

On the test ground of a modern railroad property an unmanned speed-train (that normally can be remote-controlled) is out of control due to a technical defect. This speed-train is heading towards nine railroad workers that are maintaining the tracks.[8] Since these workers are wearing a new type of hearing protection, they would not notice the speed-train on time and hence would be run over by it. Carl, an employee of the rail track control center, recognizes the upcoming accident. However, it is not possible to stop the train on time any more.

Carl can choose between exactly two options:

Option 1: Carl could run to a nearby bridge on which a heavy worker is standing and push this worker from the bridge. Thereby this worker would fall on the tracks and collide with the speed-train. Due to the collision with the heavy worker (Carl himself would not be heavy enough to stop the train) the speed-train would stop before it reaches the nine workers. The heavy worker would lose his life due to the collision.

Option 2: Carl could do nothing. In this case the nine workers would be run over by the speed-train and lose their lives in this accident.

And here is the exact wording of Six Options:

On the test ground of a modern railroad property an unmanned speed-train (that normally can be remote-controlled) is out of control due to a technical defect. This speed-train is heading towards nine railroad

---

[8] Usually, only five lives are at stake in trolley-style cases. We raised the number to nine lives to keep it parallel to the six-option case, in which we need a higher number to implement a variety of intermediate options, as suggested by Unger (Section 2). Moreover, the net number of lives that can be saved by redirecting the train (Option 5 below) is still four lives (5 versus 9 lives), which is the standard in the literature.

workers that are maintaining the tracks. Since these workers are wearing a new type of hearing protection, they would not notice the speed-train on time and hence would be run over by it. Carl, an employee of the rail track control center, recognizes the upcoming accident. However, it is not possible to stop the train on time any more.

Carl can choose between exactly six options:

Option 1: Carl could run to the nearby, *left bridge* on which a heavy worker is standing and push this worker from the bridge. Thereby this worker would fall on the tracks and collide with the speed-train. Due to the collision with the heavy worker (Carl himself would not be heavy enough to stop the train) the speed-train would stop before it reaches the nine workers. The heavy worker would lose his life due to the collision.

Option 2: Carl could push a button that would open a trap door and thereby causing two workers on top of the *right bridge* to fall on the tracks. The speed-train would collide with the two workers and be stopped before it reaches the nine workers. The two workers would lose their lives due to the collision.

Option 3: Carl could throw *Switch 3* and thereby redirect a train carrying three workers from the lower parallel track onto the main track. The speed-train would collide with this train and be stopped before it reaches the nine workers. The three workers on the train would lose their lives due to the collision.

Option 4: Carl could throw *Switch 2* and thereby redirect an empty train from the upper parallel track onto the main track. The speed-train would collide with this train and be stopped before it reaches the nine workers. On its way to the main track the empty train would run over four workers (wearing the novel hearing protection). The four workers would lose their lives due to the collision.

Option 5: Carl could throw *Switch 1* and thereby redirect the speed-train from the main track onto a parallel track before it reaches the nine workers. On the parallel track the speed train would run over five workers (wearing the novel hearing protection). The five workers would lose their lives due to the collision.

Option 6: Carl could do nothing. In this case the nine workers would be run over by the speed-train and lose their lives in this accident.

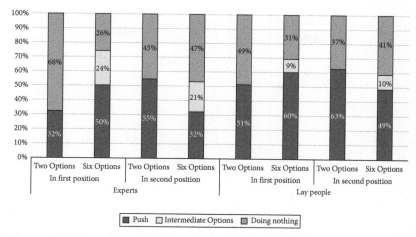

Figure 11.3 Participants' choices as a function of scenario, order of presentation, and level of expertise.

Both case descriptions were accompanied by an illustration (Figure 11.2) of the respective initial situation. The test question asked participants to indicate which of the available options Carl should choose. On the final page, we asked a number of demographic questions and questions concerning the participants' level of philosophical education and expertise.

3.3 Results

The results of the experiment are summarized in Figure 11.3 and Table 11.1.

3.3.1 All participants

3.3.1.1 *Effect of additional options*

Two Options first vs. Six Options first. Before we compare the number of participants who chose the push option, as compared to doing nothing, in Two Options presented first versus Six Options presented first, we need to decide whether and how we take the intermediate options in Six Options into account. Depending on one's first-order moral views, the intermediate options could maybe be divided and simply added to the two extreme options for the purposes of analysis in one way or

Table 11.1 Participants' choices (absolute numbers) as a function of scenario, order of presentation, and level of expertise.

	Experts				Lay people			
	In first position		In second position		In first position		In second position	
	Two Options	Six Options	Two Options	Six Options	Two Options	Six Options	Two Options	Six Options
Push	22	33	36	22	36	45	47	34
Doing nothing	46	17	30	32	34	23	28	29
Option 2	–	2	–	1	–	2	–	4
Option 3	–	3	–	3	–	3	–	1
Option 4	–	4	–	1	–	0	–	1
Option 5	–	7	–	9	–	2	–	1

another. For instance, Frances Kamm (2007) would presumably only consider doing nothing and redirecting the threatening trolley as morally permissible. Hence, one could add the numbers for doing nothing and redirecting the trolley on the one side (and label this category as *permissible options*), and the numbers for all other options on the other side (and label this category as *impermissible options*). Then, one could analyze whether the proportions of participants choosing permissible versus impermissible options differ between Two Options and Six Options.

To avoid such tricky classification issues, we will perform the most conservative analysis, namely adding all choices of intermediate options to the option of doing nothing, and then testing whether the proportion of participants choosing the push option is still significantly higher in Six Options than in Two Options. This approach stacks the deck in favor of the participants and thus provides an unambiguous measure for testing whether their judgments exhibit an irrational pattern, namely, an increase of the ratings for the push option if more competing options are available (see Section 4.1 for discussion).

When participants were presented with Two Options first, 42% (58 out of 138) chose the push option, while 58% (80 out of 138) preferred not to push. When Six Options was presented first, 55% of the participants chose the push option (78 out of 141) and 45% (63 out of 141) preferred not to push. We built a binary logistic regression model to assess the influence of level of expertise, the number of available options, and the interaction thereof. The model $(\chi^2_{3,\ N=279} = 11.56,\ p = .009)$ is described in Table 11.2 and provides suggestive evidence that level of

Table 11.2 Coefficients of the model predicting whether a participant chooses the push option.

	B	S.E.	Wald	df	Sig.	Exp(B)	95% C.I. for Exp(B)
Included							
Level of expertise	−0.6.	0.245	5.989	1	0.014	0.549	[0.339; 0.887]
Number of options	0.543	0.245	4.902	1	0.027	1.721	[1.064; 2.783]
Expertise * options	0.389	0.49	0.63	1	0.427	1.476	[0.564; 3.86]
Constant	−0.069	0.123	0.314	1	0.575	0.934	

Note: $R^2 = .04$ (Cox and Snell). Model $\chi^2_{3,\ N=279} = 11.558, p = .009$.

Contrast coding: lay subjects = −.5, philosophers =.5; Two Options = −.5, Six Options =.5.

expertise and number of options have an influence on choosing or not choosing the push option, with philosophers being less likely to choose the push option, as compared to lay subjects, and participants being more likely to choose the push option in Six Options than in Two Options (p =.014 for level of expertise and p =.027 for number of options). The interaction between level of expertise and number of options was not significant (p =.427), suggesting that the influence of the number of options does not differ between lay and expert subjects.

3.3.1.2 Order effects

Two Options. When participants were presented with Two Options first, 42% (58 out of 138) chose the push option, while 58% (80 out of 138) preferred doing nothing. When Two Options was presented after Six Options, 59% (83 out of 141) chose the push option, while 41% (58 out of 141) preferred doing nothing. We again built a binary logistic regression model to assess the influence of level of expertise, order of presentation, and the interaction thereof. The model ($\chi^2_{3, N=279}$ = 14.09, p =.003) is described in Table 11.3 and provides suggestive evidence that level of expertise and order of presentation both have an influence on choosing or not choosing the push option in Two Options, with philosophers being less likely to choose the push option in Two Options, as compared to lay subjects, and participants being more likely to choose the push option in Two Options if Two Options is presented after Six Options (p =.022 for level of expertise and p =.005 for order of presentation). The interaction between level of expertise and order of presentation was not

Table 11.3 Coefficients of the model predicting whether a participant chooses the push option in Two Options.

	B	S.E.	Wald	df	Sig.	Exp(B)	95% C.I. for Exp(B)
Included							
Level of expertise	−0.565	0.246	5.269	1	0.022	0.568	[0.351; 0.921]
Position	0.69	0.246	7.862	1	0.005	1.994	[1.231; 3.231]
Expertise * position	0.459	0.492	0.869	1	0.351	1.583	[0.603; 4.155]
Constant	0.005	0.123	0.002	1	0.968	1.005	

Note: R^2 = .05 (Cox and Snell). Model $\chi^2_{3, N=279}$ = 14.093, p =.003.

Contrast coding: lay subjects = −.5, philosophers =.5; Two Options first = −.5, Six Options first =.5.

significant ($p =.351$), suggesting that the influence of order of presentation does not differ between lay and expert subjects.

Six Options. When participants were presented with Six Options first, 55% (78 out of 141) chose the push option, while 28% (40 out of 141) preferred doing nothing and 16% (23 out of 141) chose an intermediate option. When Six Options was presented after Two Options, 41% (56 out of 138) chose the push option, while 44% (61 out of 138) preferred doing nothing and 15% (21 out of 138) chose an intermediate option. To assess whether the order of presentation has an influence on participants moral judgments we will use the same classification for the intermediate options as we did before, namely, treating the push option as one category and all other options as the other category and then testing whether the proportion of participants choosing the push option differs as a function of order of presentation.

We again built a binary logistic regression model to assess the influence of level of expertise, order of presentation, and the interaction thereof. The model ($\chi^2_{3,\,N=279} = 11.3$, $p =.01$) is described in Table 11.4 and provides suggestive evidence that level of expertise and order of presentation both have an influence on choosing or not choosing the push option in Two Options, with philosophers being less likely to choose the push option in Six Options, as compared to lay subjects, and participants being more likely to choose the push option in Six Options if Six Options is presented before Two Options ($p =.027$ for level of

Table 11.4 Coefficients of the model predicting whether a participant chooses the push option in Six Options.

	B	S.E.	Wald	df	Sig.	Exp(B)	95% C.I. for Exp(B)
Included							
Level of expertise	−0.543	0.245	4.902	1	0.027	0.581	[0.359; 0.94]
Position	−0.6	0.245	5.989	1	0.014	0.549	[0.339; 0.887]
Expertise * position	−0.275	0.490	0.314	1	0.575	0.76	[0.29; 1.986]
Constant	−0.097	0.123	0.63	1	0.427	0.907	

Note: $R^2 = .04$ (Cox & Snell). Model $\chi 2_{3,\,N=279} = 11.3$, $p =.01$.

Contrast coding: lay subjects $= -.5$, philosophers $=.5$; Six Options first $= -.5$, Two Options first $=.5$.

expertise and p =.014 for order of presentation). The interaction between level of expertise and order of presentation was not significant (p =.575), suggesting that the influence of order of presentation does not differ between lay and expert subjects.

3.3.2 Expert participants

3.3.2.1 Effect of additional options

Two Options first vs. Six Options first. We will use the same classification for the intermediate options as we did before, namely, treating the push option as one category and all other options as the other category. When expert participants were presented with Two Options first, 32% of them (22 out of 68) chose the push option, while 68% (46 out of 68) preferred not to push. When Six Options was presented first, 50% of the expert participants chose the push option (33 out of 66) and 50% (33 out of 66) preferred not to push. This difference was significant, $\chi^2_{1, N=134}$ = 4.31, p =.038, V =.18, providing suggestive evidence that expert participants are more likely to choose the push option, as compared to doing nothing, in Six Options first.

3.3.2.2 Order effects

Two Options. When expert participants were presented with Two Options first, 32% (22 out of 68) chose the push option, while 68% (46 out of 68) preferred doing nothing. When Two Options was presented after Six Options, 55% (36 out of 66) chose the push option, while 45% (30 out of 66) preferred doing nothing. This difference was statistically significant, $\chi^2_{1, N=134}$ = 6.72, p =.01, V =.22, providing suggestive evidence that presenting Six Options first increases the probability of participants choosing the push option in a subsequent presentation of Two Options.

Six Options. When expert participants were presented with Six Options first, 50% (33 out of 66) chose the push option, while 26% (17 out of 66) preferred doing nothing and 24% (16 out of 66) chose an intermediate option. When Six Options was presented after Two Options, 32% (22 out of 68) chose the push option, while 47% (32 out of 68) preferred doing nothing and 21% (14 out of 68) chose an intermediate option.

To assess whether participants' choices in Six Options are affected by being presented with Two Options first, we will use the same classification for the intermediate options as we did before, namely, treating the push option as one category and all other options as the other category and then testing whether the proportion of participants choosing the push option differs as a function of order of presentation.[9] When Six Options was presented first, 50% of the expert participants chose the push option (33 out of 66), while also 50% (33 out of 66) preferred not to push. When Six Options was presented second, 32% of the expert participants chose the push option (22 out of 68), while 68% (46 out of 68) preferred not to push. This difference was significant, $\chi^2_{1, N=134} = 4.31$, $p = .038$, $V = 0.18$, providing suggestive evidence that presenting Two Options first decreases the probability of expert participants choosing the push option in a subsequent presentation of Six Options.[10]

3.3.3 Lay participants
3.3.3.1 Effect of additional options
Two Options first vs. Six Options first. First, we will use the same classification for the intermediate options as we did before, namely, treating the push option as one category and all other options as the other category. When lay participants were presented with Two Options first, 51% of them (36 out of 70) chose the push option, while 49% (34 out of 70) preferred doing nothing. When Six Options was presented first, 60% of the lay participants chose the push option (45 out of 75) and 40%

---

[9] If we include the intermediate options as a third category, the same inference could be drawn ($\chi^2_{2, N=134} = 6.90$, $p = .031$, $V = .16$), namely, that the data provide suggestive evidence that order of presentation affected participants' choices.

[10] The fact that the statistical values for the comparison of Six Options first vs. Six Options second are identical with the ones for the comparison of Two Options first vs. Six Options first does not seem to be a coincidence. A closer look at individual responses revealed that philosophers were perfectly consistent in their responses when first judging Two Options and then Six Options: Every single philosopher who chose the push option in Two Options also chose the push option in Six Options, and whenever a philosopher did not choose the push option in Two Options, she did not do so in Six Options either. This perfectly consistent pattern suggests that philosophers might have expertise in giving consistent responses (see also Section 4).

(30 out of 75) preferred not to push. This increase in choosing the push option in Six Options was not significant, $\chi^2_{1, N=145} = 1.08$, $p = .30$, $V = .09$.

3.3.3.2 Order effects

Two Options. When lay participants were presented with Two Options first, 51% (36 out of 70) chose the push option, while 49% (34 out of 70) chose doing nothing. When Two Options was presented after Six Options, 63% (47 out of 75) chose the push option,[11] while 37% (28 out of 75) preferred doing nothing. This difference was not significant, $\chi^2_{1, N=145} = 1.87$, $p = .17$, $V = .11$.

Six Options. When lay participants were presented with Six Options first, 60% (45 out of 75) chose the push option, while 31% (23 out of 75) preferred doing nothing and 9% (7 out of 75) chose an intermediate option. When Six Options was presented after Two Options, 49% (34 out of 70) chose the push option, while 41% (29 out of 70) preferred doing nothing and 10% (7 out of 70) chose an intermediate option.

To assess whether participants' choices in Six Options are affected by being presented with Two Options first, we will use the same classification for the intermediate options as we did before, namely, treating the push option as one category and all other options as the other category, and then test whether the proportion of participants choosing the push option differs as a function of order of presentation.[12] When Six Options was presented first, 60% of the lay participants chose the push option (45 out of 75), while 40% (30 out of 75) preferred not to push. When Six Options was presented after Two Options, 49% (34 out of 70) chose the push option, while 51% (36 out of 70) preferred not to push. This difference was not significant, $\chi^2_{1, N=145} = 1.91$, $p = .167$, $V = .11$.

---

[11] The proportion of participants choosing the push option (51%) is relatively high, especially in comparison with earlier seminal findings (~10% in Mikhail, 2007). However, the numbers in more recent studies are usually higher (e.g., ~40% in Capraro and Sippel, 2017), and Cao et al. (2017) recently found that participants preferred the push option in a two-option scenario when 15 lives were at stake. In light of these findings, we speculate that our relatively high numbers are based on the fact that 9 lives instead of 5 lives—as usual—were at stake.

[12] If we include the intermediate options as a third category, the same inference could be drawn ($\chi^2_{2, N=145} = 2.05$, $p = .36$, $V = .08$), namely, that the data provide no evidence that order of presentation affected participants' choices.

4. Discussion

Let us begin by discussing the general findings for all participants before we focus on expert participants in particular.

As Unger (1992, 1996) predicted, we found that adding intermediate options to the push dilemma increased the number of participants who preferred the push option. Whereas doing nothing was preferred to the push option in Two Options (when presented first), the latter was preferred to the non-push options in Six Options (when presented first). Given the main purpose of this chapter and the fact that we have not conducted further experiments that would allow us to identify the underlying psychological mechanisms, we will refrain from speculating about the psychological explanation of this effect (see, e.g., Huber et al., 1982 for an explanation of a classic effect of this kind).

We also found an effect of order of presentation, which was already predicted by Unger (1992, 1996) as well. When Two Options was presented first, fewer participants chose the push option, as compared to when Two Options was presented after Six Options. And when Six Options was presented first, more participants chose the push option, as compared to when Six Options was presented after Two Options.

Concerning the best psychological explanation for order effects in moral judgments, several proposals have been put forward (cf. Horne et al., 2013; Lombrozo, 2009; Schwitzgebel and Cushman, 2012; Wiegmann and Waldmann, 2014). Since the design of our experiment does not allow us to identify the underlying psychological mechanisms or to decide between competing explanations, we will largely avoid this discussion here.

However, the specific setup of our experiment, in combination with the finding that order effects were equally strong in both directions, suggests a rather simple explanation. In contrast to most other studies that investigate order effects, the two scenarios that we used in our experiment both contained the identical options of doing nothing and push (as previously discussed). Hence, participants who either chose doing nothing or push in the first scenario could also make the very same choice in the second scenario. A plausible hypothesis would thus be that participants' need for consistency in their judgments can account for the order effects we found. Since consistency is also an important philosophical value, this explanation might be especially fitting in case of our expert moral philosophers (see also Campbell and Kumar, 2012).[13]

We will organize the remainder of our discussion around the two findings concerning expert participants that are most striking from the perspective of the expertise defense. First, expert participants were more likely to choose the push option when more options (six vs. two) were available. Second, we also found order effects in expert ethicists in both directions, from Two Options to Six Options and vice versa, again concerning choices of the push option.

4.1   Finding 1: The influence of irrelevant options on expert judgments

Concerning the expertise defense, the main significance of the effect of several options is that the additional intermediate options in Six Options arguably constitute an irrelevant factor in the experimental restrictionist sense, that is, a factor that is irrelevant to the proper moral evaluation of this case (in a sense to be further specified below). Nevertheless, our data provide suggestive evidence that the intuitive judgments of expert ethicists were influenced by the presence of additional intermediate options.

To be sure, the additional options are not per se irrelevant to the question which of the options in Six Options is morally optimal. Some moral philosophers might argue that one of the intermediate options is in fact morally better than either doing nothing or the push option (see, e.g., Kamm, 2007). A potential reason might be that Option 5, for example, still saves four lives in comparison to the nine people that would be killed in case of doing nothing, yet without using any of the victims as a means. Thus, there are prima facie morally relevant considerations that might justify preferring one of the intermediate options over both doing nothing and pushing. In that sense, the intermediate options are *not* an irrelevant factor concerning one's moral evaluation of the case. Without begging substantial philosophical questions, we therefore cannot say

[13]   See also footnote 9.

that the 22% of our expert participants who chose an intermediate option in Six Options were influenced by a morally irrelevant factor.

However, the significant increase in expert ratings for the push option in Six Options, when presented first, as compared to Two Options, when presented first, *is* the result of an irrelevant factor. For with respect to that difference, the presence of additional intermediate options is indeed morally irrelevant.

Why is the presence of additional intermediate options a morally irrelevant factor here? One's choice of either doing nothing or the push option in Two Options, if rational, is the result of a direct moral comparison of the two options in terms of the number of lives saved and their further morally relevant features, which are explicitly stipulated in the case description. Moreover, the option of doing nothing and the push option are exactly the same in Six Options, and thus both options are available for direct moral comparison in Six Options, just as they are in Two Options. The only morally relevant feature that actually speaks in favor of the push option is the number of lives saved (other morally relevant features rather tend to speak against the push option). In this respect, the push option clearly dominates all other options, because it would save the net sum of eight lives—more than any other option. Thus, the only defensible moral reason that would favor the push option over all other options—that it saves the most lives—applies to Six Options just as clearly and unambiguously as it applies to Two Options.

Therefore, if the choices of our expert participants were rational, and given the random assignment of expert participants to the two conditions, we would expect only two possible outcomes. First, we might get lower expert ratings for the push option in Six Options (when presented first) than in Two Options (when presented first) if some expert participants also attach moral weight to features other than the number of lives saved, for example, to the fact that someone is used as a mere means, and therefore choose an intermediate option over the push option in Six Options. Second, we might get basically the same expert ratings for the push option in Six Options (when presented first) as in Two Options (when presented first) if all expert participants who attach a decisive moral weight to the number of lives saved would do so in a purely consequentialist vein, that is, by ignoring all other features of the available options. What we would not expect, however, is a third kind of outcome, namely, that the expert ratings for the push option are significantly higher in Six Options (when presented first) than in Two Options (when presented first). For this would require that some expert participants who *would not* attach a decisive moral weight to the number of lives saved in Two Options, and thus opt for doing nothing in the two-option scenario, nevertheless *do* attach a decisive moral weight to the number of lives saved in Six Options, despite the fact that the option of doing nothing is equally available in the six-option scenario. Given that the push option dominates all other options in terms of the number of lives saved in both Two Options and Six Options, this would be an irrational outcome pattern in our group of expert participants. The fact that we nevertheless observed significantly higher expert ratings for the push option in Six Options (when presented first) than in Two Options (when presented first) thus indicates the workings of a morally irrelevant factor in our expert ethicists, namely, the presence of additional intermediate options, which is the only difference between the two cases.

The rationale that underlies this argument is captured by the so-called *regularity principle*, which is a minimum condition in most existing models of rational choice (cf. Huber et al., 1982; Luce, 1959; Tversky, 1972). What the regularity principle says, in a nutshell, is that "[…] the addition of an option to a choice set should never increase the probability of selecting an option from the original set" (Rieskamp et al., 2006, p. 644). Thus, adopting the regularity principle as a basic principle of rational choice generates an even stronger and more general reason why the intermediate options in Six Options work as an irrelevant factor in the experimental restrictionist sense: because any significant increase of the ratings for *either* pushing *or* doing nothing in Six Options (when presented first), in comparison to Two Options (when presented first), would thereby be rendered irrational—irrespective of one's particular first-order ethical views.

One possible objection might be that the additional intermediate options in Six Options make the morally relevant differences between the available options more salient (cf. Wiegmann and Meyer, 2015), which may then justify a moral preference for the push option over doing nothing in Six Options. However, all information about the morally relevant features of doing nothing and the push option is equally present in both Two Options and Six Options, and so an increase of ratings for the push option in Six Options (when presented first) in comparison to Two Options (when presented first) would still constitute a rational shortcoming of some sort. Moreover, the morally relevant differences between doing nothing and the push option should already be maximally salient to our expert ethicists in particular, due to their many years of professional training in moral philosophy, where assessments of this kind are very much "routine business."

Another possible and even stronger objection might be that one can actually *learn* something new from the additional options in Six Options, and that this new information might justify a different moral assessment of the push option in direct comparison to doing nothing.[14] But first, it is quite unclear which morally relevant fact about these two options one might learn from Six Options that one cannot also learn from Two Options. And second, it seems especially implausible that our expert ethicists would learn something new from Six Options that they did not already know before (see Section 4.2 for further discussion, where we call this the *learning hypothesis*).

4.2 Finding 2: Order effects in expert judgments

A second striking finding is the order effects in expert ethicists from Six Options to Two Options and vice versa with respect to the push option. As a reminder, when Two Options was presented first, a clear majority of expert participants judged that the agent should do nothing, whereas a narrow majority of expert participants preferred the push option when Two Options was presented after Six Options. When Six Options was presented first, the push option was preferred by half of all experts, whereas the majority preferred not to push when Six Options was presented after Two Options. This result is in line with the findings

---

[14] Thanks to Joshua Knobe for the objection.

about order effects in expert ethicists by Schwitzgebel and Cushman (2012, 2015).

What are the implications of these order effects for the expertise defense against the experimental restrictionist challenge? The order in which Two Options and Six Options are presented seems irrelevant to their correct moral evaluation. Concerning our results, there is no good reason why one's verdict about Two Options should be different if one sees Six Options first or vice versa. Thus, our expert participants are susceptible to an irrelevant factor in the experimental restrictionist sense (Section 4.1), namely, order of presentation.

One might argue that the reversal of expert preferences in Two Options when presented first versus Two Options when presented after Six Options is not due to the influence of a morally irrelevant factor, but rather to the fact that the experts learned something new from Six Options, and then applied this new knowledge to the Two Options case (cf. Horne and Livengood, 2015). Let us call this objection the *learning hypothesis* (cf. Unger, 1996; Weijers et al., ms).

Our first reply is that one would have to make a number of important specifications before the learning hypothesis can be properly assessed: it would have to be specified what exactly the experts might learn from their exposure to Six Options, and why this newly acquired knowledge might justify higher expert ratings for the push option in Two Options.

Apart from that, the fact that the order effect was not stronger in lay people than in expert ethicists speaks against the learning hypothesis. For if there really were something to be learned from Six Options, one would expect that our lay participants—who had no prior experience with trolley-style cases, and presumably much less experience with moral problem cases in general—would learn something new, rather than our expert participants, who should already be highly familiar with the relevant moral considerations and scenarios.

However, the strongest objection to the learning hypothesis is that we did not only find an order effect in the direction from Six Options to Two Options, but an equally strong effect in the reverse direction from Two Options to Six Options. Since Two Options contains much less information or potential knowledge than Six Options, it seems quite implausible that one can learn something new by first considering Two

Options that would justify the subsequent pattern of expert ratings in Six Options.

5. Conclusion

In the experiment reported in this chapter, we investigated the moral intuitions of expert participants and lay participants concerning two questions.

First, we tested whether adding intermediate options to the push dilemma would increase the proportion of participants who prefer the push option. While there is suggestive evidence for the effect in general (all participants taken together) and for expert participants in particular, there was only a non-significant trend for lay participants.

Second, we tested whether presenting the classic two-option version of the push dilemma and the six-option version in varying order has an effect on participants' intuitive judgments. When the two-option case was presented after the six-option case, the number of participants who chose the push option increased significantly, as compared to the condition in which the two-option case was presented first. And when the six-option case was presented after the two-option case, the number of participants who preferred the push option decreased significantly, as compared to the condition in which the six-option case was presented first. Again, these results hold for all participants taken together and also for expert participants, while there was only a non-significant trend for lay participants.

In descriptive terms, both kinds of effects—the effect of additional intermediate options and the effect of order of presentation—were stronger in expert participants than in lay participants, but this expert–lay difference itself was not statistically significant. For this reason, we only made the conservative assumption that both effects were not weaker in experts than in lay people. We then argued that both effects are due to the influence of a morally irrelevant factor—irrelevant options and order of presentation—which has unfavorable implications for the expertise defense against the experimental restrictionist challenge. In line with previous research, we found no evidence that the intuitive judgments of philosophical experts are more resistant to the influence of irrelevant factors than those of lay people.

Acknowledgments

We would like to thank James Beebe, Eugen Fischer, Bryan Frances, York Hagmayer, Hanjo Hamann, Matthias Katzer, Antti Kauppinen, Markus Kneer, Joshua Knobe, Victor Kumar, Clayton Littlejohn, Dustin Locke, Edouard Machery, Angra Mainyu, Jonas Nagel, Shaun Nichols, Philip Nickel, Sven Nyholm, Jana Samland, Hanno Sauer, Andreas Spahn, Michael Waldmann, Pascale Willemsen, and several anonymous reviewers for very helpful comments and discussions. Many thanks also to our audiences at the *Philosophy & Ethics Departmental Seminar* at Eindhoven University of Technology in June 2016, at the *Bonn/Cologne Research Colloquium on Epistemology* at University of Cologne in June 2016, at the *Legal Studies & Ethics Department* of the Frankfurt School of Finance & Management in October 2016, at the *ZiF Workshop "Is and ought: The Ethical and Legal Relevance of Moral Psychology"* at the Zentrum für interdisziplinäre Forschung (ZiF) of University of Bielefeld in May 2017, at the workshop *The Experimental Philosophy of Morality and Causation— Perspectives from Philosophy, Psychology, and Law* of the Experimental Philosophy Group Germany at Ruhr-University Bochum in June 2017, and at *The Eighth (2017) Workshop of the Experimental Philosophy Group (UK)* at University of East Anglia in July 2017. Alex Wiegmann's work on this chapter was supported by a grant of Deutsche Forschungsgemeinschaft (*The Psychology of Moral Dilemmas*, project number 167159114). Joachim Horvath's work on this chapter was supported by a grant of Deutsche Forschungsgemeinschaft for the Emmy Noether Independent Junior Research Group *Experimental Philosophy and the Method of Cases: Theoretical Foundations, Responses, and Alternatives (EXTRA)*, project number 391304769.

References

Alexander, J. (2012). *Experimental Philosophy: An Introduction*. Cambridge: Polity Press.

Alexander, J., Mallon, R., & Weinberg, J. (2009). Accentuate the Negative. *Review of Philosophy and Psychology*, *1*(2), 297–314. https://doi. org/10.1007/s13164-009-0015-2.

Alexander, J. & Weinberg, J. (2007). Analytic Epistemology and Experimental Philosophy. *Philosophy Compass*, *2*, 56–80.

Beebe, J. R. & Monaghan, J. (2018). Epistemic Closure in Folk Epistemology. In T. Lombrozo, J. Knobe, & S. Nichols (Eds), *Oxford Studies in*

Experimental Philosophy, Volume Two (pp. 38–70). New York: Oxford University Press.

Bengson, J. (2015). The Intellectual Given. *Mind, 124*(495), 707–60. https://doi.org/10.1093/mind/fzv029.

Buckwalter, W. (2016). Intuition Fail: Philosophical Activity and the Limits of Expertise. *Philosophy and Phenomenological Research, 92*(2), 378–410. https://doi.org/10.1111/phpr.12147.

Campbell, R. & Kumar, V. (2012). Moral Reasoning on the Ground. *Ethics, 122*(2), 273–312. https://doi.org/10.1086/663980.

Cao, F., Zhang, J., Song, L., Wang, S., Miao, D., & Peng, J. (2017). Framing Effect in the Trolley Problem and Footbridge Dilemma: Number of Saved Lives Matters. *Psychological Reports, 120*(1), 88–101. https://doi.org/10.1177/0033294116685866.

Cappelen, H. (2012). *Philosophy without Intuitions*. Oxford: Oxford University Press.

Capraro, V. & Sippel, J. (2017). Gender Differences in Moral Judgment and the Evaluation of Gender-Specified Moral Agents. *Cognitive Processing, 18*(4), 399–405. https://doi.org/10.1007/s10339-017-0822-9.

Carter, J. A., Peterson, M., & Bezooijen, B. van. (2015). Not Knowing a Cat is a Cat: Analyticity and Knowledge Ascriptions. *Review of Philosophy and Psychology, 7*(4), 1–18. https://doi.org/10.1007/s13164-015-0279-7.

Carter, J. A., Pritchard, D., & Sheperd, J. (ms). *Knowledge-How, Understanding-Why and Epistemic Luck: An Experimental Study*.

Chudnoff, E. (2013). *Intuition*. Oxford: Oxford University Press.

Crandall, B. & Getchell-Reiter, K. (1993). Critical Decision Method: A Technique for Eliciting Concrete Assessment Indicators from the Intuition of NICU Nurses. *Advances in Nursing Science, 16*(1), 42–51. https://doi.org/10.1097/00012272-199309000-00006.

De Cruz, H. (2015). Where Philosophical Intuitions Come From. *Australasian Journal of Philosophy, 93*(2), 233–249. https://doi.org/10.1080/00048402.2014.967792.

Deutsch, M. (2015). *The Myth of the Intuitive: Experimental Philosophy and Philosophical Method*. Cambridge, MA: MIT Press.

Devitt, M. (2011). Experimental Semantics. *Philosophy and Phenomenological Research, 82*(2), 418–35. https://doi.org/10.1111/j.1933-1592.2010.00413.x.

Ericsson, K. A., Charness, N., Feltovich, P., & Hoffman, R. (Eds) (2006). *The Cambridge Handbook of Expertise and Expert Performance*. New York: Cambridge University Press.

Feltz, A. & Cokely, E. (2009). Do Judgments About Freedom and Responsibility Depend on Who You Are? Personality Differences in Intuitions About Compatibilism and Incompatibilism. *Consciousness and Cognition*, *18*(1), 342–50. https://doi.org/10.1016/j.concog.2008.08.001.

Feltz, A. & Cokely, E. (2012). The Philosophical Personality Argument. *Philosophical Studies*, *161*(2), 227–46. https://doi.org/10.1007/s11098-011-9731-4.

Hales, S. (2006). *Relativism and the Foundations of Philosophy*. Cambridge, MA: MIT Press.

Hitchcock, C. (2012). Thought Experiments, Real Experiments, and the Expertise Objection. *European Journal for Philosophy of Science*, *2*(2), 205–18. https://doi.org/10.1007/s13194-012-0051-0.

Hitchcock, C. & Knobe, J. (2009). Cause and Norm. *Journal of Philosophy*, *106*(11), 587–612.

Hofmann, F. (2010). Intuitions, Concepts, and Imagination. *Philosophical Psychology*, *23*(4), 529–46. https://doi.org/10.1080/09515089.2010.505980.

Hooker, B. (2000). *Ideal Code, Real World: A Rule-Consequentialist Theory of Morality*. Oxford: Oxford University Press.

Horne, Z. & Livengood, J. (2015). Ordering Effects, Updating Effects, and the Specter of Global Skepticism. *Synthese*, 1–30. https://doi.org/10.1007/s11229-015-0985-9.

Horne, Z., Powell, D., & Spino, J. (2013). Belief Updating in Moral Dilemmas. *Review of Philosophy and Psychology*, *4*(4), 705–14. https://doi.org/10.1007/s13164-013-0159-y.

Horvath, J. (2010). How (Not) to React to Experimental Philosophy. *Philosophical Psychology*, *23*(4), 447–80.

Horvath, J. & Wiegmann, A. (2016). Intuitive Expertise and Intuitions about Knowledge. *Philosophical Studies*, *173*(10), 2701–26. https://doi.org/10.1007/s11098-016-0627-1.

Huber, J., Payne, J. W., & Puto, C. (1982). Adding Asymmetrically Dominated Alternatives: Violations of Regularity and the Similarity Hypothesis. *Journal of Consumer Research*, *9*(1), 90–8. https://doi.org/10.1086/208899.

Kahneman, D. & Klein, G. (2009). Conditions for Intuitive Expertise: A Failure to Disagree. *American Psychologist*, *64*(6), 515–26. https://doi.org/10.1037/a0016755.

Kamm, F. M. (1998). Grouping and the Imposition of Loss. *Utilitas*, *10*(3), 292–319.

Kamm, F. M. (2007). *Intricate Ethics: Rights, Responsibilities, and Permissible Harm*. New York: Oxford University Press.

Kauppinen, A. (2007). The Rise and Fall of Experimental Philosophy. *Philosophical Explorations*, *10*(2), 95–118.

Klein, G., Calderwood, R., & Clinton-Cirocco, A. (1986). Rapid Decision Making on the Fire Ground. *Proceedings of the Human Factors and Ergonomics Society Annual Meeting*, *30*(6), 576–80. https://doi. org/10.1177/154193128603000616.

Liao, S. M., Wiegmann, A., Alexander, J., & Vong, G. (2012). Putting the Trolley in Order: Experimental Philosophy and the Loop Case. *Philosophical Psychology*, *25*(5), 661–71. https://doi.org/10.1080/0951508 9.2011.627536.

Lombrozo, T. (2009). The Role of Moral Commitments in Moral Judgment. *Cognitive Science*, *33*(2), 273–86. https://doi.org/10.1111/j.1551–6709.2009. 01013.x.

Luce, R. D. (1959). *Individual Choice Behavior: A Theoretical Analysis*. New York: Wiley.

Ludwig, K. (2007). The Epistemology of Thought Experiments: First Person versus Third Person Approaches. *Midwest Studies in Philosophy*, *31*(1), 128–59.

Machery, E. (2012). Expertise and Intuitions About Reference. *Theoria*, *27*(1), 37–54.

Machery, E. (2017). *Philosophy Within Its Proper Bounds*. Oxford: Oxford University Press.

Machery, E., Mallon, R., Nichols, S., & Stich, S. (2004). Semantics, Cross-Cultural Style. *Cognition*, *92*, 1–12.

Machery, E. & O'Neill, E. (Eds) (2014). *Current Controversies in Experimental Philosophy*. London: Routledge.

Mikhail, J. (2007). Universal Moral Grammar: Theory, Evidence and the Future. *Trends in Cognitive Sciences*, *11*(4), 143–52. https://doi. org/10.1016/j.tics.2006.12.007.

Nado, J. (2014). Philosophical Expertise. *Philosophy Compass*, *9*(9), 631–41. https://doi.org/10.1111/phc3.12154.

Nado, J. (2015). Philosophical Expertise and Scientific Expertise. *Philosophical Psychology*, *28*(7), 1026–44. https://doi.org/10.1080/095150 89.2014.961186.

Nado, J. (2016). The Intuition Deniers. *Philosophical Studies*, *173*(3), 781–800. https://doi.org/10.1007/s11098-015-0519-9.

Nagel, J. (2012). Intuitions and Experiments: A Defense of the Case Method in Epistemology. *Philosophy and Phenomenological Research*, *85*(3), 495–527. https://doi.org/10.1111/j.1933–1592.2012.00634.x.

Nichols, S. & Knobe, J. (2007). Moral Responsibility and Determinism: The Cognitive Science of Folk Intuitions. *Noûs*, *41*(4), 663–85.

Palan, S. & Schitter, C. (2018). Prolific.ac—A Subject Pool for Online Experiments. *Journal of Behavioral and Experimental Finance*, *17*, 22–27. https://doi.org/10.1016/j.jbef.2017.12.004.

Rieskamp, J., Busemeyer, J. R., & Mellers, B. A. (2006). Extending the Bounds of Rationality: Evidence and Theories of Preferential Choice. *Journal of Economic Literature*, *44*(3), 631–61. https://doi.org/10.1257/jel.44.3.631.

Rini, R. A. (2014). Analogies, Moral Intuitions, and the Expertise Defence. *Review of Philosophy and Psychology*, *5*(2), 169–81. https://doi.org/10.1007/s13164-013-0163-2.

Rini, R. A. (2015). How Not to Test for Philosophical Expertise. *Synthese*, *192*(2), 431–52. https://doi.org/10.1007/s11229-014-0579-y.

Schulz, E., Cokely, E., & Feltz, A. (2011). Persistent Bias in Expert Judgments About Free Will and Moral Responsibility: A Test of the Expertise Defense. *Consciousness and Cognition*, *20*(4), 1722–31. https://doi.org/10.1016/j.concog.2011.04.007.

Schwitzgebel, E. & Cushman, F. (2012). Expertise in Moral Reasoning? Order Effects on Moral Judgment in Professional Philosophers and Non-Philosophers. *Mind & Language*, *27*(2), 135–53. https://doi.org/10.1111/j.1468–0017.2012.01438.x.

Schwitzgebel, E. & Cushman, F. (2015). Philosophers' Biased Judgments Persist Despite Training, Expertise and Reflection. *Cognition*, *141*, 127–37. https://doi.org/10.1016/j.cognition.2015.04.015.

Sorensen, R. (2014). Novice Thought Experiments. In A. R. Booth & D. P. Rowbottom (Eds), *Intuitions* (pp. 135–47). Oxford: Oxford University Press.

Sosa, E. (2007). Experimental Philosophy and Philosophical Intuition. *Philosophical Studies*, *132*(1), 99–107.

Sosa, E. (2009). A Defense of the Use of Intuitions in Philosophy. In M. Bishop & D. Murphy (Eds), *Stich and his Critics* (pp. 101–12). Oxford: Blackwell.

Swain, S., Alexander, J., & Weinberg, J. (2008). The Instability of Philosophical Intuitions: Running Hot and Cold on Truetemp. *Philosophy and Phenomenological Research*, *76*(1), 138–55.

Sytsma, J. & Livengood, J. (2016). *The Theory and Practice of Experimental Philosophy*. Peterborough, ON: Broadview Press.

Sytsma, J. & Machery, E. (2010). Two Conceptions of Subjective Experience. *Philosophical Studies*, *151*(2), 299–327. https://doi.org/10.1007/s11098-009-9439-x.

Thomson, J. J. (1985). The Trolley Problem. *The Yale Law Journal*, *94*(6), 1395–415. https://doi.org/10.2307/796133.

Tobia, K., Buckwalter, W., & Stich, S. (2013). Moral Intuitions: Are Philosophers Experts? *Philosophical Psychology*, *26*(5), 629–38. https://doi.org/10.1080/09515089.2012.696327.

Tobia, K., Chapman, G., & Stich, S. (2013). Cleanliness is Next to Morality, Even for Philosophers. *Journal of Consciousness Studies*, *20*(11–12), 195–204.

Tversky, A. (1972). Elimination by Aspects: A Theory of Choice. *Psychological Review*, *79*(4), 281–99.

Unger, P. (1992). Causing and Preventing Serious Harm. *Philosophical Studies*, *65*(3), 227–55. https://doi.org/10.1007/BF00354612.

Unger, P. (1996). *Living High and Letting Die: Our Illusion of Innocence*. New York: Oxford University Press.

Waldmann, M. R., Nagel, J., & Wiegmann, A. (2012). Moral Judgment. In K. J. Holyoak & R. G. Morrison (Eds), *The Oxford Handbook of Thinking and Reasoning* (pp. 364–86). Oxford: Oxford University Press.

Weijers, D. (2015). To Push or Not to Push? Should That be the Question? Retrieved February 28, 2018, from http://www.danceofreason.com/2015/02/to-push-or-not-to-push-should-that-be.html.

Weijers, D., Unger, P., & Sytsma, J. (ms). Trolley Problems Reconsidered: Testing the Method of Several Options.

Weinberg, J., Gonnerman, C., Buckner, C., & Alexander, J. (2010). Are Philosophers Expert Intuiters? *Philosophical Psychology*, *23*(3), 331–55.

Wiegmann, A. & Meyer, K. (2015). When Killing the Heavy Man Seems Right: Making People Utilitarian by Simply Adding Options to Moral Dilemmas. In D. C. Noelle, R. Dale, A. S. Warlaumont, J. Yoshimi, T. Matlock, C. D. Jennings, & P. P. Maglio (Eds), *Proceedings of the 37th Annual Meeting of the Cognitive Science Society*. Austin, TX: Cognitive Science Society.

Wiegmann, A. & Waldmann, M. R. (2014). Transfer Effects Between Moral Dilemmas: A Causal Model Theory. *Cognition*, *131*, 28–43. https://doi.org/10.1016/j.cognition.2013.12.004.

Williamson, T. (2005). Armchair Philosophy, Metaphysical Modality and Counterfactual Thinking. *Proceedings of the Aristotelian Society*, *105*(1), 1–23.

Williamson, T. (2007). *The Philosophy of Philosophy*. Malden, MA: Blackwell.

Williamson, T. (2011). Philosophical Expertise and the Burden of Proof. *Metaphilosophy*, *42*(3), 215–29. https://doi.org/10.1111/j.1467–9973. 2011.01685.x.

Index

For the benefit of digital users, indexed terms that span two pages (e.g., 52–53) may, on occasion, appear on only one of those pages.